ORIGINARIO PRODUCTIONS

Brewmaster's Bombardier & Belly Gunner

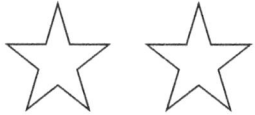

The World War II Letters of Bill & Bob Biner

Joseph Edward Fulton, Editor

ISBN 10 - 0979607213
ISBN 13 -978-0-9796072-1-9

Published by Originario Productions
Kings Valley, Oregon USA

http://originarioproductions.yolasite.com/
Contact: chiefjoephsxc@gmail.com

Cover design by Alicia Meza and Mariette Collora.
Bumi Design, LLC, Seattle, Washington
alicia@bumidesign.com

Other books by Joseph E. Fulton:

From Beardstown to Andersonville:
The Civil War Letters of Newton & Tommy Paschal
Published by Heritage Books, Inc. 1998, 2011
Dam Right! Fred Lynch, Oscar Kendall & The Lynch
Brothers Diamond Drilling Company
Published by Originario Productions, 2017

This book was dedicated to
Robert Joseph Biner

In appreciation for his service to our country, and his love for our family, on the 90th anniversary of his birth, January 31, 2013.

Acknowledgements

The letters in this collection were saved and cherished by my grandmother, Harriet Veronica Lynch Biner, and my mother, Elizabeth Jeanne Biner Fulton. I was fortunate to inherent the letters following their deaths in 1978 and 2009 respectfully. It is now my honor to publish them so that other family members and World War II readers and researchers can enjoy them as much as I have.

The transcribing of these letters from hand-written and tiny V-mail texts to a computer file was made infinitely easier by the assistance of my sisters Charlene Collora, Mary Fulton and Leslie Boniface; my niece Nicole Collora Wood; my wife Debra Hascall and my daughters Chloe and Rhea Fulton. Debra and my sister Mary also served as the primary proof-readers.

My brothers Will, Chuck, Dan, Bob, Fred and Tom Fulton and my sisters, all supported the publication of this collection so that it could be presented to Uncle Bob on the occasion of his 90th birthday.

A special acknowledgement goes to my uncle, Robert Joseph Biner, for his permission to publish the letters that he wrote home during his time as a belly gunner in World War II. I would also like to thank Barbara Biner Jimenez, the oldest surviving daughter of Lt. William Daniel Biner, for allowing me to publish her father's letters, which he wrote while serving as a bombardier in WW II.

Barbara graciously shared her father's military papers with me and Uncle Bob was kind enough, and patient enough, to sit for several interviews at his home in Yorba Linda, California during the summer of 2011. I would like to acknowledge his son Billy Biner, for recording the interviews for posterity, his son Tim for converting the film to a format that I could use, and his daughter Mary for helping us all stay fed and comfortable during the interviews.

Sheila Biner Brown, cousin to Bill and Bob, and the daughter of their favorite Biner uncle, George Biner, shared her memories from the time Bill Biner was in training near Los Angeles.

Fredericka "Fritzi" Biner Bernazani, the sister of Bill and Bob Biner, offered valuable insight and information, correcting me with good humor whenever I had something wrong about her parents or siblings. Thank you Aunt Fritzi.

And last, but not least, unless referring to her 4'6 stature, to my fellow family historian, Louise Andos Biner, the loquacious, indefatigable and diminutive wife of Bob Biner: I am glad "The Runt" found someone smaller than himself, and I am equally glad that I found someone as obsessed with family history as I am. I could never thank you enough for all the information you have shared with me over the years!

Joe Fulton, January, 2013

Gonzaga Guards Will Cause Trouble for Idaho

Right guard spot in the Gonzaga university football team is amply taken care of by this pable pair of players. Left is Bill Biner, who will spell Wendell Feldhahn, the starting player.

Top left: "Billy" Biner, the boxing brewmaster. Top right: Dan & Mate Lynch, Bill & Bob's maternal grandparents, at a mining camp with sons Kendall and Fred Lynch. Bottom photo shows Bill Biner on the left as a Gonzaga University football player.

Introduction

On December 7, 1941 Bill Biner was a student and collegiate football player at Gonzaga University in Spokane. His brother Bob was a high school senior in nearby Ellensburg, Washington. The Biner family lived in a modest Ellensburg home at 209 North Sprague Street. On that fateful day, the day that will live in infamy, their maternal grandparents, Dan and Mate Lynch, were visiting from Seattle. Little Ellensburg, like every other town in America, was abuzz with the news of the Japanese attack on Pearl Harbor. As the discussion turned toward the possibility of Bill and Bob being drafted to fight, Grandpa Lynch told them not to worry.

"We'll just drop a few bombs," proclaimed the old Irishman, "and the whole island will burn up."

As his grandson Bob would exclaim many years later, "How little did he know!"

Four days later, on December 11, 1941, Adolf Hitler made one of the most fateful blunders in his brief but deadly attempt to create a German empire. He declared war on the United States of America.

On January 21, 1942, William Daniel "Bill" Biner, enlisted in the U.S. Army Air Corps at Geiger Field in Spokane. Almost a year to the day later Robert Joseph "Bob" Biner enlisted in Seattle.

Both brothers initially hoped to be pilots and they certainly wanted to avoid infantry duty. Each had to pass a rigorous exam in order to be accepted as cadets in the Air Corps. Bill would become one of the most successful bombardiers of the war. Bob's diminutive frame made him the perfect belly gunner. And despite their dangerous roles, both boys would return home alive and well at the end of the war. More than 400,000 other American servicemen would not.

Whether stationed at various training camps or flying missions in the European theatre of action, both brothers kept in close contact with their parents, William Henry "Billy" Biner and Harriet Veronica Lynch Biner, who moved from Ellensburg to Seattle, Port Orchard and finally Pocatello, Idaho during the war. Billy Biner, a former champion boxer, was a brewmaster who roamed from one position to another as breweries struggled to stay afloat during the tough times of agricultural rationing.

With the boys off to war the only child left at home was their young sister Fredericka, or Fritzi. Their older sister Betty lived in Seattle in 1942; moved to Kennewick, Washington in 1943 and after a short stint as a teacher went to work in the Lend-Lease program.

The Lynch clan, originally from Waterford, Ireland, were miners by trade. Drawn to Michigan's "Copper Country" in 1865, the family followed the mining migration to Butte, Montana, British Columbia and Alaska; and most were in the state of Washington when America entered WW II. Grandpa Dan was a diamond drill supervisor for the Lynch Brothers Diamond Drilling Company of Seattle, which was owned by three of his younger brothers, Bill, Dick and Pat. The Lynch Brothers did the initial core drilling for nearly every major dam in the Pacific Northwest, including the Grand Coulee.

The Biner family, brewers and carpenters by trade, arrived in Montana Territory in the 1880s. They later moved to Tumwater, Washington where the family patriarch, Theophil Biner, an immigrant from Switzerland, helped a Montana friend, Leopold Schmidt, rebuild the Olympia Brewery in 1905-6. After operating breweries in British Columbia and Mexico, several members of the family settled in southern California and Bill visited them as often as he could while attending training schools at various bases in the Southwest during the first few months of 1942.

Julia Biner, younger sister of Bill & Bob's father, was married to Hollywood movie producer Paul Meredith Jones, who went out of his way to "wine and dine" his soldier nephews, often in the company of well-known movie stars, whenever they made it to Los Angeles.

These two personable brothers, both devout Catholics and committed connoisseurs of beer, were no different from hundreds of thousands of other young men who answered the call of President Franklin Delano Roosevelt and became active players in what has been christened "The Greatest Generation." They helped rescue Europe from the grips of that infamous madman, Adolf Hitler. They were heroes, but first and foremost they were sons and brothers. It is fortunate that their letters were lovingly preserved by their worrisome mother and doting sisters. Their letters paint a vivid picture of the long months of training required to earn a position in the U.S. Air Corps, which was coveted by men whose only other option might be infantry duty. And the letters also reveal the casual innocence and bravery of the young men who took on the dreaded German Luftwaffe.

In this age of emails and texting, letter writing has become a dying art, making it all the more special when such a collection is preserved. It is my honor, as the son of their late sister Betty, to share these soldier's letters with the public 75 years after they were written.

Part One: 1942

When Bill Biner entered military service on January 21, 1942, he was in his third year as an English and History major at Gonzaga University in Spokane, Washington.   Like his father and grandfather, (who was known to some as "Frenchie" Biner), Bill was proficient in French, which would come in handy during his two tours of duty.   By becoming a cadet, he was able to continue his education, although in subjects less to his liking.   Initially sent to Williams Field in Arizona, he went on to nine weeks of pre-flight training in Santa Ana, California; eight weeks of primary pilot training in King City, California and 12 weeks of bombardier training in Hobbs, New Mexico. Between his two tours of duty he became a bombardier instructor in Midland, Texas.

Bill was 5'9 and weighed 168 pounds when he entered the service.   He was twenty pounds heavier, mostly from bulking up physically, but perhaps also from his fondness for beer, following his two tours of duty. With brown hair, blue eyes and a ruddy complexion, Biner was handsome and charismatic.   He looked every part the dashing soldier.

His first tour, while stationed in North Africa and Italy (May 1943 to Feb. 1944) included the Rhineland Campaign.   His second tour, while stationed in France and Holland (Sept. 1944 to

July 1945) was in the Central European Campaign and included the epic Battle of the Bulge.

According to his military records, Captain William Daniel Biner, *"Was a B-17 Bombardier and a B-26 Navigator- Bombardier. Served two tours overseas totaling 19 months, in the Mediterranean and the European Theatre of Operations with the 12th Air Force, 15th and 9th Air Forces, 97th Heavy Bomb Group and 323rd Medium Bomb Group, based in North Africa, Italy, France and Holland. Has flown 83 combat missions and 475 combat hours. Has flown 1030 hours' military flying time. Acted as Flight Lead Bombardier on 25 combat missions in medium bombers and as Squadron Lead Bombardier on ten B-17 combat missions."*

Pretty heady stuff for a decidedly fun-loving young man as is evidenced by his first, and very brief, letter home.

Feb 3, 1942
(Aboard the San Joaquin Daylight)
Dear Folks,
Just a few lines as the train is rocking and not because I am in the lounge. The Ballet Russe[1] is on the train – O mama!   Love, Bill

---

[1] The original Ballet Russe performed between 1909 and 1929. Bill is referring to The Ballet Russe de Monte Carlo, a follow-up troupe that toured the USA

Bill was able to enjoy a few days in Los Angeles visiting relatives before he reported to his training camp in Arizona. Shortly after his arrival President Franklin D. Roosevelt signed Executive Order #9066 (Feb. 19, 1942) which led to the military internment of over 100,000 Japanese Americans. A relocation assembly center was located northwest of Williams Field near the ghost town of Mayer, Arizona. Two relocation centers and one isolation center were built in Arizona.

Williams Field[2]
Highley (Chandler) Arizona
Sunday- Feb. 15, 1942
Dear Folks,

This is a day of rest so I will try to write a little more. I got a letter from Aunt Julia[3] before I got one from home. I guess you were worried about the address though.

extensively, introducing Russian ballet to Americans during World War II. Judging by Bill's excitement it was full of attractive women.

[2] Williams Air Force Base, near Mesa, Arizona, was originally named the Mesa Military Airport. In October, 1941 it was renamed Highley Field and in February, 1942 it was renamed again in honor of Lt. Charles Williams, an Arizona native who was killed while test piloting a Boeing PW-9A over Hawaii in 1927.

[3] Julia Biner Jones was the youngest sister of Bill's father. Julia married the movie producer Paul Meredith Jones. She died in 2006 at the age of 103, having outlived most of the people mentioned in these letters, including her nephew Bill.

I certainly want to be back in L.A. Paul[4] makes Scotch & sodas in malted milk shakers (they are that big) and out of Haig & Haig.[5] He has the cutest and best stocked bar I have ever seen. Grandma[6] slipped me a ten spot before I left and I found another one in a letter from Julia Ann.[7] It will certainly come in handy. We get $25 on the 20th. I don't think we will get a full $75 this month because of deductions.

Thanks for the Valentines Fritzy.[8] I will send you something one of these days. Julie Ann[9] sent me one too.

---

[4] Paul Meredith Jones (1897-1966) was an American movie producer and the husband of Julia Biner. Prior to meeting Julia he spent a lot of time hanging out with his best friend, W.C. "Bill" Fields. During the times that Bill visited his Uncle Paul and Aunt Julia they were living at 4638 Arcola in Los Angeles with their daughter and Julia's mom. Also in the house were two African American servants; a butler, Oscar Young (1901-1958) and his wife, who had the unusual first name (for a woman) of Douglas.

[5] Haig & Haig is the oldest distillery of Scotch whiskey.

[6] Bill is referring to his paternal grandmother, Juliana Truffer Biner. Julia was born in Randa, Switzerland in 1861, and died in Los Angeles in 1950.

[7] Bill is almost certainly referring to his Aunt Julia; whose middle name was actually Marie.

[8] Fritzy (or more commonly Fritzi) is one of many nicknames for Bill's younger sister Fredericka Biner.

[9] Julie Ann Jones, Bill's young cousin and the only child of Paul & Julia Biner Jones. She was just four years old at the time.

Half the men in our company are in the hospital with dust colds and over the typhoid shots. We will be taking our classification exams tomorrow, I guess then we will find out if we will be pilots or navigator-bombardiers, armaments, weather forecasters, engineers, photographers. All get commissions, but different pay. Also I don't want some of the jobs.

Arizona is fine but the drill ground is dusty, and it is colder than hell at night and early in the morning when we do exercises in the dark. I have four blankets and wear long woolens under my pajamas and brown sweater. Sometimes I am warm at night. This tent life is not so hot.

The only place we can smoke is in our tents. They can give us the book if any officer catches us smoking any other place. So many demerits will wash a man out and they certainly aren't hard to get. As yet I have none but I am knocking on wood. If you don't salute an officer to satisfy him, you get them. I've never felt so restricted in my life. I will be glad when we get out of quarantine. We should be in Santa Ana by that time. We will get our uniforms then.

In the picture enclosed, the fellow on the right is a slow talking Irishman name John Patrick Donovan Jr.[10] from Moscow, Idaho. He has his bed

---

[10] John Patrick Donovan Jr. (1918-1999) enlisted in the Air Corps at Geiger Field in Spokane on Jan. 22, 1942.

next to mine and is funnier than the devil —
especially when the bugle blows at 5:40 in the
morning. The other fellow is in our tent and I
forgot his name. The picture was taken in
Martinez, California, [11] where we caught the
Streamliner to L.A. What a train! What a lounge
car! What a Ballet Russe!

Some doughnuts or anything would be swell. The
food is terrible. I sat at the Post Exchange half
the time. If I could get to town once, the first
thing I'd get would be a thick steak.

I had to command a platoon again the other day
and did better than the first time. The only thing
I did wrong was keeping step. I was keeping one
step and the platoon another. Everyone has to be
in the same step. I would give a command on my
right foot while the platoon was on the left and
things would get way complicated.

There is a little fellow in our tent from Dallas,
Texas I would like Betty[12] to meet. He is a good
looking little guy from S.M.U.[13] and says "My
daddy" and "You' all" and "Sho nuff" and can
imitate Donald Duck to a tee. Another guy is
engaged to a gal in Denver who has had her

---

[11] Martinez is a historic and picturesque town near San
Francisco, most famous as the hometown of the great
naturalist John Muir.
[12] Bill's older sister and the editor's mother, Elizabeth
Jeanne Biner (1918-2009).
[13] Southern Methodist University in Dallas, TX.

picture in *Life* and *Look* and a dozen other magazines as an All American college beauty. He has a large picture of her over his bed and every lieutenant stops to admire it. Maybe that's why our tent always passes with flying colors when we have an inspection.

We have Mass at 9:00 on Sunday, Mother, so quit worrying. Did I tell you we had to shave every morning and shower every afternoon and get our hair clipped every week? Also our hands and nails must pass inspection at all times!

You people have more time than me to write so why don't you? I don't think you should wait to hear from me. Just write anytime.

Love, Bill

Artist and inventor, George Biner, helped nephews Bill & Bob enjoy their free time while in Air Corps training camps. He was their dad's brother.

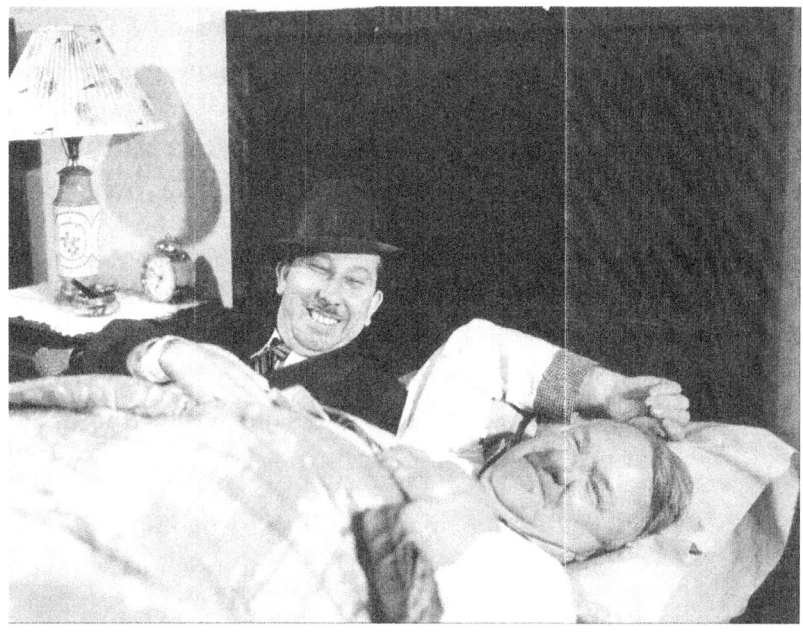

Movie producer and director Paul Meredith Jones (left), in bed with his best friend and former roommate, the legendary comedian W.C. Fields. Jones, who produced the famous "Road" movies starring Bob Hope and Bing Crosby, was married to Julia Biner, the sister of Billy Biner, and the aunt of Bill and Bob Biner. Jones was a generous man, full of good humor and memorable anecdotes about Hollywood celebrities. While Bill and Bob were in training, their Uncle Paul went out of his way to show them a good time whenever they had the opportunity to visit Los Angeles. Bill Biner, in particular, seemed to enjoy seeing so many movie stars in the company of his gregarious and good-natured uncle. *(Photo courtesy of Julia Ann Jones Cusick)*

Williams Field
Highley (Chandler) Arizona
February, 1942

Just a few lines as I have very little time of my own. Its march here and march there, and everything neat as a pin (the way I like it). We have to get our hair cut once a week. We look like a bunch of Germans.

I had to buy sunglasses today, it is so hot here. I am sunburned from neck to forehead. I don't know when we take our physical because of the long waiting line. In the meantime, we march.

Everyone wears one piece overalls of green fabric with insignia on back. I will save a pair for Bob if I can. If I pass my physical I will leave here for some other field in about three weeks. Keep on praying that I pass because this is really the life. There are five hundred Chinese pilots here.[14] They are the only ones flying – we are marching.

Love,

Bill

---

[14] More than 3,500 Chinese trained at Williams Field. 896 became pilots while the remaining 2600 received a variety of flight and technical training. Because of their small stature extra cushions were added to the seats of training craft. The United States Army also employed dozens of Chinese interpreters.

March, 1942

Dear Betty,

Thanks a million for writing so often. It's nice to get letters in a place like Williams or here.[15] We got our uniforms yesterday and you should see the figure we cut now. We will get some pictures Sunday.

Getting a kick out of meeting all the relatives but wish I could meet them in their natural habitat. This quarantine is beginning to bore something terrible.

Aunt Julia didn't buy a radio but loaned a portable till we get out and buy our own.

I certainly feel for you over the soldier situation, but if you can get any dough ahead you ought to come down here next summer. If I can get some dates you know I will oblige. No more for now. Have a math class coming up in a minute.

Love, Bill

March 20, 1942

Dear Folks,

Thanks a million for the ten spot, it will come in mighty handy. Tomorrow at 2:00 some of us get a

---

[15] Although he doesn't have it on the letterhead, Bill was likely referring to Santa Ana, California.

24-hour pass and we are going to L.A. Hip! Hip! Hooray!

Primary school opens next week but still don't know what I am to be. We took another placement exam here and the results will make us a pilot, navigator, bombardier – or private. This suspense is killing me and I'm getting fed up. We seem to be on the ground floor of an experiment. Those who took the exam at Williams went to primary anyway. We have to be the first to take the chance on missing out. I still want to be a pilot.

Hope you like the pictures. Thanks very much for the candy. Can't get my mind on a letter tonight. Radio blaring, L.A. tomorrow, big inspection and exam the next day. Will write right away again.

Love,

Bill

March 25, 1942

Dear Folks,

Got your cookies yesterday and the letter today – both were extremely pleasant. Glad you like the pictures. Notice how the sun makes me squint but doesn't bother the others?

Got our notice today. Three of us in the room made pilot training and will leave Saturday for places unknown to us yet. We won't know until the moment we leave but it will be somewhere in California. George Richard[16] hasn't been classified yet so suppose he will be left behind. Now all I have to worry about is "washing out" of primary.

Had a grand time in L.A. over the weekend. The four of us spent the evening at the Jones' and had a better time than we would have had stepping at the night clubs. At the close of the evening Paul and Julia took us to the Brown Derby[17] for a couple of drinks. Saw William Frawley[18] there but that's all. The boys sure got a kick out of Paul. He certainly is a great fellow and entertainer.

During the evening he brought in four mammoth all-day suckers for us as a present and then a carton of cigarettes a piece. Before we left he gave Donovan a bottle of Scotch because Jack had such a thirst. Donovan and Richart disappeared about 4 in the morning – we had a suite downtown –and Hugh and I didn't see them again until we got back Sunday afternoon. They had set off down the coast and spent all day in Newport with a bartender and spouse from Long Beach. Hugh

---

[16] George A. Richart Jr. (1922-1992) from Colorado joined the US Air Corps on November 18, 1940. He survived an aircraft crash in Vacaville, California.
[17] The Brown Derby was a popular restaurant frequented by Hollywood celebrities.
[18] William Frawley (1887-1966) was an American actor most famous for his portrayal as Fred Mertz in the popular TV show *I Love Lucy*.

and I couldn't even rouse them with wet towels for the dress parade at 5:00.

Alice[19] and her husband picked Hugh and me up about eleven and drove out to Albert Biners. Uncle and Aunt May [20] were in Frisco but saw all the girls. They are queens alright. Hugh was quite impressed. Then Alice and Ed drove us back to camp.

Going into L.A. the four of us had five different rides. The people hadn't seen any cadets before and they let out about 2,000 that day. The stares we got weren't hard to take at all for our conceit.

You wouldn't know this country now, Dad.[21] I have never seen a town spread out so much in my life. They build like mad around here. Just what

---

[19] Alice Biner (1916-2001) was Bill's cousin, a daughter of his uncle Gus Biner. Her husband was Ed Haskell (1912-1968).
[20] Albert Biner (1885-1959) was an older brother of Bill's father. He was married to May Kreider (1887-1971). Bill is referring to Albert & May's four daughters, who ranged in age from 20 to 30 at the time.
[21] The Billy Biner family had lived in southern California during much of the Roaring Twenties. Prohibition limited opportunities for brewers in the states, so Billy took a job as brewer for the Mexicali Brewery in Mexicali, Mexico. He lived across the border in Calexico, California with his wife Harriet and daughter Betty. His parents, Theophil and Juliana, lived in Los Angeles and that is where his sons Bill and Bob would be born in 1920 and 1923.

is going on in the brewery, anyway? Did Flynn[22] and the rest really get sacked? I certainly feel sorry for the Poolers.[23] What will they do now?

Thanks a million again for the ten spot. I think pay day is tomorrow; if it is I will send it back pronto.

Love to all,

Bill

---

[22] William F. "Billy" Flynn (1912-1944), was a truck driver for the Ellensburg Brewery. He was the son of Tom Flynn and Mary Burke. Billy Flynn enlisted on Sept. 19, 1942. He served a year in the Aleutians. Flynn died from an unspecified illness in the Spokane General Hospital on Dec. 20, 1944. He is listed as a WW II war dead for the state of Washington and is buried in Ellensburg's Holy Cross Cemetery.

[23] John F. Pooler (1882-1948) and his family were close friends with the Biner family in Ellensburg. John Sr. was the business manager of the Ellensburg Brewery. John's daughter Betty and Billy's daughter Betty remained life-long friends. John Pooler Jr. also served in World War II and is mentioned numerous times by the Biner brothers. Like John Pooler Sr., Billy Biner would also lose his job as brewmaster at Ellensburg when the brewery shut down due to government rationing of malt barley. The parent company decided to use its allotment of barley at a different brewery in Montana.

Bill Biner at training camp with his buddy Pappy Heinz. Bill drew the lines pointing to the two.

March 31, 1942
Mesa Del Ray
Dear Grandmother and Grandfather,[24]

Just got to primary flying school after two months in two reception centers, and we start flying tomorrow.

We are underclassmen here for the first four weeks. After leaving here - if I make the grade - I will go to basic school, and then on to advanced. About seven months from now I will get my wings if everything turns out alright.

---

[24] Bill is writing to his maternal grandparents, Daniel Samuel Lynch and Mariette Kendall Lynch, who lived in Seattle.

All you would have to do to ease your mind about the outcome about the war would be to come down to one of these schools and see the boys in action. At the rate we are going now, we can lick anyone.

Have seen just about all of the Biners now and so far have had a great time traveling around. The weather down here is certainly all it is cracked up to be and when this war is over I think I'll come back. We have beautiful living quarters and excellent food and sometimes I almost pinch myself to see if I am dreaming. It was such a short time ago that I was in Seattle celebrating the New Year and with no idea of what was to come.

Mother has some pictures I took at Santa Ana – a dump – and if she hasn't sent them to you to see why don't you ask her? Hope you all are fine and that goes for the rest of the Lynch clan.

Love, Bill

PS Your prayers are requested for my success.

April, 1942

Dear Folks,

This place is really heaven after living where we did for eight weeks. I don't know how to describe the place except to say that we live in a sort of super colossal tourist camp airport. All our rooms spread out fanwise from a central building in one story, patio style with trellises and roses and green lawns and knotty pine furniture. Really something.

The mess hall is also something out of a movie with insignia all over and wonderful food. The only fly in the ointment is that we are underclassmen for the first four weeks, and do we have to eat our pride!

We are "dodos"[25] and whenever one dodo wants to go anyplace he has to take along another dodo as navigator and both have to double time (run) in step. There are many things like that but just that one brings up many difficulties.

This is where I'll really need the prayers. We haven't been up yet but I am itching to get started and more than ever I want to make good. We have little silver Ryan monoplanes[26] here and they are taking off every minute. I feel like I can fly already.

King City[27] is just a little dump but the U.S.O. sends down girls from different colleges so things may not be so bad. Our P.X.[28] on the post is a

---

[25] A cadet still waiting for his first flight was called a dodo or sometimes a penguin.

[26] Designed by the Ryan Aeronautical Company, the Ryan STs were used as a trainer by the Air corps. They were a two-seat, low-wing aircraft.

[27] King City is located in Monterey County, California, about 50 miles southeast of Salinas.

[28] The P.X. was a retail store operated on an army base.

beauty. Replete with bowling alley and everything.

No more for now. Time to fall out again. Each new place has a faster and longer schedule.

Love to all,

Bill

April 6, 1942 Mesa Del Ray

Dear Folks,

Easter Monday and a very gloomy one. I wanted to send Fritzy some eggs or something but you can't buy those things on an army post. She will just have to be satisfied with the wings. Also forgot Betty's [29] birthday so she and Fritzy can fight over which one they want.

Got into King City yesterday and didn't realize there was a town deader than Ellensburg but that is what it is. They have one movie house, so I saw *Tarzan's Treasure* [30] and caught up on my sleep in the lodge seat. The pressure around here is beginning to tighten. Today we had a lecture in physics for one hour that covered what had formerly taken a week to cover. That gives you an idea of what "speeding-up" our defenses means.

---

[29] Betty, Bill's older sister, celebrated her 24th birthday on Feb. 20, 1942.
[30] *Tarzan's Secret Treasure* was a 1941 film starring Olympic swimming gold medalist Johnny Weissmuller.

Starting tonight we are having a class in electricity. This class is called during the two hrs. we have at night to do our studying for the day classes! Outside of a hr. for drill and one for exercise (I do mean exercise) and half a day on the flight line, I have nothing to do!

Aunt Julia sent me The Moon is Down[31] at Santa Ana and I haven't been able to read the forward so don't send any books. I have had three lessons so far, it rained last Friday, Sat. and Sunday so no flying, but have over two hours in the air now. The first time up I had to handle the controls and was never so scared in my life. When we got down I almost followed the example of some and asked for a transfer to the "ranks." However, am getting more used to it as I go along and I actually relaxed today and enjoyed things. You have so many things to think about up there at once that it's hard to orient yourself at first.

It's altogether different from what I thought it would be and it certainly is beautiful up there. I'll have to get some pictures taken in my flying suit. You wouldn't recognize me.

No more for now. If you don't get so many letters from now on you'll know the reason. I owe letters

---

[31] The Moon is Down was written by John Steinbeck and sponsored by the Office of Strategic Services (OSS). The novel was used as propaganda to encourage resistance movements in Nazi-occupied Europe. It was published in 1942.

all over the country right now and don't know how I'm going to answer them all.

Love, Bill

P.S. Who the hell is Bill Lambert?[32]

April 11, 1942

Dear Folks,

It looks like we will be flying seven days a week from now on. Every other week they seem to pare the program down. The upper class was informed yesterday that they were to be graduated on the 24th instead of the 30th. That also threw their plans for a celebrity studded party into a cocked hat – Bob Crosby band etc.[33]

I suppose you've noticed all the big entertainers are going down to Santa Ana now that we've left. Speaking of entertainers, I forgot to mention that Burgess Meredith[34] was a private at Williams

---

[32] Orrin "Bill" Lambert (1924-1993) was a high school friend of Bob Biner from Ellensburg. The son of Charles and Vernell Lambert, Bill Lambert enlisted on Feb. 2, 1943.

[33] Bob Crosby (1913-1993), the younger brother of Bing Crosby, served 18 months in the U.S. Marines entertaining troops with his popular Dixieland jazz band.

[34] Burgess Meredith (1907-1997) was an award-winning actor. He became a captain in the U.S. Army Air Corps but was discharged in 1944 to portray the famous war correspondent Ernie Pyle in the movie *The Story of GI*

Field and also at Santa Ana while I was there. Saw him washing his Cadillac at Williams one day and didn't recognize him. While at Santa Ana he dated Paulette Goddard.[35]

Some days I like this flying business and other days I don't. Most everyone seems to feel the same way. I guess if we were taking it a little more leisurely it would be better, but the pressure has made a lot of them up and quit. Some that were the most cocky at Santa Ana too.

Love, Bill

April 20, 1942

Dear Folks,

Just a few lines because honestly, I haven't any time. They have taken our free hour away and given us another class in its place – physics and meteorology. I don't know how long I am going to

---

Joe. Meredith was an outspoken liberal who was blacklisted by Senator Joseph McCarthy during the anti-communist hysteria of the 1950s. He is best known to Baby Boomers as the Penguin in the campy 1960s TV show *Batman.*

[35] Paulette Goddard was an American film actress. She was married to Charlie Chaplin from 1936-42. She wed Burgess Meredith in 1944. Eight years following her 1950 divorce with Meredith she married the German writer Erich Maria Remarque, author of <u>All Quiet on the Western Front</u>. Goddard died in 1990, leaving a $20 million bequest to New York University in honor of Remarque.

be able to keep this up. We have something to do from 5:20 in the morning till 10:20 when lights are out, and my nerves tingle. Flying every day is enough in itself without classes and drill and exercises and study.

My average in navigation is 77. My average in engines is 75. 80 is passing and I can't seem to get the hang of it. I passed my six hour check flight this afternoon and then went up and shot five landings. I felt like a wet rag when we came down. If things turn out alright and I learn how to relax when I get down low, I should solo in a day or two. I have a wonderful instructor and if I should "wash out" it won't be his fault. There are so damn many things to watch all at once that the sweat stands out on me.

I can do quite a few maneuvers up about 3000 feet though. Stalls, and spins, and steep turns and I like to do S turns over highways and follow a meandering river. Taking off and landing is all that bothers me. Next weekend I will write a long discourse on just what goes on around the flight line but haven't time now.

Sorry I missed your birthday, Dad, but will see what I can do about it in the future.

Love to all, Bill

P.S. I have to pay for the stationary.[36]

April 26, 1942

Dear Folks,

Just got Betty's letter and appreciated it as usual. I said I would give you a little dope on flying, so here goes.

The first six hours of flying we learn all the essentials such as climbing, gliding, stalling, spins; shallow, medium and steep turns; takeoffs and landings. At the end of six hours a check rider puts us through our paces – if we pass, we go on to solo and more intricate maneuvers. I soloed last Friday but my landings are very poor. Tomorrow I have to take a "progress check" with another instructor. If he can't help me out I'll probably be on my way back to Santa Ana. More than a third of the class has "washed" and I don't intend to. I seem to do better when I'm alone than when I'm with the instructor. He makes me nervous when I land – always hollering something to distract me and I'm never sure how much on the controls he is. When I know for sure that I'm doing all the work I can do much better.

---

[36] The stationary that Bill is using has a printed letterhead with an Air Corps insignia and reads "Aviation Cadet William D. Biner, United States Army Air Corps"

Besides the main field here, we have three practice fields in the valley – all at different altitudes. When we were dodos we used to go out to them on the elephant trains[37] and practice; now that we are upper classmen we fly from the main field. Facing the field is what we call the "flight line." In two of the hangars there are cadet Ready Rooms. These have large plate glass bay windows where we wait for the call over the loudspeaker to report to the dispatcher for flight clearances. After three supervised solos we can check out a plane as many times as they will let us. So far I have had only one supervised solo. If I do well enough on my check tomorrow, I will have my second. If I don't I will probably have to take a check from some lieutenant and that means a "wash." If I can't fly, I just can't, and there isn't much anyone can do about it. I intend to do my best though. Setting a plane down on a little field at 75 mph is quite a job in timing, let me tell you; and they have to be three-point.[38]

Huey and I hitch-hiked to Salinas this afternoon and a girl playing in "Life with Father"[39] picked us

---

[37] This probably means that they walked in single file fashion.

[38] A three-point landing is a landing in which the two main wheels and the nose wheel or tail wheel all touch down simultaneously.

[39] *Life with Father*, written by Clarence Day, was the longest running non-musical Broadway play. It was adapted to film in 1947. The name of the actress who picked up Bill and his friend Huey remains unknown.

up. She was going to Carmel but we didn't have enough time for that. There wasn't time to do anything in Salinas either, so we came back. I would give a month's pay for a week off.

No more for now.

Love, Bill

April 29, 1942,

I didn't want to write until I knew definitely what was going to happen, and now I know. Yesterday I washed on my twenty hour check but think it is all for the good. I can fly an airplane alright, but the reason I washed was because I was too tense all the time. The lieutenant said it would be better if I quit before I killed myself and someone else.

The other day when I was up in a solo ship I nearly collided with another cadet about 400 feet off the ground – too low to jump safely. We missed by about twenty feet, going at 150 mph. I don't know yet what stopped me from hitting him; one second sooner and it would have been too bad.

Anyway, I've gotten in twenty hours of flying (about ½ hour a day) and I can fly any of these private planes safely after this training so I'm not so bad off. The officer said I was too dangerous to fly army planes, where you have to be relaxed at all times.

I don't know what is going to happen to me now. I'm just loafing around at the present waiting to meet the board and find out my disposition. I have put in for a 24 hour pass to San Francisco over the weekend – if we get paid this week.

Frankly, I don't care what happens now that I can't be a pilot. Maybe they'll be bombardiering or something where I can still get a commission, but I worried about the flying so much that my grades in ground school aren't very good.

It would open your eyes if you came down here and saw the boys coming off the flight line. Right now they are putting in 3 and 4 hours of flying a day and the nineteen and twenty year olds look like 30-year-old men. So if you think I am the only one that worried, you are mistaken.

There are 100 or so planes up in the air all day long, and in a little valley like this you are dodging planes continuously. You have to keep your head moving from side to side, backwards and down and up, every movement – watching – besides keeping the motor in a constant speed and going through the different maneuvers.

I'll be doing figure eights over trees or a farm house and all at once another plane pops up, coming at me and I have to go into a steep climbing turn to get out of the way. Or, like one day I was out, flying about 2000 feet and a plane came spinning out of the sun and right down behind my tail. Apparently the dummy hadn't cleared himself before going into the spin and therefore didn't see me. Just like driving a car, it's the other fellow you have to look out for.

There are about 45 out of our class who have washed so far, and they have been living the life of Riley. [40] No formations or ground school to meet and getting time off to go to Carmel and swim. Just waiting around for orders to come. I don't want to go into the ranks but if I can be of any help there, that will be alright. Those damn Japs are getting under my skin. However, I would like to be the guy that presses the button that sends bombs down on Tokio.

No more for now. Will write again soon.

Love to all, Bill

Bill did not get his wings. In early May, 1942 he tells his Mother that he "met the board and I think I have been recommended for a bombardier. At least I am still a cadet and now it's up to them where I will go."

Santa Ana
May 20, 1942
Dear Folks,

---

[40] "Living the Life of Riley" is an Irish American saying that probably started during World War I and simply means "an easy life."

I am once more ensconced at Santa Ana, but this time in tents. The camp has doubled in size and it's hotter and dustier. I haven't felt so miserable and low since the day I got here – with all my buddies in King City. On the way down I spent a day & night with the George Biner's[41] and had a good time.

We started our classification tests today and I expect to be here for at least ten weeks. I guess I will just have to put up with it. Will let you know what happens when I have a better time to write. Also have a few items of interest I'll send next time (news I mean). My new address is A/C WD Biner, Squadron 46, A.F.R.T.C.[42] Santa Ana

Love, Bill

June 5, 1942

Dear Folks,

Finally got out of the hospital and my cheeks are pretty raw. Not doing any marching but also

---

[41] George Michael Biner (1897-1971) was a younger brother of Bill's father. George contracted polio as a soldier during World War I. However, he went on to be a successful artist, brewer and inventor. He supervised the laying of the tile for the dome of the Los Angeles County Library, invented a labeling machine for breweries and was the co-founder of Biner Ellison which pioneered the production of liquid filling machines.
[42] Air Force Reserve Training Center.

haven't been classified yet. Am in Squadron 45 now, all unclassified men, but should be moving into a bombardier squadron next week.

That girl I mentioned meeting came down to visit me in the hospital but luckily they wouldn't let her in because she wasn't wife or kin. By driving down she has sort of put me in a spot. In other words, she will probably expect me to date her over weekends and I certainly have no time for that. I don't know why I always have to get involved.[43]

I would like to be home for Bob's graduation. (I would just like to be home.) I'm even envying the men who are getting medical discharges now. If Betty would like any advice I would suggest she try to get work down here this summer. Have her write Carolyn[44] about possibilities. It seems that any girl that can type or take short-hand can get a good job.

There are ten thousand cadets stationed here now and things are in such a mess you begin to wonder if the congressmen aren't running it.

About Bob joining up. The best thing he can do is wait, go to school, take C.P.T.[45] and if he <u>likes</u>

---

[43] The girl Bill refers to is unknown. Perhaps she was the young actress he hitched a ride with in late April.
[44] Carolyn Biner was Bill's cousin and the daughter of Albert Biner, one of his dad's brothers.
[45] Possibly Cockpit Procedure Training.

flying, stay with it. C.P.T. will exempt him from the draft. If I had it to do over again I would do the same. Stay out just as long as you can, Bob and get all the school you can.

What is most important, get a year of physics in this first year, and if and when you are called, you have a chance on getting a commission in armaments. But you have to have two years of college. I can't stress staying in school hard enough. It is very important around here if you wash out. By the way, Tom Harmon just washed out. Don't think he even soloed.

The whole thing in a nutshell, if you can stay out for a couple of years, the war is likely to be over. And take it from me, you are not missing anything. Congratulations on graduating, Bob, and stay away from this reserve business. It's just another enlistment gag and they will call you just as soon as they have room down here.

Love to all,

Bill

June 8, 1942

Dear Folks,

Just a few lines to go along with the picture. The fellow with me is Nelson Black who was with me at King City. I had a couple of dances with

Carolyn here at the Palladium[46] where Henry James[47] is playing. Happened to bump into her right after the picture was taken. (All this happened before the operation). James has the best band I ever heard. He has California by the ear right now.

Went to L.A. over the weekend and went out with the George Biner's to a party. Had a pretty good time. Next week I am going to Paul & Julia's. They have invited me for the week end and I don't see why I should turn it down. Besides, I won't have to take Dorothy out now. Maybe if I put it off long enough she will forget me. I hope.

Still haven't been classified and right now I am working on the public relations office for a job. I'll tell them I ran the *Spokesman Review,* if I have to, to get on. I'd do anything to be a foreign correspondent.

Hope Bob takes my advice. Even if he is drafted he can get in the air corps if he can pass the exams.

Love to all, Bill

---

[46] The Palladium Ballroom on Sunset Blvd in Hollywood opened in 1940.

[47] Henry James (1916-1983) was a bandleader from Georgia and one of the most popular musicians of the 1940s. Frank Sinatra was a vocalist for the Henry James Band. James reportedly tried to change Sinatra's name to Frankie Satin, but the singer refused.

June 15, 1942

Dear Folks,

Received your letter today and have summoned up enough energy to answer it.

I had a very good weekend with Paul & Julia and Dorothy somebody – Betty knows her, a friend of Julia's. We went to Preston Sturges'[48] club "The Players" and stayed till it closed. The Players is a new club and since Ciro's[49] is closed, has taken over the limelight.

I bumped butts with Errol Flynn[50] on the dance floor, and Claire Trevor[51] (who looks 100% better off screen); sat next to Pat Dane – "Johnny Eager's" sweetheart;[52] had breast-of-guinea hen;

---

[48] Preston Sturgis (1898-1959) was one of America's greatest and most innovative filmmakers. Paul Jones produced (and had a cameo in) his 1941 comedy *Sullivan's Travels* which later inspired the Coen brother's 2000 hit film *Oh Brother Where Art Thou?*
[49] Both *The Players* and *Ciros* were nightclubs on Sunset Strip, popular with Hollywood celebrities.
[50] Errol Flynn (1909-1959) was an Australian actor with a reputation as a ladies' man. He starred as a dashing hero in such films as *Captain Blood; The Adventures of Robin Hood* and *The Adventures of Don Juan.*
[51] Claire Trevor (1910-2000) was a popular American actress who won an Academy Award for her role in the 1948 film *Key Largo.*
[52] Patricia Dane (1919-1995) was an American actress. Bill refers to her role as "Garnet" in the 1941 film *Johnny Eager* starring Robert Taylor, Lana Turner and

and drank scotch and water till 2:00 AM when two lieutenants could buy only beer after 10:00 PM. Saw the big producers, writers and directors making fools of themselves with their young dates.

All in all, it was a very fancy evening and I thanked my lucky stars I didn't have to pay the check.

One of the nicest things about these visits is to see how well Grandma[53] still is. She was out on the patio when I got there, having a drink and smoking a cigarette. She bounds in and out of a car with more alacrity than I. Coming from Mass Sunday we were talking about Seattle. Grandma pulled a fast one. She said, "The fog was so thick you couldn't Seattle." I had never heard it before and it tickled me. Also, she was very proud of Dad's letter to her. You ought to write her more often, Pop.

I got classified Saturday as a bombardier and should move to another company (squadron) sometime this week. Mother, when a man joins the army they don't release him for something else. The army has its own Public Relations dept. Anyway, they wouldn't take me because they need me in the air corps.

(Wednesday)

Van Heflin in an Academy Award winning performance.
[53] Juliana Truffer Biner.

This is the first time I've been able to finish this since Monday. I am now in Squadron 95. Remember that. Saw Joe Webster[54] and Tom Horton[55] last night. They are both in the same barracks and looking very good. Don't worry about me having girl trouble, Mother; but I guess you wouldn't be happy if you didn't.

Have to close this now. Pretty busy.

Love to all, Bill

June 30, 1942

Dear Folks,

Got your letter and you are very correct. I am busier than a cat on a tin roof. Our classes start at 7:00 in the morning and end just before supper. After supper it's homework till lights out. The FBI is probably investigating me now. All bombardiers have to be investigated because we handle the

---

[54] Joseph A. Webster (1917-1992) was the son of William & Mary Webster. The Webster's were family friends from Ellensburg. They operated Webster's Café, a popular hangout for teenagers. Bill briefly dated Betty Webster, Joe & Tom's sister. Joe became a colonel in the Air Force and saw action in WW II and Korea. He is buried in Ellensburg's Holy Cross Cemetery.

[55] This is possibly Bill's cousin, Lt. Charles T. Horton, from Portland, who was also a member of the Air Corps. His grandmother, Nora Harris Horton, was a first cousin to Bill's grandfather, Dan Lynch.

bombsight.[56] I don't know of anything that will trip me up.

Spent last weekend in Balboa[57] with the gang and had a wonderful time in the ocean and dancing etc. Balboa is real California. I may go to Laguna this week. It is only sixteen miles from here. Haven't seen Mr. Pooler yet but got his address from Uncle George. Also had him get me a birth certificate I had to have to be a bombardier. I wonder how they figured I got into the air corps.

If that mine ever comes in Dad, grab a little place in Balboa and get a tan and some ocean fishing. Never saw a place quite like it before. Well, no more for now.

Bill

___

July 6, 1942

Dear Folks,

No fooling, this school we are going to here is the toughest thing I ever ran into. We don't get through until 6:30 in the evening and the classrooms fairly steam in the sub-tropic weather

___

[56] Bill is referring to the top secret Norden bombsight which was used in high altitude precision strategic bombing by the U.S. Army Air Force during World War II.

[57] Balboa is a narrow peninsula along the Pacific Coast south of Los Angeles. It is now a neighborhood of Newport Beach, California.

we are having right now. My face is a brilliant chocolate color now and Sunday I got a bad burn down at Laguna. Speaking of Laguna, you wouldn't know it now, Mother. There are so many beautiful homes hanging all over the hills. The real estate must be terrific.

I am scheduled to be here at least another five weeks and maybe eight, before going to advanced school. It will be another twelve weeks at advanced before I get my commission. Anyone who thinks being a bombardier is easy ought to try it. Five men in my barracks have quit already. One of the many things we have to do before leaving here is to be able to identify a Jap ship seven miles away and instantaneously. We can't drop bombs on our own boats like the Wops[58] and English have done.

S.A.A.A.B. is simply Santa Ana Army Air Base. Couldn't anybody figure that out?

Glad the beer is such a success and also glad to hear of Betty's good fortune in Seattle. Sorry I didn't get to see Mr. Pooler but Uncle George forgot to send the address. No more for now.

Love to all, Bill

---

[58] Wop was a derogatory term for Italians. It stood for "Without Papers" and originally referred to Italian immigrants without the proper paperwork. During the war it was commonly used when referring to any Italians.

July, 1942

Well, we are well into our school now but more confused than ever. We have to study navigation as well because only the B-24 and B-17 carry navigators. On all other ships the bombardier has to be the navigator too. Also, something might happen to the navigator on the two big ships.

I'm sorry I can't say a thing about our bombsights. If you saw them, and the way they are guarded from even the colonels on the post, you would realize my position. We are very privileged characters. The instructors informed us that there would be about 30 of us made instructors when we graduate. All I can hope for is that I catch on quickly. Because, boy that is just what you have to do. Right now I wouldn't trade my position with any pilot in the air force. The little they have to do on a bomber compared to our duties is amazing. Someday I'll be able to tell you.

Bob is in a funny situation. The three of you will have to figure it out I guess, but my advice would be to start school and get in as much math as possible. We don't have a bit down here and Santa Ana was only elementary. I believe Bob could make it alright if he applied himself. Besides, school would be something that would help in anything he got into. A few dollars that he would make working doesn't mean very much once he is in the army.

However, three good heads ought to figure out the solution. I want Bob to make his own decisions.

No more for now. Lights out.

Love, Bill

July 22, 1942

Dear Betty,

Here is the letter I promised last night. I know I have been pretty slow but I'm so darn busy it would take an hour explaining all my duties and I haven't the hour to spare.

The school here is terrific. We took a year of college physics in exactly three weeks. We are taking so many subjects I don't know what to start studying at night. We have two entire hours to get our homework done in. I'm passing in everything so far but keep your fingers crossed. It sounds like you have an interesting job. Have you dated any of the ensigns yet? Have you phoned Jeanne yet?[59] She works in an insurance office. You ought to have lunch together and maybe she could get you a date with one of her friends.

---

[59] Bill had asked his sister Betty, in a postcard sent the day before, to give Jeanne (apparently Jeanne Murphy, a love interest), "a ring (East 0424 is the phone) and tell her I'm still waiting to hear from her. On second thought, bawl her out."

This letter is for Aunt Mollie[60] also. Those goodies were really appreciated Aunt Mollie. Mother never did send your address and I threw the one on the package away. So this is the first opportunity to express my gratitude. Don't try and send anymore however, because you need the sugar and we are getting good food now.

Betty, how about you and me making some arrangements for a California trip for Mother and Dad this fall or winter? We could make it a fifty-fifty deal or anything you wish. I want them to come down pretty badly though, and with grandma worrying over Uncle Gus' <u>intended remarriage</u> she might get pretty low. Don't say anything to Dad. I will write myself.

No more for now, Betty, but will try and answer sooner next time. My love to Grandma and Grandpa (Lynch).

Ever, Bill

___

July 22, 1942

Dear Folks,

Just a few lines as I have four tests tomorrow and only an hour and a half to study for them. My correspondence is so far behind I don't know how I

___

[60] Mollie Wiitanen was the wife of Bill's uncle, Fred Lynch, the brother of his mother Harriet. Mollie was raised in Douglas, Alaska where she met Fred, who would become a famous Irish tenor for KOMO radio.

will ever catch up. I wrote Betty last night for the first time since her new job.

Spent Saturday night with the George Biner's and maybe it was my last. The rumor is going around that this is to be a "closed post" from now on. Not even visitors at the gate. The morale is low enough now without an added blow.

Uncle George wants me to tell you of the new romance in the family, Dad. I guess Uncle Gus[61] is planning a new marriage. I don't know what the set-up is but I guess he is serious about it. You ought to have heard George's discourse on "young love."

I haven't seen Joe Webster or Tom in weeks. This school takes up every spare minute I have. We have about five more weeks to go here and then out of the hole and into the air again.

Am sending along a letter I got from Hugh. I feel pretty low when I think I should be getting my wings with them at the end of next month. However, maybe I will be lucky enough to have one of them fly my bomber for me. Well, I have to

---

[61] Gustave Biner (1886-1962) was an older brother of Bill's father. He was married to Florence Tetreaut and they raised ten children. His brother George seems to have the idea that Gus plans to divorce Florence and marry some Irish girlfriend. Gus and Florence did not get divorced.

close. Don't be mad if I don't write quickly enough from now on. Time is awfully valuable.

Love to all,

Bill

July 30, 1942

Dear Folks,

I've put the books aside for a while to dash this off. Just finished another course (Maps & Charts) but I don't know how I came out. We are taking so much all at once it's like throwing mud on a barn. Some of it sticks but most of it falls off.

All I know about Uncle Gus is that he is getting a divorce and remarrying. She is some Irish woman who hangs out in the same place he does. This is what George told me. Other than that, you will have to write George.

I am sitting outside the barracks writing this in the sun. Getting quite proud of my tan. You can send me donuts for my birthday if you want to. Otherwise I don't need anything. There are no army stores in Ellensburg; otherwise you could send me some socks.

How did Bob like Kay Murphy?[62] She is the best looking of the three girls, but they all look

---

[62] This is possibly the younger sister of a girl that Bill was interested in, Jeanne Murphy from Seattle. In the

somewhat alike. Mother included. Speaking of Bob, I have something for the runt I will send along one of these days.

We are working on real bombing problems now and they certainly are tough. There's more to this than looking through a sight. Wish I was back with Hugh and the gang. They are in the best part of their training right now.

I may go into L.A. to see some of the G. Biner's again. I have a good time with them. Went to Laguna last Saturday. No more for now. Have to go out in the dust and drill for an hour.

Love to all,

Bill

P.S. Now Sqd. 91

August 5, 1942

Dear Mother & Dad & all,

Got the box yesterday but the cookies were pretty badly shaken apart. Nevertheless, they were welcomed. But Mother there is no use in insuring

---

1940 census there is a William and Nellie Murphy in Seattle with three teenage daughters; Jeanne, Kathleen (Kay?) and Helen. Since Bob moved to Seattle to attend school perhaps he was hooked up with the sister of Bill's girlfriend.

food to me. It is just money wasted. Thanks again.

Had a wonderful weekend with the George Biner's. It turned into quite a party in my honor. [63] "Pappy" Heinz, a Dutchman from Chicago[64] and a kid from San Francisco were with me. Pappy stayed all night but the other fellow and his date naturally didn't. I have a picture of Pappy & me taken at the Casa Manana where Cab Calloway[65] was playing. After all these years I killed two birds and saw the Mills Brothers[66] at the Florentine Gardens in the same night. Quite an event for me.

Got a beautiful Ronson lighter from George and Helen[67], a sewing kit from Sheila[68] and a

---

[63] Bill turned 22 on August 3, 1942.

[64] The editor regrets to say that he has failed to determine the exact identity of "Pappy" Heinz, although he was clearly one of Bill Biner's best friends during the war. There is no record of a Heinz in any of Bill Biner's military papers. Bob Biner, Bill's brother, cannot recall a Pappy Heinz. There is a John Hines in Bill's bomb group during his second tour, but there is no way to know if this is the Pappy Heinz he refers to in so many of his letters. The editor would appreciate any information leading to the identity of Pappy Heinz.

[65] Cab Calloway (1907-1994) was an African American jazz musician, singer and bandleader. Among his many famous hit songs was "Minnie the Moocher."

[66] The Mills Brothers was a popular African American jazz quartet from Ohio.

[67] Helen Kathryn Chandler (1907-2000) was the wife of George Biner.

combination shoe polisher and clothes brush from Tommy[69]. Also had a birthday cake with an American flag on it. Pretty swell of them, don't you think? I went to bed about 4:00, leaving Pappy and the host & hostess in the kitchen mixing tall ones and telling tall ones. It is the most carefree household I have ever been in. George isn't working, but apparently has made enough lately to tide him over for quite a while. The whole family kids him about going on the bum. Saw a sketch he drew of Grandpa[70] and it is really great. Have you seen it?

However, I still wish I had spent the weekend at home with all of you. The surprise is still a surprise, but can tell you it isn't Geiger Field. That would be a surprise to me. Be sure to compliment John through the Pooler's for me. The fellow is doing alright by himself.

Love, Bill

---

[68] Sheila Biner was Bill's cousin and the daughter of George and Helen Biner.

[69] Tommy Biner was Bill's cousin and the son of George and Helen Biner.

[70] Bill is referring to his paternal grandfather, Theophil Biner, who was born in 1855 in Randa, Switzerland and died in 1926 in Los Angeles.

August 11, 1942

Dear Folks,

Late answering your letter once again but our schedule seems to increase in tempo as we enter the final stages. We should leave here before the month runs out.

I have finished my math and physics – passed both – have only meteorology to get by now. These, along with code, are our main subjects. I hate to admit it but I am becoming a whiz at code. Have a little system worked out now and picked up another 50 cents today. Every other day we have a "code check" and I bet some fellow who thinks he is good and the highest grade wins. It's pretty hard to beat a 100% and that's what I usually get. Oh me!

Got a card from BettyWebster for my birthday and one from the Moredhorsts's.[71] Not to forget the one from Freddie[72]. Pretty good eye you have, Fritzy old pal. The pipe arrived and it certainly is a beauty. The only Kirsten[73] in the squadron, and

---

[71] The Moordharst family lived next door to the Biner family in Ellensburg. Lillian and Ray Moordharst had two young daughters, Robin and Virginia, who were nine and eight years old respectively at this time. Ray was a butcher.

[72] Freddie is another nickname for Bill's little sister Fredericka, though not used as often as Fritzy.

[73] Kirsten of Seattle designs premier smoking pipes. It is still in operation.

the only one I have seen of the same color. Thanks a million. With my pipe and lighter I am pretty well equipped. I use a Texan's tobacco. He sleeps in the bunk under me.

Glad to hear you got a raise, Dad; it's about time. With only two dead-beats on your hands now you ought to be able to see daylight pretty soon. Got a card from Bob enroute. [74] He said it was his last good time before the army got him. Is it possible that the draft will get him soon? Hope he can start school and C.P.T. this fall and get out of it. See that he takes math also. It certainly is important.

Think I will see all the relatives this week. It may be the last weekend I get out here. Pappy Heinz and I were confined last Sat. and Sunday and had to walk punishment tours because Uncle George brought us back late. It was a good thing though. I got a good rest when I wasn't marching up and down with a rifle. Had five hours to walk off. Forgot how many miles we estimated. Plenty though.

See by the papers that the Washington Redskins are training in San Diego now. Wonder if the

---

[74] Fresh out of high school Bob went on a road trip with a couple of buddies to Yellowstone National Park. They packed the car with rejected bottles of beer from his dad's brewery.

Hare boys[75] are with them again. I'm going to try and get in touch with them. Incidentally, Nick Daviscourt,[76] one of our ends, is down here now.

I think I'll get a pair of gabardine slacks this Sat. in town. They are officers but we can wear them and they certainly look neat. I'll be able to wear them for quite a few months yet.

Have some past newspapers I will mail when I get enough gathered. Have you noticed the publicity the bombardiers are getting now? Will let you know how this weekend goes. Thanks again for the pipe.

Love to all,

Bill

September 2, 1942

Dear Mother & Dad,

They informed us last night that we are to leave this afternoon. I don't mind leaving but where they are sending us is the rub. We are going to Hobbs Field, New Mexico– a hundred and fifty

---

[75] Ray Hare (1917-1975) and Cecil Hare (1919-1963) were running backs at Gonzaga University and both played for the Washington Redskins. Bill was their teammate at Gonzaga. He was a left guard.

[76] Nick Daviscourt Jr. (1918-1970) was a friend from Ellensburg and the son of Nick Daviscourt, Sr. (1887-1960), a nationally known professional wrestler from Ellensburg.

miles from nowhere, and brand new. There will only be eighty cadets and it will be the first class to go there, so maybe we will get a little break. However, it means living in tents probably. No swimming pool or air-conditioned barracks!

Another thing, I can't ask you to come down for graduation because of the long trip. It is right on the border of Texas. You can get a map and look it up. We may be able to get a ten-day furlough and I could meet you in L.A. though. We will just have to wait and see what the future has in store.

Apparently, Fritzy didn't have the presents when you wrote last. The chocolate should have beaten the card, and the set should have arrived the day after the card.

We leave this afternoon by train and we won't get there until Saturday. Gives you an idea of the distance. If you have enough time and would like to see the U.S.A. you can still come, but if not I will understand perfectly. Please don't feel disappointed because I have a feeling my bad luck has run out by now, and from now on in everything will turn out O.K.

My new address is: A/C Biner, W.D., AAFAFS Hobbs Field, Hobbs, New Mexico

AAFAFS is for your benefit: Army Air Force Advanced Flying School.

Will send some cards enroute – and hope you work things out O.K. with the brewery, Dad.[77]

Love to all, Bill

September 3, 1942

(From a postcard written aboard the train and postmarked in Winslow, Arizona. It shows a cowboy tackling a steer in the desert which was taken from an original oil painting by the noted cowboy artist and poet, L.H. "Dude" Larsen.[78])

Dear Folks,

We are "deep in the heart of Arizona" and going fast. This part of the state isn't too bad. We are up pretty high and climbing all the time. Someone just said we were near Flagstaff. You could fool me.

Love, Bill

---

[77] He could not work things out as the Ellensburg Brewery closed due to the rationing of malted barley.
[78] Lewis H. "Dude" Larsen (1909-1997) was a cattleman, artist, poet and politician who lived in Kanab, Utah.

Hobbs, New Mexico[79]

September 6, 1942

Dear Folks,

We got in here about midnight Friday and we slept in the Pullmans. It's really brand new. The contractors are still at work and will be for another three weeks. Our barracks are pretty good. There are two to a room and the rooms are good size. Ten rooms to a barrack. In any other post they would be "bachelor officer's quarters."

I don't know, but from what I can gather, being the first eighty cadets here, some of us have a good chance at becoming instructors. I only hope I am good enough to qualify. There are only two planes on the field so far, but we don't start flying for two weeks yet so that doesn't mean anything. I looked one over last night and the maze of instruments in the bombardier's nose scared me a little. Never saw so many electrical gadgets and switches before. The bombsight wasn't in, of course, but that will only add to the complications.

---

[79] Hobbs Army Airfield opened in September, 1942 and Bill was part of the first class of 80 cadets and 20 instructors. This turned out to be the only class of bombardiers trained at the base. 69 of the 80 graduated on November 21, 1942. The airfield then became a multi-engine pilot training school. Hobbs was decommissioned in 1948.

I believe our training on the bombsight and other class work begins tomorrow at 7:00. We also go to school after supper for two or three hours.

This is beautiful flying country, can't see a hill for hundreds of miles. There are innumerable oil wells around us and each one burns waste gas at night. As a result, the country looks like it is on fire. The Texas border is only five miles away, but we can't go across because of an oil boom-town[80] and its riff-raff. Our C.O., a colonel who flew in the first war, said he was getting one of the hotels in Hobbs to put in a Cadet Club for us, also, we are to have our own private dances, etc. As yet none of us has been to town so can't give you any information.

We filled out five questionnaires yesterday. One was for our commission. We'll start getting measured for uniforms pretty soon. Right now I am anxious to get a look at that bombsight and see if I can master it.

Spent a few hours in El Paso, Texas on the way down and it is quite a large town. The oil and cattle millionaires have some beautiful homes high up on the hills in town. From the drive there you can see hundreds of miles down into the Mexican Rio Grande valley. Quite a sight. We

---

[80] Bill is probably referring to Denver City, Texas, in the heart of the massive Wasson Oil Field, where oil wells were first drilled in 1935.

also went across into Juarez and came back glad we were Americans, if even we were at war.

Chow time is only a few minutes off and I had better get dressed. Forgot to tell you that I got your letter yesterday with the good news. That was one of the best letters I've had in months. Don't worry about coming down – we'll work out something. Tell Bette Webster I'm sorry I can't see her – and I really am. Also that I will answer her last letter.

The ten is for Bob. I owed it to him too long. How is the runt behaving himself lately?

Love to all, Bill

P.S. Don't use all the war-paint at once, Fritzy.

September 30, 1942

Dear Folks,

Just a few lines during a few spare moments caught on the fly. Speaking of flying, that's what we are doing a lot of now that we have doubled our working hours. Went on two mission's yesterday afternoon alone.

Don't worry about our flying here Mother. At the other bombardier schools there are a great many more planes, and also advanced pilot training planes. Where you have the two combined you have an occasional mid-air collision. Here, there is only about a one-in-a-million chance of that. If I had the time and paper I could explain the situation, but until I see you please take my word for it.

Passed my physical for commission today – tomorrow we get fitted for uniforms. Monday we had our ring sizes taken. Our class rings are really nice. There is not a little pride in us over the fact that we are to be the only class to graduate from Hobbs, and that we are being graduated a month earlier than the other schools.

There is a rumor going around that we may get furloughs and another that we are to move and open up a new field. Nothing official, of course! However, I would give anything for a furlough.

If my bombing continues to improve they will ship me on a B-17 to Berlin right away or make an instructor out of me. Boy, I sure love this. It has piloting beat seven ways to Sunday.[81] Five have washed out so far se we are hitting the ball pretty hard. It would break my heart to miss out now. I can feel those wings and bars on me now.

I don't know what you should do, Bob. If I were in your shoes I would stick to the math and physics.

---

[81] Meaning "No matter how you look at it, the outcome will always be the same." In other words Bill thought that being a bombardier was far better than being a pilot.

It won't be so tough then at Santa Ana, (which isn't really bad), and take it from me, if you ever get there, put bombardiering as your first choice. You can always go back to pilot training, but I don't think you will. You would be put in pursuits and they are death traps, and nothing can equal this egg dropping. I have seen all the angles and I know from experience. These big ships are like Pullman cars and the bombardier is the cheese.

Love, Bill

P.S. How's the new job coming, Dad? Hear you are an "eager beaver" with a white coat.[82]

October 12, 1942

Dear Bette,

Well old gal, I really am sorry for not answering you sooner, but the days just slipped by unnoticed. We are flying day and night, besides attending long classes on navigation and the like, and somehow I don't know where September went.

In nineteen more days I will be candidate for commission as 2nd Lt. USAAC. However, we won't

---

[82] Bill Sr. had accepted a job as assistant brewmaster for Sick's Seattle Brewing & Malt Company following the closure of the Ellensburg Brewery. Sick's brewed the popular Rainier Beer. The building that housed the brewery remains a Seattle landmark and is located beside Interstate 5. It is now the headquarters of Tully's Coffee.

be able to get them until the 27th of November, finished or not. The other schools graduate their 42-16 class on that date and ours goes through Congress with theirs. We are a month ahead of any school in the country and also have the lowest circular error. Pretty hot bombardiers I would say. The engineers have been rebuilding "shacks" (10'x10' wooden buildings) ever since we arrived. I blew the slats off two of them myself today. "Shacks" are little diamond-shaped chicken-coops, one for the center of each target. They look like pinpoints from 12,000 feet and a bombardier's dream is to hit one with every bomb in the plane. A fellow in the next room from me hit 4 out of 5 two weeks ago but he hasn't hit one since I think. However, if a fellow puts one inside the 100 foot circle every time he is considered "hot."

I really like this 100% better than piloting and I hope Bob can get into it if he has to join. I would like to be his instructor. We are to move to Deming, N.M. when we graduate, but the rumors have it that we might get a furlough first. It is another new field and they don't expect a new class until December. In the meantime, I am keeping my fingers crossed. Going home for a week or two is too good to be true. Also, I haven't graduated yet. A couple wild bombs and I will be on the outside, looking in. I can't let that happen. Keep on praying Betty.

I'm glad Dad likes his new job. I really think it will amount to something. Uncle George has a soft job in an aircraft plant and gets $500 a month for it. He certainly wishes he could be back in uniform though. [83] Uncle Paul is 3A with the army now.[84] I sure miss them all. Never knew two families who had so much fun all the time. I don't think the George Biners have ever worried about a thing except maybe the new threatened shortage of bottled spirits. It was always a tonic to visit them. The Jones' likewise – better than going to any of Paul's movies was a visit with them.

Your shirt came back from its first laundry visit here a different color. It is now a pale cream and quite unmilitary. These southwest laundries just don't know how to handle a good piece of merchandise. Speaking of clothes, we were measured for ours a week ago - $150 worth. And then they wonder why we are broke. Also, an old gold and ruby class ring set us back $26. Looks like I'll thumb my way home.

How's the Navy cadet? Corresponding faithfully? Wish someone would write me.

Love, Bill

---

[83] George was a veteran of World War I but contracted polio upon his return from combat duty.

[84] With a draft rating of RE-3A, Paul Jones was not eligible for reenlistment. This was probably due to his age at the time. He originally enlisted during World War I.

October 19, 1942

Dear Folks,

Finally got around to writing again. Just came down from a 12,000-foot mission where I dropped ten bombs. Have only seven more bombs at 12,000 and will be through with my day bombs. Will have only night bombs to finish up on before graduating. Still keeping my fingers crossed though, they washed two more yesterday, and I believe two more will get it today.

Our commandant has put a furlough request into Santa Ana for us from the 10th to the 27th when we are supposed to be commissioned. If any other place than Santa Ana had to pass on it, I would say it was a cinch. But, as it is, one can only be optimistic and hope. All the officers here are in favor of it, but Santa Ana is West Coast Hdqs.

No Mother, the army did not buy our class rings. We had to lay out $26.50 for them, but I think it was worth it. Had my picture taken last week, but in Hobbs, where no one ever heard of rushing, it will take another ten days before I can get them. I may even be on the verge of leaving for home by then. I only had three prints to choose from so don't expect a very good picture.

Served Mass yesterday for the first time in years and had stage fright.[85] Managed to get by somehow, though.

Got a letter from Betty's Biner and Webster the other day. Betty B. seems to like her job pretty well. By the way, where is the Pooler family now? Still in Ellensburg? Joe Webster got sick-leave and spent some time home, the lucky stiff.

Well, one more week after this and I'm all set. Keep praying and maybe I'll see you all in a little while.

Love to all,

Bill

P.S. What are you doing now, Dad? Also, Jack Costello[86] is only thirty miles from our next post (Deming). He is at Fort Bliss, El Paso, Tex.

October 26, 1942

Dear Folks, just came down from a night mission and read your letter. Thought I'd answer it right away. Saturday our flying officers told us that we were to be commissioned next Sunday, given a

---

[85] Bill served as an altar boy, assisting a priest in the celebration of a Catholic Mass.

[86] John A. "Jack" Costello was a classmate of Bill Biner at Gonzaga High School in Spokane. The son of John and Elizabeth Costello, Jack enlisted in Spokane on July 2, 1942.

ten-day furlough and then to report to Salt Lake. However, Blue Monday has rolled around and the latest news is that we have to wait until late in November before the big day.

I still haven't seen any written order or anything so I cannot plan a darn thing. Our uniforms are here and our wings, but they don't seem to be doing us much good. I wish we could hear something definite for a change, but that's the army. I'm only hoping they have started this new talk to disguise our real movement. It seems everyone in town knew that we were to leave next Sunday.

Jeanne is now working for the Navy in Seattle - $140 a month. With her salary and my future one it would come to $465 a month. Maybe I ought to do something about it. (Do I hear you scream?)

Have only two more exams; one tomorrow and one Wednesday, and then I'll be through – I hope. These last weeks will certainly drag if we have to stay.

I don't know what kind of watch bombardier's wear either, unless it's like the one I already have. We all like fancy pajamas though. I haven't had any since I left primary. Also, I could use an officer's spread eagle for my cap, or shirts or sox. Whatever you would like to get.

No more for now. Have to rest the old eyes. They've been under quite a strain lately.

Love to all, Bill

At this point there is a gap in Bill's letters. He graduated from Hobbs, along with 68 other cadets, on November 21, 1942, and became a commissioned officer (2nd Lt.) as a bombardier. During his two months at Hobbs, Bill logged 51 hours and 40 minutes of flight time. This was confirmed on his records by Major Keith S. Wilson.

By order of Colonel Bailey, on a special orders extract signed by Captain William K. Houston, Bill was assigned to the 2nd Air Force, 18th Replacement Wing at the Army Air Base in Salt Lake City. He was to report without delay.

Although the following letter was not dated it appears to have been written on November 23, 1942 as Bill was on his way to Salt Lake City where he would then be directed to Gowen Field in Boise, Idaho for tactical training. He would remain at Gowen Field until February 5, 1943.

Hotel Whitman
Pueblo, Colorado
Dear Folks,

We all decided to stay overnight here in Pueblo. The train ride was getting to be tiring and this looked like a nice town, and is, of about 65,000. Quite a change from New Mexico. We are on our way to Salt Lake but will only be there long enough to be assigned to a new field. My chances on getting up into the Northwest look pretty good and I'm keeping my tongue in my cheek.

We had a nice ceremony Saturday morning and then we were so busy until we left that I didn't think we would ever get away. Papers and red tape galore.

You have the barracks bags by now no doubt. The clothes in the white laundry bag I would like washed. The other stuff I am getting out of the way. Fritzy can have her pick of the flight caps. I also promised Tommy one of the dark ones. Anything that you can use, go ahead. Maybe the shirts and pants will fit someone: Dad or Grandpa. Good roughing material.

Colorado is a pretty state and I am looking forward to the Grand Gorge[87] scenery tomorrow. Will write again when I can and will send my next permanent address as soon as I am able.

Love to all,

Bill

---

[87] Bill is referring to the Rio Grande Gorge along the Arkansas River in southern Colorado. He would have passed through it on his way to Salt Lake City from Pueblo.

Gowen Field, Boise, Idaho
November 30, 1942
Dear Folks,

At last I am somewhat settled here but still in quite a daze. Tactical is altogether different from what we have been through before; but one thing is still unchanged – four hours of ground school every day.

We have nice quarters, (a room to myself) and dandy officer's club (where I am writing this) and an officer's mess that beats anything I have ever seen. I am eating again now, and really enjoying this. We can go in any hour out of the twenty-four and have anything we want. After being a cadet so long I feel like I am being pampered.

We fly B-17's here – just what I wanted. However, I would have taken anything to get up to Ephrata, Wash. As it was, I missed going by one name. Boise is a swell town and you can't beat this field for comfort, but Ephrata with all its inconveniences is still closer to home. There is a chance I might go to Walla Walla from here though. Keep your fingers crossed. We work long hours here and are on the go day and night, but it is really O.K.

What has Bob decided on? Tell him that the top 20% of all classes receive regular commissions and the others are flight officers with all our privileges. Also, if he goes to Sun Valley, he has to stop off here and see me. We aren't very far from there.

Here's hoping you have a house by now.

Love to all, Bill

Dec. 14, 1942
Dear Mother & All,

Received your letter and the surprising news about Dad's sudden exit from Sick Enterprises[88]. Deals like that make my blood boil. I like the idea of his trip to L.A. though. If he doesn't land anything there he ought to try Paul out on the idea of impersonations. Seriously though, if he does get anything have him get it in <u>writing.</u>

Bob has my heartiest congratulations and sympathy. He ought to do well in his branch and if he thinks he might like pilot training tell him to try it out. However, it might mean a second stretch of Santa Ana, and I don't think he would go for that. Tell him to take some galoshes along. It is the rainy season and adobe mud is something unique in mud. Also, have him see about his eyes like I did – it will pay dividends.

---

[88] Perhaps Bill Sr. was under the impression that he would become head brewmaster, but was passed over. Hence the reference to "get it in writing."

Do you think Dad will be home for Christmas? I got kind of sore when I was put in vault O.D.[89] Christmas Eve. But when I think of where some of the boys will be Christmas I don't think I am so badly off.

I hear from Jeanne every other day and just between you and me Mother, I am working on all the angles to change my status. I may be in this country for quite a while and a change in status would up my pay to $325 a month. However, Christmas is just around the corner, I haven't had any officer's pay yet, and "times a wasting." Please keep this under your bonnet, Mother.

The laundry came today with the candy. Thanks a million for everything. And don't worry, Mother, everything is going to be alright.

Love, Bill

Gowen Field Officers' Club
Boise, Idaho
December 19, 1942

Dear Bette,

I am rushed as usual but I have owed you a letter for so long now, that I couldn't put it off any longer. Besides, I have to keep in your good graces – it is the Christmas season!

---

[89] Bill was probably scheduled to be the "O.D.", (Officer of the Day), to guard the concrete vault that protected the top secret Norden bombsight.

I thought that after I was commissioned I would have more time to myself, but actually have less than when I was at Hobbs. I guess this school keeps up until I actually go overseas. It's beginning to get me down though.

It's hard to answer your question about presents. About the only thing I can think of are good dress gloves, scarves, etc. Good Housekeeping Mag. usually has good Christmas suggestions, also Esquire. Why not browse through them? Anything bulky is definitely out, because we usually live out of our flight bags (of which the army has given me two). Whatever you send him, your love-light I mean, I am sure will be appreciated. How about a lock of your hair? Helpful, ain't I?

I'm having a H--- of a time myself. Not having been to town for a week, and with my travel and ration money between a good Christmas and a poor one, I don't know what to do. I hear the stores are generous with charge accounts though. I suppose Mother told you about my being bomb sight vault O.D. Christmas Eve? It lasts until 4:00 Christmas Day. Some fun, eh?

How's your love life coming along? Or am I being brazen? I'm not afraid to say that as soon as the opportunity presents itself I believe I'll go off the deep end. However, there are so many problems; I don't rightly know where to begin.

What do you think about the latest kick in the pants Dad got? I certainly hope he gets something in or around L.A. It's almost time he and Mother got a break. It's going to be a bad Christmas for Mother, but there will be good ones again. Remember how they used to be? We always had so much – and there were always so many who didn't.

No more for now, old girl. Merry Christmas.

Love, Willie[90]

December 1942 (*A Tuesday but otherwise day uncertain*)

Dear Folks,

No pens available so excuse, please, the pencil. Received your letters yesterday and was glad to get them. The "affair of the missing barracks bags" makes me mad, tough. They should have been there two weeks ago. It cost me $3.60 to send them and that also makes me mad. I'll run thru my papers and see if I can find the receipts.

We are pretty busy here and sleep at all hours. However, I am putting on too much weight. Will have to do something about that. Had some good news given to me yesterday. I am to be bomb

---

[90] Since Bill only signs his name as "Willie" when writing to his sister Betty, one can conclude that this was her nickname for him.

vault officer of the day from 3:30 Christmas Eve until 3:30 Christmas Day. Just my luck to have mine come up at that time. "Twas the night before Christmas and all thru the vault, not a saboteur strayed, 'fore Biner was about."

I was firing .50 caliber machine guns today and my ears are still ringing. Those guns are small cannons. And there are a slew of them on our B-17's. Not getting in much flying lately on account of the weather, but plenty of school. Brought some long-handled drawers[91] to keep out the cold. My blood certainly thinned on me.

What I hear from the Queen[92], Mother, is for my knowledge alone. Suffice to say, I hear plenty and often.

Will try to be better at this writing and <u>please</u> stop worrying.

Love to all, Bill

---

[91] Long johns.

[92] Bill is referring to Jeanne Murphy, a girl from Seattle that he was wooing at the time. Bill's sister Fritzi remembers Jeanne as, "A society girl." She worked for the Navy.

Part Two: 1943

The first few letters that Bill wrote to his family in early 1943 do not have dates on them. He would write the day of the week, but not the actual date. The first five letters were most likely written in January and February 1943, while Bill finished his training at Gowen Field in Boise and the Walla Walla Army Air Base. Bill left Gowen Field on February 5th. He was stationed in Walla Walla, Washington from February 6th through March 3rd.

Bill Biner's younger brother, Robert Joseph "Bob" Biner, or "The Runt" as Bill called him, entered in the United States Army Air Corps on February 12, 1943 in Seattle. He was 20 years old. At the time he was living with his maternal grandparents, Dan and Mate Kendall Lynch, and attending classes at Seattle College (now Seattle University). His first letter was written four days before he joined the Air Corps. He writes to his older sister Betty, who was teaching in Kennewick, Washington.

Bob Biner would become a Staff Sergeant. Following deployment he was stationed at Old Buckenham Air Field near Attenborough and Norwich, England in the Eighth Air Force, Second Air Division, and 453rd Bomb Group. He remains a member of these associations 70 years later. Bob flew in a B-24 Liberator first as a belly gunner and later, when the belly turret was removed to make room for a bombsight, as a waist gunner. He flew 17 missions, all of them over Germany, in the climatic period between November, 1944, and February, 1945.

For the remainder of this book Bill and Bob's letters will be interspersed and presented chronologically. Bob's letters will be differentiated from Bill's through italic font.

Gowen Field Officers' Club
Friday (January 1943)
Dear Folks,

I know you are burning up and I don't blame you, but things have been pretty unsettled lately. They flew us out to Walla Walla suddenly and kept us there until last night and then sent us back by train. "Us" are the combat crews in my outfit who were to take second phase training there.

As soon as we arrived we could see that it was only going to be temporary and we didn't know where we were to go, hence my reluctance to write until something definite happened. The way it stands now, we are to start our first phase all over again because our pilots don't have enough time (hours). It doesn't hurt my feelings because as a post, Walla Walla is a stinker.

What has been happening in Seattle of any importance that concerns the family? Everything is Jake with me[93] and am still hanging around until Bob shows up as co-pilot for our crew. We don't have one now, and from the look of things we'll be here until he does get through. Incidentally, the flight officers are beginning to come to the field, and the only difference is their blue and gold bar. So he needn't worry about being an officer.

Please forgive me and tell me all the news. Especially the job situation.

Love to all, Bill

Gowen Field
Tuesday *(in January)*
Dear Folks,

You are probably angrier with me than ever right now but it can't be helped. When I say that I haven't had my clothes off in two days I speak the truth. Our crew has been flying 3 hrs. on and three off for three days now. We have missed meals and sleep. When it is a toss-up whether we eat or sleep, we usually crawl on a cot and sleep. I would certainly welcome a flock of bad weather all of a sudden.

I expect a visit from Jeanne pretty soon and it won't be so hot if I have to fly all the time.

---

[93] "Everything is Jake with me" is believed to be of Australian origin and means, "all is satisfactory." It is seldom used today.

I was certainly glad to hear that you landed a job Dad.[94]   Never could picture you working in a shipyard. Maybe this one will turn out better than the others. Let's hope so.

Got a letter from my long lost pal Ted[95] and a picture of a seven month old boy, who, in Ted's own words, "has his brother and brother-in-law drooling with envy."   It seems the others have enough girls to start a WAAC[96] regiment. Right now he is in Port Alberni[97] in the intelligence dept. but still a P.F.C.[98]

There isn't much of anything to relate except that I got a card from Bill Flynn. He's at Rapid City, South Dakota where I may go for my final training. Also that I'm about three weeks behind on letters to L.A.

---

[94] Bill Sr. landed a job as a brewmaster for Silver Springs Brewery in Port Orchard, Washington. The six-story brewery was known as, "The tallest building in Kitsap County." Silver Springs was originally Kitsap Beer. He would be there for only a few months before securing a job as brewmaster for Aero Club Beer at the East Idaho Brewing Company in Pocatello, Idaho.

[95] Ted Burns was Bill's best boyhood pal. They grew up together in Nelson, British Columbia when Bill's father was the brewmaster for the Kooteney Brewing Company in Trail and Nelson, B.C. from 1928-36. Ted's parents ran the resort at nearby Ainsworth Hot Springs.

[96] Women's Auxiliary Army Corps.

[97] Port Alberni is located on Vancouver Island in British Columbia, Canada.

[98] Private First Class.

Tell Bob to have a little patience and he'll see all the army he wants.[99]

Love to all, Bill

Gowen Field Officers' Club
Friday *(In January)*
Dear Bette,

I should feel like a heel for not writing sooner, but I'm not going to use the old one about working hard and long. The fact is, we aren't working hard, but the hours are long and I've been living round-the-clock for a month now.

To give you an idea of my condition, my pilot and I went to the dispensary this morning to take a typhus shot and two minutes after taking mine, I keeled over in a dead faint. I probably would have been grounded for good if it wasn't for the fact that I hadn't had any breakfast or sleep. I hope that is the first and last time I'll ever faint. (At least in the Air Corps).

Expect a visit from Jeanne any day now. Looks like I'll have to pull a few strings and get out of some of these flights. We've decided to put things off until this mess is over. Whether it is the best thing to do now, I haven't quite decided.

---

[99] Robert Joseph Biner enlisted in the United States Army Air Corps on February 12, 1943 in Seattle. He was immediately sent to Fresno, California to commence his basic training.

Sorry I didn't stay in "Walla Walla" longer, but may go back next month. Those figures didn't deserve all the praise you gave them – I think you were putting it on a little thick, weren't you? The fact is, you presented my toughest problem and I had to do all my shopping late one afternoon just before the deadline. By the way, when is your birthday?

It's my turn to thank you now. The pajamas were welcome even if they were a little big. The book is very good, ate all the nuts, use the soap now and again when I begin to crawl and I needed the dictionary. I like to impress the Queen with my vocabulary. Thanks a million Shorty, but next time buy a rug or lamp for the apartment.

Well, no more for now. Write when you can.

Love, "Willie"

P.S. Guess you were also relieved to hear of dad's new job, eh?

Feb. 8, 1943
2333 N. 57th
Seattle, Wash.
Dear Bette,

I hope you don't think that I wait for a present before I ever write, but the truth is there is nothing for me to write about here. The case came Thursday and the lighter came Sat, they're both swell, and thanks a lot. How did you know those were just the things I wanted?

Bill sure must be taking a beating over there in Boise. That loss of sleep must be pretty hard on a guy. I'm sorry to hear wedding bells aren't going to ring.[100] I was almost counting on having a sister-in-law. By the way, Bill sent me a neat bag. One of those canvas bags like the pilots carry around. They unfold and you can hang your suit up with the bag. They look like this: (Bob makes an arrow to a drawing of a bag). I'm beginning to think my family spoils me. (I'm using both sides of the paper because we haven't much left).

How is your love life getting along now that the poor guy is an ensign? Women are the most cruel and cunning animals alive. I suppose you have a battle plan all worked out to trap the poor devil. (But I wish you luck.) I was really surprised to hear about Red Pattillo.[101] I gave her credit for more brains, but there's no understanding a female. Personally, I feel sorrier for Mickey. Bill

---

[100] Apparently Bob had heard that Bill and Jeanne Murphy indefinitely postponed any plans of marriage.
[101] Franny Pattillo, nicknamed Red because of her hair, was the daughter of Marie Fitterer Pattillo. She was a girlfriend of Bob's when the two attended high school in Ellensburg, where Fanny was living with her grandparents, Frank & Margaret Fitterer. Apparently "Red" had just got engaged with another classmate named Mickey.

Lambert[102] was drafted and he leaves for Fort Lewis on Friday.

Mother sure worries a lot about Bill. I don't know what we're going to do when he gets sent over and I leave for training. If I knew I wouldn't be miserable as a private, I think I would quit the AC[103] just to take a part of the load off her mind.

Don't pay any attention to what Weezy[104] says; she always talks about more than she knows. The sooner Mother moves to Port Orchard the better it will be for me. Then I can room and board out someplace. The way it is now, it's all I can do to keep from declaring open war at Grandma and Gramps.[105] Thanks again for the presents and write again sometimes.

Love, Bob

Gowen Field Officers' Club
Monday *(Feb. 1, 1943)*
Dear Folks,

---

[102] Orrin "Bill" Lambert (1924-1993) was a high school friend from Ellensburg. The son of Charles and Vernell Lambert, Bill Lambert enlisted on Feb. 2, 1943.
[103] Air Corps
[104] Louisa Ann "Weezy" Weaver was a high school friend in Ellensburg, the daughter of Ray & May Weaver. She married Doug Griffin.
[105] Bob was living with his grandparents, Dan and Mate Lynch, in Seattle. Although his grandfather was remembered as a tall, jovial leprechaun, his grandmother was much more difficult to be around.

Here I am late again, but nevertheless – here I am.

We finally put all our time in here, had to fly six hours at a stretch to do it last week. We finally started taking box lunches up with us. Also got in a little "stick-time" the other night. That is, I flew the ship for a while, also yesterday morning.

We are ready to pull out tomorrow or the next day, don't know just where yet, but I think it will be Walla Walla. However, we may not stay there over a week after we get there.

I've got something for Bob's birthday, wasn't able to get it until today but I think it is worth waiting for. Jeanne couldn't get off to come down here but she may be able to make it to Walla Walla if I stay there long enough.

Had some good news the other day – found out I have $141 income tax to pay. I'm afraid to think what it will cost next year. Enclosed is a card I want Dad to sign and send to the address on the card. I am having $100 taken out of my check each month and sent there. One allotment is already on its way.

Has Bob heard when he is to be sent to Santa Ana? I have an extra summer flying suit that I am trying to exchange – if I can get his size. If not maybe, he can get it cut down to his size.

Well, no more for now. I'll let you know what's cooking when it cooks.

Love to all, Bill

W.W.A.A.F. Officers Mess
Walla Walla, Washington[106]
Thursday *(February 11, 1943)*
Dear Folks,

Am fairly well settled now and able to give you an idea of what we do here. This is the bombardier's phase, and so, on every mission we drop bombs and machine gun targets. So every mission is a lot of fun as far as I'm concerned. Next phase will be fun too, when all we do is cross-country work. That is where the navigator gets his workout.

Our bombing range is eighty miles away, we skirt Kennewick and Pasco on the way out, and it only takes a few minutes to get there. Our crew is on the noon to midnight shift and next week we get one 24 hour pass a week so I ought to have a little free time while you are here.

I have to leave pretty soon and fly a Link trainer. An hour of Link in civilian life cost $30 and I get it for nothing. It comes under the pilot's training, but some day we may have to take over the ship and fly by instruments, so they give it to bombardiers too. I've already done a little flying

---

[106] Bill was stationed in Walla Walla from February 6 to March 3, 1943.

in the 17 but not enough to satisfy me. Actually, they fly very easily.

I hope we have better weather when you are here Mother, but I guess we can't have everything. Well, let me know when you expect to arrive and I'll make reservations at the Marcus Whitman.[107] Rooms are scarce.

Love to all, Bill

After a quick visit from his parents Bill was off briefly to Roberts Field in Redmond, Oregon, which served as a bomber base for the Army Air Corps. He then moved on to Rapid City, South Dakota and over the next two months Bill and his crew practiced lengthy flights and night flights as the final preparation before actual deployment overseas. Ironically, they never practiced bailing out with a parachute. Meanwhile Bob was just beginning his basic training.

---

[107] The beautiful Marcus Whitman Hotel opened on September 1, 1928. Still in operation and a popular landmark in Walla Walla, Washington it was named for Marcus Whitman, one of the earliest Euroamerican settlers in eastern Washington. In 1847 Whitman and his wife Narcissa were killed by Cayuse Indians who blamed settlers for intentionally spreading a disease (measles) that was decimating natives but not whites.

Feb 27, 1943
Train

Dear Mom & Dad & Fritz,

I don't know when this will reach you because I don't think they are letting us off the train until we reach Fresno. We didn't have a thing to eat until 9 PM and was I hungry.

We slept two in the lower and one in the upper but I had a good sleep even though I was a trifle crowded. We're about 350 strong now. We packed up about 250 in Portland.

I want you to know I was proud of you at the depot, Mom. You made it a lot easier for me.

There is no more news for now, but as soon as I find out whether I pass or not, I'll let you know.

Love, Bob

P.S. The numbers after our names mean the amount of rations we are allowed. 1 1/3 = 4 meals or 4 bucks.

Pvt. Robert J. Biner
779ᵗʰ T.S.S, B.T.C #8
Barrack #170, Fresno, CA
February 28, 1943

Dear Mom, Dad and Folks,
Well, we arrived in Fresno today 1:30 am. We stayed in the Pullman until 5:30, when they

picked us up. The town is nice looking from what we saw going through.

I don't know how long we have to stay here, but we think it will be around 3 weeks. We've done everything today. We got all of our clothing issues and such. We also took a physical; it was rather light but I don't think I showed up too well. I am on the list for further examination. The doctor acted rather doubtful.

The days here are pretty hot, but the nights are nice and cool. I had a dose of my usual good luck today. While I was getting my uniform (pvt), someone stole my pillow. No one in the barracks took it because I looked. I'll have to buy a new one now and it'll set me back quite a bit.

The food here is certainly nothing to write home about. We had to stay on the train all the way down. All my clothes fit me like a bag. They just don't make them that small. We probably won't be able to leave the camp all the time we're here, but I guess I'll just have to learn to like it.

We are the second bunch of cadets to arrive here. The others came last week. There about as many soldiers here as cadets, and that makes it kinda tuff on us, because they get leave and don't have to drill, and they treat us like dirt. If you want my opinion on the first day of army life, I'll tell you, I don't like it.

Tell Mrs. Butt[108] the stationary is sure coming in handy, and tell Grandma, too. I'll write to you as soon as I get another chance.

Love, Bob

P.S. Give Bumps[109] a hug and a kiss.

March 2, 1943

Dear Mom, Dad and Folks,

Well my third day of army life has come to a close, and I already feel like an old hand. We drilled today (all day) in the sun. In our spare time we did calisthenics and I don't mind telling you I'm really tired.

To get anything around here, you wait in line. We even line up to wash our "mess kits". This camp is really clean. We can't even throw cigarette butts on the ground. We have to go around in groups collecting little bits of paper. We have swell showers and a nice day room. Everything at the P.X. is very reasonable. We get all the gum and

---

[108] Charlotte Greeby Butt (1901-1998) was the next door neighbor of Bob's grandparents in Seattle. The daughter of British immigrants George and Ann Greeby, Charlotte married William J. Butt (1898-1995), a veteran of WW I. Mr. & Mrs. Butt both lived to be 97 and are buried in Seattle's Evergreen Washelli Memorial Park.

[109] Bumps was yet another nickname for the youngest Biner child, Fredericka, who was also known as Fritz, Fritzy, Ignatz and Freddy to her big brothers.

candy we want. We can buy a whole box of bars for 75 cents.

We hear hundreds of rumors all around about the few boys that really make the Air Corps. I haven't been ordered to report for my second physical yet, but I hope they take me pretty quick because the suspense is killing me.

I have certainly picked up a wonderful sunburn on my face. The sun here is really terrific. (Especially when we are drilling). The reason you are getting so many letters is because I have a little spare time now, but if I make primary they might not come so often.

I am sending my bag back. That's orders. My tennis shoes are in them and if I make primary I may want you to send them back along with the pajamas, etc. I just haven't got room for them in the barracks bags. They rouse us out at 5:30 in the morning and were on the go from then on. I have to mail this letter while there still time. Kiss Bumps......Love, Bob

---

Wed, March 3, 1943
Fresno, Cal
Dear Bette,

The 4th day of camp and I feel like it's been a month. I've had a taste of everything, army food (rotten), drilling, and a G.I. issue of clothing that fits like a sack. My army zoot suit,[110] otherwise known as a fatigue outfit, is the only thing I am liable to be wearing for the next two weeks.

We get the basics of drilling, classification lists and a minor physical. Keep up those prayers because I really need some help. You hear all kinds of rumors about the odds of ever getting a commission. I don't think I did too well on my physical, but I'm praying that everything will come out o.k. We have a pretty nice camp here; we have good showers, P.X., recreation rooms and a tavern. This is a fairly new camp; it was built as a concentration camp for Japs.[111] We were about the 2nd group of cadets to arrive and were nothing but privates unassigned. Most of the guys in my barracks are pretty nice. We rise in the morning about 5:30, stand in line to wash, stand in line for breakfast, and then stand in line to wash our mess kits. We spend half of our time standing in line.

The days here are hot and the nights are cold. I am already looking forward to the day they let us

---

[110] The Zoot Suit was the preferred attire of some "cool cats" in the 1940s, particularly within the African American and Hispanic American communities. It consisted of baggy pants with tight cuffs and an oversized suit coat.

[111] Bob's base, known as Hammer Field when he trained there, had been a temporary detention center for Japanese Americans from May 6th to October 30, 1942. At its peak over 5000 people were held there. After processing most were removed to permanent camps.

out of the barracks and into town, but that won't be before a couple of weeks are up.

Has mother come to visit you yet? Is Bill still in Walla Walla? You will have to write a letter now, because I am getting a little blue. I'm not homesick yet, and I have no special girl to write to.

It's 1300 o'clock now and the sergeant will be coming around any minute now with some more duty work for us, so I'd better finish this letter.

Love, Bob

P.S. Don't forget to keep up the prayers. This marching is sure ruining my feet. We have no Catholic Chaplain here, but a Catholic Priest comes from town each Sunday.

Pierre, S.D.[112]
March 9, 1943
Dear Folks,

Just a few lines caught on the fly. I have been looking for forwarded mail, but so far there has been none. We are down here in much the same capacity as we were in Redmond. Namely, an alternate base from which to fly. Just got back from a trip to Minneapolis & St. Paul; Fargo, and Bismarck, N.D. Minneapolis and St. Paul are quite the place. We took off this morning and got back

[112] Bill was sent to a base in Rapid City, South Dakota on March 4, 1943 and was stationed there until April 29, 1943.

this evening eleven hours later. We were in the air the entire time, and as usual, none of us got up early enough to eat breakfast, so we were pretty hungry when we got back.

Took a trip through Iowa and Kansas Tuesday and spent a few hours in Sioux Falls, S.D. on the way back. The crew had the picture taken there so will send some when they arrive.

How is Bob coming along? I'm anxious to hear how he makes out in his new life. Also, to find out why they sent him to Fresno. If by chance you haven't mentioned it yet, don't tell Jeanne I am expecting a leave next month, for reasons of my own.

Just write to my address in Rapid City if you can't get mail here before the 15th, because that is where we will be then.

Love to all, Bill

March 17, 1943

Dear Mom, Dad, and Folks,

Your letter arrived yesterday, Fritz, and it was very nice. The picture looks exactly like me, when my uniform is on. You should write longer letters and more of them. It is raining again today. The only thing we did today was calisthenics. We also attended a few lectures. I'm the only one in the barracks who has a bed partner. I have to sleep with my rifle all week. I dropped a stack of them in drill. I also have trouble keeping in step. The tall guys in front set the pace, and my short legs have to take two steps to keep up with them. We passed in drill inspection in front of the Colonel yesterday. I've never seen so much marching in all my life.

The pictures haven't been developed yet. Did you get a letter asking for five? I really need it in a bad way. I only have 10 cents to my name. I don't know why we're staying here so long. They are giving us the training as if we were always going to be privates. The proportion of cadets who make anything are very low. A lot of the "wash-outs" around here are doing K.P. I am really getting disgusted with the army. Nothing is ever done right. There are two ways of doing things. The right way and the army way. We wouldn't have any fun if we didn't have something to crab about. I am getting in pretty good physical condition anyhow.

Say hello to Dan Drew[113] for me, and tell him I will write as soon as I can find time. The shoes are getting a little easier on my feet.

---

[113] Dan Drew was Bob's boss at Drew-English, Inc. Fine Shoes in Seattle.

Yes, Maw, I did get a short G.I. haircut, but you can't see it because we have to wear hats all the time anyhow. There isn't much to talk about now unless you want to hear me beef.

I'm not homesick yet. That's probably because things are happening so fast, or else it's the lack of home news. If I had some money, I'd eat at the P.X. tonight. The stuff they feed us at the dump here is terrible, and when it is half good, they don't give us enough. I don't do that very often though.

I'm running out of ink so I'll finish it in a different color. The package hasn't arrived here yet. Write soon.

Love, Bob

March 18, 1943

Dear Mom, Dad, and Folks,

Don't expect too much from me in this letter. I got another shot today. I can't even raise my left arm. The sarge got my pictures last night. I couldn't pay for them, but he let me take them anyhow. I will send a few of the better ones, and the rest when I have more room.

Lectures, drilling, clean-up, drilling, shots and more lectures. That's all we do. They keep us on the run all the time, even in our own time. I was going to do my washing tonight but they sprung a lecture on us. I've been going to do my washing ever since I got here. Did you send that package yet Mom? You letter arrived today Mom. It was dated the 16ᵗʰ. Cookies would be very nice if you could send some that would stay fresh in case we were transferred before it arrived. We may leave any day now. Maybe you ought to wait until I get settled. Don't send anything unless it is insured. There are too many mistakes made around here.

Today was clear; tomorrow it will probably be rain. No one can talk to me about the wonderful weather in California. It is 5 to 10 and it'll be lights out in 5 minutes. I just got back from the wash room. We didn't have the lecture after all. The barracks is decorated like a Christmas tree.[114] They won't dry tonight, however. I can't think of anything else to say so I'll cut it short.

Love, Bob

March 20, 1943

Dear Mom, Dad and Folks,

The package came yesterday but I didn't have time to write. We had a G.I. party last nite,[115] "cleaned up the barracks." Today we had a personal inspection. Everyone in our barracks did ok. The flight that came here two days ahead of us left today. That doesn't mean we will leave in

---

[114] With his wet laundry.
[115] General inspection.

two days tho. I hope the money arrives today. If it doesn't I won't be able to make use of the pass I hope to get.

The weather has cleared up considerably. Now the only drawback is chapped lips. The shoe outfit came in handy. I've been using the other guys all the time. We have to polish them every day. The paper and pencils are just what I wanted. Thank you.

We had a pretty good meal this noon, so I feel pretty good. The last few days we've been listening to lectures most of the time and have done very little drilling. The latest "Latrine-o-gram" is we'll be going to some school from here, where we will spend about five months. We never know for sure just where or what we will do from one day to the next. The rumor now is we will spend all day tomorrow-Sunday doing K.P. I hope it is false. There are a lot of "washed out" cadets stationed here, and it is very discouraging to listen to them. As long as I have a chance I'm going to give it everything I have.

I talked the Sgt. out of making me sleep with the rifle. They call me "Junior" around here, but I don't know why. I am writing this letter during lunch hour, so I'll have to make it fast. We've been having lectures on how to use gas masks, rifles, tommy guns, and hand grenades. We are supposed to go to the rifle range one of these days. We also had to take a sniff of real gas. We were put in a room with our gas masks on. Then we were told to take them off and go directly out the door. The room was filled with tear gas. I took one whiff and could hardly make it to the door. The room was filled with lachrymator gas, (tear gas). My eyes burned for 10 minutes. I'll write again as soon as I get a few spare minutes.

Love, Bob

P.S. Did you get the pictures?

Sun. March 21, 1943
Fresno, Cal
Dear Mom, Dad and Folks,

I just came back from mass. It was held in one of the lecture halls. They are building a church here, but probably won't be finished by the time we leave. They are also building a theatre.

We got a pass last night again. Bill cashed a check so we were able to have a pretty fair time. We went bowling and then to a dance. We don't have much time to dance tho, because we are "Cinderella Boys".[116] The sad part of it is I have already spent the five dollars that is on the way. I borrowed $2.50 from Bill to pay the Baron for the pictures.

---

[116] Perhaps Bob means they were expected to be back at the base by midnight.

Everything here is about as expensive as Seattle. They also have sales tax. What I'm trying to say is I'll need another five to tide me over until the end of the month. I'm really not spending foolishly, but when we spend the whole week on the drill field we have to go out on Sat.

It is raining again; this is the rottenest weather I've ever seen. We could talk the Baron out of another pass today but it is even too miserable to leave the barracks.

Another bunch of cadets are coming today. We can have the fun of yelling at them "you'll be sorry" just like the other guys did at us. We didn't believe all the things they told us, but everything was true. Enclosed is a verse of a song that was composed and printed by our flight that expresses our sentiments exactly. There are a few more, but I haven't room for them.

I'm sending a few of the pictures to Betty and few other friends. We took 36 altogether. They issued rain coats the other day, but they only had the large sizes, so we small boys still go unprotected. Some of the boys are down in the other side of the barracks harmonizing. We really have a nice time on Sunday. No lectures, drilling, inspection, details or anything.

Enclosed is a poor sketch of our real artist, Leon Bishop. [117] He is really good. He is going to draw a portrait of me one of these days. I think I'll be able to do as well as he, when I get a little practice.

Say hello to the Lynches, K.O,[118] Fred and all and tell them I'll be writing one of these days.

Love, Bob

March 22, 1943

Dear Bette,

Sorry to wait so long answering your letter, but I have been pretty busy this past week. A week ago yesterday I went to a park outside of town. We took some snap-shots, so I'll send you a few. I received a letter from Bill yesterday. He must be having a swell time, but he'll probably be moving out pretty soon.

Last week we had lectures and handling such things as grenades, rifles and gas masks. We had to take sniffs of the real gasses. We were also put into a room filled with tear gas. We had our gas

---

[117] Bob enclosed a sketch he drew of Leon Bishop sitting on his bunk sketching. Bishop (1923-2005), was from Seattle. He was wounded in action and received an honorable discharge. He then attended the School of the Art Institute of Chicago and became a respected watercolorist.

[118] A nickname for his uncle, Kendall Oscar Lynch.

masks on, and then we took them off and we were to go directly out the door. I took one smell and could hardly make it to the door. Today we went to the rifle range. We shot the new Thompson sub-machine gun. It shoots around 600 rounds per min. We were given 20 rounds. I hit the target eight times and three of them were bulls-eyes. That is a pretty fair score in comparison with the others.

It rains one day and shines the next. It's the screwiest weather I've ever seen. Everyone has a cough in his chest and a sunburned face. I've been out 4 nights in the last two weekends, so that makes it a little easier to take. This is a nice town, and it isn't too crowded, except for the soldiers. All the women look Spanish.

The latest rumor is we will be shipped out some time this week, but we never know for sure. We are practically through with the basic training, so there isn't much to keep us except lack of space somewhere else. We should go to some college next, for about five months.

Are my prayers doing you any good? Is he breaking down? You can keep them up for me, because I still have to pass that all important physical and mental. There is nothing I need now, because we have just about everything at the P.X. Cookies are very nice tho. But don't send me anything until I get a permanent place. Don't forget to write. Love, Bob

Bob left Hammer Field in Fresno on March 23, 1943 and two days later arrived for his college training courses in Cedar City, Utah.

Juliana Truffer Biner, Swiss immigrant and paternal grandmother of Bill & Bob Biner.

Bob Biner and his quarters in Cedar City, Utah.

Wed, March 25, 1943

Dear Mom, Dad and Folks,

Just a short note telling you I have arrived. The place is called Cedar City, Utah. It's about half the size of Cle Elum[119]. I will be here five months if everything goes well, including the physical. We arrived this morning. The one thing I'm going to like about it is the food. It is pretty good. We will be going to a small Branch Agricultural College. The elevation is about 5000 ft.

I'll write a longer letter as soon as I get time. In the meantime, I'm flat broke. If you haven't sent the second five, you can send ten, here.

Love, Bob

A/S Robt. Biner
316 AAF, C.T.O.
Cedar City, Utah

March 26, 1943

Dear Mom, Dad and Fritz,

Well you probably received the first notice. I'll give you a few more details. We left Fresno last Tuesday night and we had no idea where we were going until we were half way here. As I said before, it's about half the size of Cle Elum, and I like it about as much.

---

[119] Cle Elum is a small town in the state of Washington about 75 miles southeast of Seattle.

We have very nice quarter. They took over a hotel. We sleep two in a bunk and two bunks per room. They furnish sheets and clean towels, which is something we don't see in Fresno. We have a bathroom with a shower and tub. The rugs are deep enough to give a pretty good shock. The college looks nice, but it's very small. This is a swell town to study in, because there is absolutely nothing else to do. The only thing is I hate thinking of being confined here for five months.

The A/S means Aviation Student. We're still classed as privates, and we only get $50 a month. We are treated as cadets tho. We are addressed as Mister, and everything is run on the honor system. The food is very good compared to Fresno, and we can have all we want. We eat off of plates instead of mess kits, and table manners are strict.

I received your letter with the five dollars enclosed, and it certainly came in the nick of time. The only trouble is it didn't last long enough.

Our barracks were split up so badly, we'll have to make a new set of friends. Only half of our barracks left Fresno. The half that left was split again. The other half went to the Dakotas. When we got here they split what was left three ways, and put us in with other groups. Bill Andrews was left in Fresno.

From what I hear, we won't get our physical and mental until we reach our next stage. It will take

*us 14 months to graduate. This town is over 80%
Mormon. There is a small Catholic Church here,
so I'm told. The Driscall boy is here,[120] but he is
not in my flight. I met him the other day. There
are also several boys who have gone to Gonzaga,
but none of them seem to know Bill. Most of them
went to night school.*

*Are you settled in the house yet? How do you like
it? You ought to be able to save a little money
now. Send me the address. We will probably start
classes next Monday. We are supposed to get
three nights off a week, but since there is no place
to go, it doesn't do much good.*

Love, Bob

---

*March 28, 1943
Cedar City, Utah
Dear Mom, Dad, and Folks,*

*This is our day of rest. We can stay in bed until
twelve if we want, but on one ever does it. Six of
the guys in our apartment are Catholics, and there
are only thirteen of us. The church is small, but
nice. It is only about 30 by 15 feet and it was
really crowded.*

*We have inspection every day, and the way they
hand out demerits isn't funny. We are supposed to
turn in our own demerits. This place is run the*

---

[120] Bob is probably referring to Jake Driscoll from
Ellensburg, Washington.

same as West Point. We will probably start school tomorrow. I have to take Math, Physics, Geography, History, English, First Aid and Military Law. In the last month we get ten hours of dual flying. It is mostly to see if we get air sick or not. The weather here has been swell. The sun shines every day, and it never gets really hot.

I got the glasses adjusted the other day for nothing. The people around here are very friendly. There is no R. X. here, so if you can get some gum for me, I would appreciate it. Cigarettes are the same price here as in Wash. None of the letters have been forwarded from Fresno yet, so there should be a little stack for me one of these days.

I have to shave every day, whether I need it or not. If we don't, we have to turn in a demerit. My slate is clean so far. There is a swimming pool here, but it doesn't open until May, so that won't do me much good for the present.

We are only about 75 miles from "Zion Nat'l Park". We will probably get to see it one of these months.

There is no news around here.

Love, Bob

A kiss for Mom and Fritz

March 29, 1943

Dear Folks,

Just got back from an all-night trip to Lincoln, Nebraska and Wichita, Kansas, and picked up your mail. We took off at eleven last night and got back at eleven this morning. You may have an idea how I feel.

We've had three days of really warm weather here now and ice has broken up in the Missouri River, near the edge of the field. We are on a plateau, so the floods they are having through the Middle West now don't affect us. There are two thousand families in Fargo who have been washed out and the water is still rising. Flew over a lot of inundated land on the way up from Sioux Falls this morning.

Tomorrow morning we take off for Cheyenne, Denver and Sioux Falls. Saturday we went to Oklahoma City and pretended to bomb the world's largest cracking plant at Ponca City.[121] It was a twelve-hour trip, non-stop and hotter than the devil. Oklahoma City is one of the cleanest and prettiest I have ever seen. There doesn't seem to be an old house in the town. All the homes are new, white and every roof has a different color.

---

[121] Cracking was the distillation of petroleum crude to produce greater quantities of liquefied petroleum gas and gasoline. The advanced cracking process in plants like the one in Ponca City gave the Allied Forces an air advantage over the Axis powers.

The oil kings have private lakes and what looks like eighty room mansions.

The day before that we flew over Kansas City, Missouri but we were pretty high, 25,000 feet and using oxygen which is very uncomfortable, so I didn't enjoy the trip. From all indications our training will be over in a day or two and then we start our leave. We are not going to get the six days at home that we thought we would, but if we get a ferry plane out of Rapid City I should be able to get almost that.

Anyway, I should be home some time the end of this week. By the way, how is the ferry schedule across the sound?[122] Would you wait until I am ready to come home to move, or have you forgotten I have a heart interest in Seattle?

Got my first letter from Bob the other day and he was pretty glum about everything. Seems that he was listening to latrine rumors and they were all bad. If I was him, I wouldn't fret so much about getting into this thing so quickly.

Don't write anymore until you hear from me again, because I probably would never get it. Here's hoping I see you all soon.

Bill

---

[122] Port Orchard is across the Puget Sound from Seattle and is most easily accessed by ferry.

Bill did meet up with his family for a brief reunion before reporting to Salinas, Kansas for processing to the war front. Meanwhile, Bob continued writing to his family almost daily from Utah.

March 29-30, 1943

Dear Mom, Dad and Fritz,

Your letter arrived today that you mailed on the 23rd, Mom. They just started forwarding them from Fresno. Well, we started school today. Everything looks as though it's going to be plenty tough, but I think I can make it all right. The classification that we took in Fresno was to determine what subject we would have to take here. I have to take them all. Some of the "brains" only have to take one or two subjects. Our schooling only counts on third of our record.

Are you in the new house yet? I hope you can get a little rest and spare time now Mom. Did you get a contract at the brewery Dad? Where is Fritz going to stay?

We really have a nice apartment here. I hope we get to keep it. It's the best one in the hotel. We have all the hot water we want. The boys are having quite a time with the rugs. You can get quite a jolt from the electricity it generates. It's getting late, so I'll finish it tomorrow.

March 30. We had a hard day today, but we really had a nice meal tonight. Chicken pot pie, and peach cobbler. We can get as many refills as we want, and all the milk we can drink. You might send your letters air mail if you want; I think that will arrive here sooner than by ordinary mail.

I received the first five bucks the night we left Fresno, but nothing else has arrived yet. I've been broke for the last few days, but don't worry about me. If you send any more money, send a money order. I don't trust those guys at Fresno.

We get Wednesday and Saturday nights off, and all day Sunday. Last Sunday, I met a guy who worked on the drill in Idaho. Ask Ken if he remembers him.[123] His name is Rodgers, and he also ran a restaurant in Patterson.[124] The one you ate at the night you were there. He didn't remember my face, but I knew him the moment I saw him.

Send me a phone number where I can get you. I was going to phone for some money, but I didn't know where to get you. By the way, we get paid on the 10th. They have a pretty good dance here

---

[123] Kendall Lynch worked for his father's diamond drilling company. The Lynch Brothers Diamond Drillers usually prepared sites for dam construction and did so for most of the dams on the Columbia River. (See addendum).

[124] Bob is probably referring to Paterson, Washington, a small town on the Columbia River south of Pasco. The 1930 census shows a 22 year-old named Henry Rodgers living in Paterson.

on Sat night, and we also have two theatres. Write soon.

Love, Bob....A kiss for Mom and Fritz

April 2, 1943
Cedar City, Utah
Dear Mom, Dad and Folks,

I haven't had much time to get off a letter in the last few days. I received your letter the other day, with the five dollars in it. It certainly came in handy. I would have received it sooner if it hadn't been delayed so long in Fresno.

We received word from some of the guys in Fresno that flight 25 was sent to Ellensburg. We left two days ahead of them. Most of the guys that came here were within 180 miles radius of Ellensburg. I miss out on all the luck.

The weather here is swell. My face is almost black. Last night we went to a play put on by the U.S.O. It is just getting started here, but I think they will make it pretty nice for us. School hasn't been so hard as yet, but we haven't started our physics class.

I get a letter from Wayne[125] quite often. He tells me they are quite busy over there. Eli has gone, and Cliff is in the hospital. He is making from 50

---

[125] Wayne Pennington, Ellensburg High Class of 1941, was in the U.S. Navy reserve.

to 100 bucks a week, and going to school. I would sure like to be in some civil job now.

This town is dead and that's all the news.

Love, Bob

April 5, 1943

Dear Mom, Dad and Folks,

I'm getting behind on my letters; they are working us pretty hard. Yesterday, I was K. P. It was my first sample, and of course, I would have to get it on Sunday. They got us up at 5 am and I worked straight through for 16 hours. It sure isn't any fun.

To top it off, they moved us out of our wonderful home. We are now in a barracks. It is twice as crowded as where we were. We jumped from 13 men to 100. It's sure a big change but it's still better than the one we had in Fresno. I got your letter yesterday with the blank checks in it. It's a nice idea, and I haven't cashed one yet, but if I do it will be for a five spot.

I'm glad to see you are finally settled. I wish you had as nice weather as we. Have you got any neighbors near you? What have you heard from Bill? You shouldn't expect many letters from him now, Mom. He is on the go all the time.

The school work is getting harder, and it will keep on increasing. I haven't heard from Betty for a long time. Did you send her my address yet?

I think we are going to have a parade tomorrow, its army day. Did you get John Poolers address yet? Our barracks is a converted warehouse. It belonged to the Union Pacific, and it is a little close to the tracks.

I'm glad they aren't working you too hard Dad. Are you having much of a job getting malt and staff? I would sure like to be working in the brewery again. It was a cinch to this life. We drilled for 4 hours the other day, and that was in addition to our classes. We sure don't have much time to study. We still have an hour of calisthenics. Along with the other exercises we do 20 pushups, chin ourselves 10 times and then we top it off by running a mile and scaling an 8-foot wall.

Well, there is no news in this place.

Love, Bob

Salinas, Kansas
April 9, 1943
Dear Folks,

You should have my telegram, as ordered, by now and know I arrived safely. We were held up in Salt Lake and didn't get into Denver until eleven-thirty, so I didn't phone DeLoughray.[126] I'll catch him on my next leave.

This is a good field and I am writing this in the newly opened Officers' Club; one of the best I've ever been in. Right now we are going through a few days of processing. That is, getting all our equipment checked and old items replaced, medical examinations, classes, etc. After this we wait around for orders.

I met an old Hobbs buddy here who left yesterday for points unknown and he had been here for a full month, so your guess is as good as mine as to how long we'll be here.

I'm glad I left Seattle like I did. I didn't want a repetition of that last time at Ken's. It's my turn to be proud of you, Mother.[127] The country down here is nice right now, but windy all the time, which makes it pretty dusty in the summer I guess.

All our crew is back with the exception of Gonsior[128], the radio man. He is certainly making

---

[126] William George "Doc" DeLoughray (1882-1965) was a first cousin to Bill's maternal grandfather, Daniel Lynch.

[127] Bill is probably talking about his mother's younger brother, Kendall Lynch, a veteran of World War I. Perhaps his Uncle Ken was saying things or acting in a way that irritated Bill's mother.

[128] Frank Gonsior was the radioman/waste gunner on the Berlin Sleeper, which was the name of the B-17

good his threat. I only hope we don't lose him though because he is one of our best men and no telling what we would get as a replacement.

I'll write again as soon as I think of something to write about.

Love to all, Bill

April 11, 1943

Dear Mom, Dad and Fritz,

I received your letter yesterday. This is the first chance I've had to answer it. The weather has changed for the worse. It has been snowing for the last ten days. It's too bad Bill had to leave so soon. Four days is better than nothing. It will probably be at least a year and a quarter before I get a furlough.

We had a showdown inspection today, and I had to turn myself in for demerits, because I had two small spots on my blouse. The discipline around here is really stiff.

The math is getting harder and harder by the day. I can do the work, but I'm too slow. I only get about ¾ of the test done in the allotted time.

I get to move back to the hotel this week. It is a lot better place to study. I went to a late mass

---

that Bill and his crewmates operated in North Africa and Europe.

today. There were only 4 soldiers there, including myself. The guys I chum with are all moving back to the hotel with me. There are 8 of us all together. Their names are Red, Butch and Bevo. Bevo is my bunk partner. We were in Fresno together. His real name is Eugene Bevoquo.[129] We are going to get some pictures taken.

By the way, if my camera isn't packed away, you might send it down. Also some film, we can hardly buy it here. We still haven't been paid. We were supposed to get it yesterday but no money. I cashed ten dollars this week.

How does Fritz like staying with the K.O. Lynches? Tell her to write me. I'm getting lonesome for her. Tell Molly to mail that letter she is carrying in her purse. Give me Bill's address as soon as you get it. Don't worry about him mom, we're all praying for him.

Love, Bob

Army Air Base, Salinas, Kansas
April 16, 1943
Dear Mother & Dad,

---

[129] Eugene A. "Bevo" Bevacqua (1920-1995) was also from the state of Washington. He became a colonel. Bob probably came up with the nickname. Bevo was the brand name of the most popular near-beer during Prohibition. It was introduced by Anheuser-Busch. Bob's own father had produced near-beer for the American market during the 1920s.

Well, I am still here, and I am apt to be here for quite a while yet – who knows. Am not doing a thing but lying around and getting fatter. Intend to work out in a gym every day from now until we go.

We have the Sweaty Betty but I haven't flown since I have been here. It is a spanking new ship and we are trying to get someone to paint the name on the nose.

I am glad to hear that my trench coat is finally catching up with me. Will probably have some use for it in the future. Enclosed is the money I borrowed from you, Dad. Don't forget the other $75 I owe you. I think I will put in another $50 allotment this month. I don't think I'll need to spend much anymore and I want you to pay off my bills and income tax – if it breaks me.

You ought to see all the equipment they unloaded on us here. I don't see how we are going to get it all on the ship. This country reminds me of Ellensburg, except there are no hills. Everything is green right now and the wind blows all the time. One thing I don't like about it is that it is <u>dry</u>. Only 3.2 beer and bum beer at that. The politicians must be cleaning up because the bootleg stuff – which I refuse to buy – is ten dollars a quart. I hear there are about twenty boys in an infantry camp near here who are blind as a result of the stuff. Nice people, these prohibitionists.

Had a letter from Bob and I think I'll supplement his G.I. pay with a fiver. He seems to be working pretty hard. Also Jack Costello – who is at officer's training camp in North Carolina.

Will write again soon. Love, Bill

April 17, 1943
Cedar City, Utah
Dear Mom, Dad and Fritz,

I received your letter the day before yesterday. They are running us pretty hard these days. We have to stand retreat about every night. Tonight we had to stand retreat and pass in review in front of the Governor of Utah.[130]

We are nicely settled in our apartment now. The rug doesn't generate as much electricity as the other, but it is better in most other respects. The weather is really beautiful and I have a nice tan on my face. You probably wouldn't recognize me now. My hair is half an inch, and that's all. No curls left. The top of my head looks like a clothes brush. They are very strict about our personal appearance.

We have a fine record here. The police have never heard a complaint nor have the people. You know

---

[130] The governor of Utah at the time was Herbert B. Maw (1893-1990), a Democrat, who served from 1941-49. Maw had been a member of the U.S. Aviation Corps during WW I.

how stuff gets around in a small town. When the people start complimenting us, it sounds pretty good.

Sunday-

Last night we had a "beer bust" here at the barracks. The officers brought all the beer and we had five half kegs.

We had a little better crowd at mass today. It is certainly a wonderful day for Palm Sunday. When you address your letters, don't forget to include Squadron 5, Flight C. If that isn't on them they go to the dead letter office and we may not get them for a couple of weeks.

Ask Betty what is the matter with her? She still hasn't written me a letter. How is the brewery getting along, Dad? Do you have a <u>phone</u>? If so what is the number? Did you find my notebook and camera?

I have been getting pretty good grades in History and English, but my math is kinda low. What do you do for recreation? Have you made any friends yet? I am sitting here racking my brain trying to think of something new to tell you, but everything we do is according to a set schedule and the town is too small to do anything on our free hours.

I'm not going to write again until I have something to say. Love, Bob

April 21, 1943
Cedar City, Utah
Dear Mom, Dad and Fritz,

The last few days have been great occasions for me. Monday I received 4 letters, and yesterday there were 3 more letters and 3 packages. Two of them were from you, and the other one was from Betty. The cookies are really nice; at least that's what the boys tell me. Betty sent some cookies, nuts and a carton of cigarettes. One of the letters was from Bill. In it was five dollars. I am beginning to feel important. Thanks also for the loose leaf. It certainly makes things a lot neater.

I am glad to see you are enjoying nice weather, so are we. We haven't had the snapshots developed yet. It's almost time for school, so I'll finish this tonight-

Well, I've just been doing a little sewing. We have to sew the 9th corps insignia on our clothes. Did Bill tell you the name of his ship was "Sweaty Bette"?

We are almost through with our Algebra already. Next week we will start Geometry, and then we will finish up with Trigonometry. There we will start in our on our Physics. We get as much math in one week as the college students get in a month. Most of the teachers are pretty nice.

We got the load of our shots today. We won't have to take any more for a year. We now have small-

pox, typhoid, and tetanus. I think I am getting fat, in spite of all the marching and calisthenics, my belly is still round. We must drink about five cokes a day, and it just goes down like water now.

I don't think I could use that bag now Mom, we have three large dressers, and a big closet. When I get to pre-flight I will probably send for it. As I said before, there is nothing to write about since we have the same old grind every day. This sure doesn't seem like holy week to me. The only time we get to church is Sunday.

Well, I have to write to Betty yet.

Love, Bob

Xxxxxxx For Mom and Fritz

P.S. You'll be getting a birthday present Dad.

April 21, 1943
Cedar City, Utah
Dear Bette,

Your package arrived yesterday. You are too good to me. Everything just hit the spot. I am guarding the stuff with my life. These wolves would clean it up in a minute if I let them. I also got a package from Mom yesterday, and the sum total (not from Mom) of 2 letters in two days. Pretty good huh?

Did you hear what they are calling Bill's plane? In case you didn't, it's "Sweaty Bette." How do you like that?

The work is really getting stiff now. We are taking 16 hrs. of math, a week, and that's in addition to all our other studies. We are also taking a preparatory course for meteorology and navigation. Mom tells me your new boss is a pretty good egg.[131] Have you got the Mormon converted yet?[132] They are all trying to convert us around here. The captain said you ought to see what goes on behind the closed doors. They ain't as pious they're cracked up to be.

---

[131] Betty had quit her teaching job after a dispute with the principal. Since all nylon was used for military purposes, fashionable young women like Betty Biner took to drawing a line down the back of their legs to make it appear they were wearing nylon stockings. The school principal told her that she could not do it, so like any good woman standing up for her rights, she quit. She quickly found an office job with the Big Pasco Lend Lease facility in Pasco, Washington. According to the Washington Public Ports Association, "Big Pasco was originally built in 1942 as a holding and reconsignment point for military supplies, mostly bound for the Soviet Union as part of the Lend-Lease program. Big Pasco was a massive facility of warehouses, rail spurs, and docks. It was deactivated in 1947." When Betty Biner's initial boss disappeared on a drunken binge in Portland, the government sent down 42 year-old Charlton "Pat" Fulton, from Everett, Washington, to take over the accounting office she worked in.
[132] Betty was dating a Mormon at the time. By the end of the year she would be dating her new boss.

They really treat us nice, but it's practically dry ten-story around here. We can't buy a thing until after six o clock, and then it's only 3.2 beer.

I am getting some more snap shots taken pretty soon if they are any good, I'll let you have one for the top of a box of Wheaties and ten cents to cover mailing fees. The weather around here is really nice. Around the middle of next month, they are going to open up the pool, so I guess I will be able to hold out a few more months. Although the box was very nice, I still expect a letter from you. We sure do a lot of marching, and I still can't keep in step. Write soon.

Love, Bob

P.S. Get John Poolers address from Betty.[133]

Army Air Base, Salinas, Kansas
Good Friday, April 23, 1943
Dear Mother & Dad,

Received your letter yesterday and this is one of four I have written today. I am trying to clean up all my correspondence before I leave. Well, we are all set to go, almost. I think we'll be around for Easter Sunday and maybe later. After that we'll

---

[133] Betty Pooler, John's sister and Betty Biner's close friend.

still be in the country for a week or so, so don't go worrying.

My trench coat arrived in good shape – thank you. About the pictures, here is a list – you, Grandma Lynch, Kendall, Fred, Julia, Helen & George, Betty Biner, Mary & Perk[134], Mrs. McCanna,[135] Ted Burns, c/o Jack Burns, Nelson, Bob Biner, Jeanne (if she has called for one by now), Gus Biner. If you want anymore, I guess they will make them for you.

Did you get the 23 dollars I sent you? Here's another ten to pay on the pictures. Am sending along Julia's bill, the one she gave me for Christmas. You can send it back when you pay her off. - $66.07. Remember, I owe George $110. I made a new allotment effective next month for $150. I only have about $5 in my account now, but it will build up pretty fast. In case anything does happen to me my pay is supposed to go for six months afterward.[136]

---

[134] Mary Cecelia Biner (1892-1990) was a sister of Bill's father. She was married to William Xavier Perkins (1878-1955), affectionately known as Perk.
[135] Mrs. McCanna ran the boarding house in Spokane, Washington where Bill lived while attending Gonzaga.
[136] For someone who keeps telling his mother not to worry, this line must have been unsettling. Bill's mother (and the editor's grandmother), Harriet Lynch Biner, was a mother hen, highly protective and prone to worry about all of her children and grandchildren.

Here's wishing you a happy Easter and I'll write again with my A.P.O.[137] in a day or two.

Love to all, Bill

April 25, 1943

Dear Mom, Dad, Fritz,

Well, today is Easter Sunday. I made my Easter duty so don't worry, Mom. The wind has been blowing all day. It reminds me of Ellensburg.

I received another package from Betty today. It was a cribbage board and cards. It comes in a little compact folder. She is certainly nice to me, but I wish she would write.

I went to the dance last night, and had a pretty fair time. Saturday is the only thing we have to look forward to. Were you at Grandma's today? I was going to phone but I couldn't remember the number. Do you have a phone or not? This is the last time I am going to ask you. How am I going to get a hold of you in a hurry?

I think I will be taking out an insurance policy pretty soon. We don't get them free until we start flying, and in the meantime, it will only cost us around $7.00 a month for the $10,000 policy. Who will I make it to?

---

[137] Army Post Office

There are two reasons why I don't write so often. I-I am pressed for time. II- There is nothing to say. Our P.E. class is really getting strenuous. They run us so hard every day, I almost get sick. In spite of it all, I have gained ten pounds since I've been in the army.

We have been short sheeting the boys in our room the last few nights. It's really a laugh when the guys come rushing in the last minute before taps. They dive in bed as the lights go and spend the next ten minutes making them up in the dark.

The picture is the only one that came out good, but when my camera arrives we will get some good shots.

Write soon. Love, Bob

P.S. I just made 100% in my first Geography test.

Cedar City
April 26, 1943
Dear Betty,

Your letter arrived today and the present came yesterday. Thanks a lot for everything. The boys have become quite interested in cribbage. I really didn't need the money. But if you get short, you can get it back. The pictures were nice, send some more.

Tell Pooler she can write as soon as she gets time. I'll give her a big thrill by getting a letter from a real soldier. Thanks for John's address. Mom told me he was in California. Did you hear that Commodore Burnett[138] and Al Goodwin were both killed in plane crashes?

How are you getting along with your Mormon? I'm not doin' so good with the ones here, but I do have one lined up for next Sunday.

I now have a total of 14 demerits, and that's not so good. If we get more than 8 a week we have to walk a tour. My studies are just so-so. My grades in English, History and Geography are good but Math as usual is too hard. I got 100% in Geography. This 5-month course is equivalent to two years of Junior college, so you can guess how fast they are pushing us.

Well, I'm on K.P. again tomorrow so I guess I'll have to get to bed. Write again soon. Thanks a lot for everything.

Love, Bob

April 26, 1943, Cedar City, Utah

Dear Mom, Dad & Fritz,

---

[138] Bob is probably referring to Air Commodore Wilf Burnett, a Canadian who flew many heroic missions for the RAF. He was actually the sole survivor of one crash when his aircraft ran out of fuel following a bombing mission to Hamburg. Burnett survived the war and died in 2006 at the age of 91.

Both of your letters arrived today, also one from Betty. She also sent a ten-dollar check. I'm sorry to hear you spent the day in Seattle without me phoning.

No Mom, we don't wear clothes like Bill wears. We wear the plain buck private's issue. We wear absolutely no insignia, no wings, no U.S., no nothing. We are just one step lower than a buck private. If I make cadets, we will have to buy our own uniform if we want anything different from what we are wearing.

The food is about as good as it ever was, but tonight we had liver and as a result I am still hungry. WE have fish for a least one meal every Friday.

Bill Lambert is in Mississippi, and I haven't written to Bill Robertson yet. I hear Robertson is getting married this month. I hope Fritz is better now. Tell the little bum to write me. She ought to be out of school pretty soon now.

I'm on K.P. again tomorrow. I sure hate that job. Our whole room got 4 gigs a piece today. It didn't pass inspection very well. If we get more than 8 demerits' a week, we have to walk a tour, and that's no fun. We have to walk them on Sunday, and I got a little Mormon date.

Well, I have to get up early for K.P. in the morning, and it's a long job.   *Love, Bob*

May 2, 1943

Dear Mom, Dad and Fritz,

I got your letters yesterday. The picture is nice mom, but you look so sad. The weather is really beautiful here; there isn't a cloud in the sky today. We are wearing our suntans now, and the only way you can tell an officer from a private is by the bars. We got paid again this month. If I can ever get to the post office, I will send a little home for safe keeping. By the time I leave here, I may have enough for a cadet dress suit.

This afternoon I have a Mormon date. I wonder if Grandpaw forgot to mail the camera. I intended on taking a few pictures today. I think it is a good idea staying away from Seattle. But if you do go in I don't see any reason why you shouldn't have a good time.

Time is really going fast. It doesn't seem like I have been here over a month. The kids are enjoying their summer vacation already. When will Fritz be out?

Gotta close, nothing to write about.

Love, Bob

Hotel Miami, Dayton, Ohio
Monday, May 3, 1943
Dear Folks,

I guess it surprises you to see where I am now. It surprised me too. We went to Palm Beach, Florida last Monday and were ready to go across when they sent us up here for modifications on our ship. Morrison Field, where we were in Florida, is an embarkation field and we were not allowed off nor would any mail we wrote there leave until after we did.

Morrison is certainly a beautiful field. Palm trees and tropical flowers and a hot sun every day and all the girls working on the post have a deep brown tan. Makes you want to stay around a little longer.

Dayton is a busy town with Wright and Patterson Field[139] running full blast. There are eighteen girls to every man here and very few soldiers. Most of the personnel at the fields are civilians.

We have our ships name painted on and it looks pretty good.

My income tax is $80 Dad and I have paid one quarterly installment of $20, so I owe $60 more. I sent it to the P.O. in Seattle and gave Grandpa's address. I have $150 going into effect at Sam

---

[139] Wright and Patterson were two fields about ten miles apart that were merged into one base following the war. Wright was named in honor of the famed aviators the Wright Brothers. Patterson was in honor of the local Ohio family that founded National Cash Register (NCR), a company instrumental in early computer technology and eventually acquired by AT&T.

Houston starting this month so you ought to be able to get my bills paid off pretty soon.

I am the finance officer of our crew and am packing $1500 around with me now but all of it is a lot of grief and red tape.

As far as Jeanne and I are concerned, Mother, I guess you could say things are all off. They are with me at any rate. I'll bet she hasn't picked up the picture yet, has she?

I think you can reach me at Morrison if you send a letter to me. Put Crew #25, DeJohn's Group on it and send it to Morrison Field, West Palm Beach, Florida. Put my name on it of course and send it Air Mail. I'll get my A.P.O. when I get back and send it to you.

Things are looking up in Europe now, so don't worry so much. We have enough guns in our ship to scare an M-4 tank[140]. I'll write and send some postcards from Palm Beach.

Love and kisses,

Bill

---

[140] The famous Sherman Tank, which was the primary tank used by the U.S. military during World War II

Bill mailed a postcard on May 4, 1943 that showed the ten-story Hotel Miami and wrote, "Dear Folks, This is our abode while in Dayton. Six percent beer here, Dad. Pretty good too."

May 6, 1943

Dear Mom, Dad, and Fritz,

I got your letters yesterday, but this is the first chance I have had to answer it. I am in charge of quarters tonight, and it is a 24-hour shift. I am in charge of the whole barracks. Everyone has to take his turn like K.P. I went to a free show last night sponsored by the U.S.O. It was "Once upon a Honeymoon".[141] I never laughed so hard in all my life.

They published an academic deficiency list the other day. Seventeen of the 30 guys in my flight were deficient. I feel pretty good, since I wasn't amongst them.

I haven't heard from Bill since I got the first letter. I hope he hasn't left yet. I was sick the other morning from something I ate. About 2/3 of the whole detachment reported for sick call, but everyone is ok now.

The camera arrived yesterday. Thanks, and I'll be taking some pictures pretty soon.

---

[141] "Once Upon a Honeymoon" was a 1942 film starring Ginger Rogers and Cary Grant.

Tell Fritz to write.

Love, Bob

May 10, 1943

Dear Mom, Dad, and Fritz,

I got your second letter today, but this is the first time I've had to answer it. I also got one from Betty.

We've sure had some fun weather here. The day before yesterday, we had a blizzard. Today it is as hot as it ever was. I went to a show Sat. nite, and one Sunday. That was about the extent of my recreation over the weekend.

Did you get the candy Mom? I received communion for you Sunday. I haven't heard a thing from Bill. He is probably enjoying the springtime in England.[142] I took some pictures yesterday, as soon as I finish the roll I'll get them developed.

One of the squadrons left for Santa Ana the other day, so we have some nice furniture in our room now. We have the softest inner springs mattresses you ever felt, a rocking chair, and a dresser with a big mirror.

---

[142] Bob did not know that his big brother was still stateside, nor could he have known that he was not bound for England, but North Africa.

I'm getting tired of this place but the time is going pretty fast.

A Mother's Day kiss for Mom.

Love, Bob

May 13, 1943, Cedar City

Dear Mom, Dad, and Fritz,

There's not much doing, but I have a little time. We have a new squadron here. Since we are upperclassmen, we thought we would have a lot of fun riding the new recruits, but they turned out to be veterans. They all have at least a year in the service. There are master sergeants, and aerial gunners amongst them, and many of them have had Foreign Service. They are all cadets now.

The work is getting harder by the day, but time is sure flying. I'm glad to hear Bill hasn't left yet. I hope he writes to me. I got a letter from Betty the other day. I wish it were I who's going home. I'm plenty sick of this war.

Bevo's wife came to visit him today. (Bevo is my bunkmate.) About a third of the guys here are married, and most of them have their wives here.[143]

---

[143] Bob must have enjoyed his personal freedom. It would be another 20 years before he got married.

They are filming a picture just twenty miles from here. I don't suppose I'll be able to get a look at it though. We sure run up a cleaning bill wearing our sun tans.[144] We have to get two pairs of pants and two shirts cleaned a week.

I'm still waiting for a letter from Fritz. I finally lost the set in my K.C. ring.[145] I'm sure sick about it. The soldering broke loose. Where's that second box you promised mom?

Well, I have to get busy on my homework.

Love, Bob

On May 14, 1943 Bill sent his parents a postcard from New Orleans that had a drawing of Antoine's Restaurant, "The Oldest French Restaurant in New Orleans in the Heart of the Vieux Carre." On it he wrote, "Dear Mother & Dad, got out of Morrison again and I can continue correspondence. We should be in Macon, Georgia getting more work on our ship but the navigator[146] and I detoured thru New Orleans. Letter following. Love, Bill"

Hotel St. Francis
St Charles at Common Sts., New Orleans
May 15, 1943

---

[144] Sun tans were light clothing, without ties, issued to the soldiers for hot days.
[145] Knights of Columbus, a Catholic fraternal order.
[146] The navigator of the crew was Scott Bascom.

Dear Folks,

The ball is over as far as New Orleans is concerned and the navigator and I have to leave for Mobile, Alabama where we hope to get a ride on a plane to Macon, Georgia where our ship is laid up.

New Orleans is a gay town but expensive as the devil. One of the great things here are the quaint and romantic restaurants where you get all the old French and Creole dishes. I have eaten so many strange seafood dishes that I expect to sprout fins at any time.

Scotty and I went swimming in Lake Pontchartrain, 600 square miles, the day before yesterday and we got the darnedest sunburn you ever saw. A little Unguentine[147] fixed it up fine though. I thought I had enough tan from Florida to take care of it but I guess I was fooled. My face and neck are a bright brown color though and the pool-room color is gone for good.

Just had dinner in Kolb's – a German restaurant – replete with large seidels[148] of dark or light beer, and enjoyed it very much. When you take that trip one of these days, you'll have to come down here and put on a few pounds. When you come, I want to come with you.

---

[147] An antiseptic ointment for burns and rashes.
[148] A seidel is a large beer mug, or stein, with a hinged lid.

I'm sorry about last Sunday, Mother, but we were stuck in Morrison and no communication is allowed out of there. We are scheduled to go to N. Africa but now I don't know where we will go. Maybe they will station us there to bomb Italy, etc.; it's hard to say. I hope so, anyway.

No, I haven't done any gambling since I left home the last time and there should have been $100 in the bank. I cashed a check for $25 today. This month's check will be the first of $150 I am starting to allot to the bank.

I'll write again when I get to Macon. Take care of yourselves.

Love to all, Bill

Bill sent a postcard the following day showing the tallest building in Mobile, Alabama and wrote: "Dear Folks, on my way back to Macon. This Mobile is about the stenchiest town I have ever been in. Aroma-de-phew![149] Love, Bill"

---

[149] Mobile, Alabama became a major industrial center during World War II. Between 1940-43 the city's population grew by nearly 90,000 as poor white and black Americans sought jobs in the shipbuilding industry and the chemical and paper plants. The huge influx of people and industry contributed to the stench Bill refers to.

May 15, 1943,

Cedar City, Utah

Dear Mom, Dad, and Fritz,

I got your letter today and the package yesterday. Mom, the cookies were really neat. They lasted about 15 minutes when these wolves got at them. The cigarettes were also welcome.

I went to the dance last night. That's about the only thing we have to look forward to. Two of the boys in my room were late for call to quarters last night. They will probably get two weeks' confinement and some tours to walk. The next guy that is late in our room will get moved down to the other barracks.

What was the cause of Bill's fall-out with Jeanne? This physics is really getting tough. No, I haven't heard from John. According to Betty, he is still in Sioux City.

The wind is blowing today. It reminds me of Ellensburg. We are having a field meet today. The squadron that wins it gets two consecutive all night passes.

As you can see by the letter, there is nothing to write about. This town is really getting under my skin. I'd give anything for a two-week furlough. Now the rumor going about is we'll spend 7 months here instead of going to Santa Ana. I hope it's just a rumor. Guess I'll have to go to a show today and get cheered up.

Dad ought to have plenty of time to raise chickens and a garden now that he is only brewing 5 days a week.

Well, I have to make another formation.

Love, Bob

May 20, 1943
Cedar City
Dear Mom, Dad, and Fritz,

Well I'm two days late answering your letter. I just haven't had time to write. I got Bill's picture the day before yesterday. It was sure swell. I hope I can wear one of those outfits one of these days. I wouldn't even mind saluting him. I also received a package from Aunt Molly yesterday. It was sure swell. She sent me nuts, 2 boxes of candy, and two boxes of cookies. Everyone is spoiling me. Well, did you see Betty? How does she like the house?

They are finally going to open the swimming pool tomorrow. The last few days have been pretty cold. I finally got some pictures developed. They turned out pretty fair. Some of them were taken in the park across from the hotel. Some of me by the tree was taken in front of the hotel. It's a pretty nice place.

The physics is really tough. I hope I won't be deficient in it this month. We have an 8 am class now, so we are going 8 hours a day for six days a week. They seem to be stepping up our schedule.

Well, it's almost 10 o clock, and I have to get some sleep.

Love, Bob

May 24, 1943

Dear Mom, Dad, and Fritz,

I got your letter yesterday, Mom. I'm starting this one now, but I don't know when I'll finish it.

We are having tests again this week. We have them at the end of every month. Tonight we have to go down and take a test on army regulations. We could sure use the time for studying.

Butch and I are quitting smoking. The first one that starts has to pay the other five dollars. I can run a mile now, but by the time I get through, five will be just as easy.

Well they finally opened the pool. It is sure going to help pass these dreary months away. I don't see how I can learn much more; my head feels like it's going to bust now.

How did you like the snap shots? I took some more this weekend. I can't get films here, so if you can get a hold of some 620 I'd appreciate it.

Well, here it is Wednesday, and it's the first chance I've had to finish this letter. We took math and physics tests today. I got an 86 in physics and an 87 in math. That just helps to bring up the average. If I can get a decent grade on the geography test tomorrow, I'll stay off the deficiency list this month. If you can imagine it, they are stepping up our schedule still more. We will be leaving for Santa Ana sooner than we expected.

The days are sure hot. To top it all off, just when it gets hot enough to swim, I get a head cold.

From the last group that left, they're washed out at Santa Ana. The doctor here says they are leaning over backwards to take them. That makes me feel a little better, but give up the prayers, I still need them.

They have deprived us of our Wednesday night open pass, so you can see how hard we study. It's so hot I can hardly sit still long enough to write this letter. I'm sure getting behind on my letter writing. Now I can understand why Bill only wrote once a week. By the way, have you heard anything else from him? Well, I have to get busy on this geography. It's more navigation and meteorology than anything else.

Write soon…Love, Bob

Lt. William Daniel "Bill" Biner

On May 26, 1943 Bill was deployed to North Africa. He would be assigned to the 342nd Squadron of the already famous 97th Bombardment Group. The 97th would be under the command of Col. Leroy A. Rainey. They were part of the 5th Bomb Wing under the command of Brig. Gen. Joseph H. Atkinson. The 5th Bomb Wing was part of the North Africa Strategic Air Force, commanded by Major General James H. Doolittle.

Bill's journey to North Africa and the heat of both battle and the Sahara, began more like an exotic vacation than a march to war and hardship, as evidenced by his next letter. According to Bill's sister Fritzi, Bill went to North Africa via Natal, Brazil and Dakar, Senegal, which was the shortest distance across the Atlantic. Meanwhile, little brother Bob was sweating it out in Utah.

May 29, 1943
Cedar City, Utah
Dear, Mom, Dad and Fritz,

I got your letter the day before yesterday. I feel guilty for not writing sooner, but they are sure rushing us now. I also got a cute letter from ingots.

I just got back from the dance. I hear they are even trying to cut out our Saturdays. Monday is Memorial Day, so we get a holiday. The only catch in it is we have to march in a parade.

The way we figure it, we just have about two months left. That should get us out about the first of August. No Mom, we didn't win the field meet. We took a measly third. On top of that, we have special duty tomorrow. Our squadron had too many late for formations.

Well, here it is Sunday again, and I still haven't finished this letter. We had to get up and march this morning. They are really cracking down on the discipline around here. We can't speak to girls on the campus. Can't smoke any place but in our rooms. When we walk up town, we have to walk at attention, and in step with whomever we are walking with. We also have a personal inspection every morning.

You ought to see our mascot. He's a little pup, called Sergeant. He barks at every civilian who walks by.

Well, tomorrow is pay day, and I'm kinda glad to see it roll around. I'll try to write sooner next time.

Love, Bob

May 30, 1943
Cedar City, Utah
Dear Bumps,

I got your letter the other day, and I was sure glad to get it. You ought to write more often. Are you the first girl in your class yet? The boys down here would really be nuts about you. Who is your latest beau? Mom told me that you and Danny and Jack[150] were out at the house last week. Is it a nice place? She never tells me anything. What do you do out there besides digging clams? Where did you get your sun tan? Have you been swimming? The work is getting tougher here every day.

How are the kids, and Uncle Ken, and Aunt Grace? Tell them I'm still going to write as soon as I can get a breather. Tell Uncle Ken I met Rodgers. One of the guys that worked on the drill for him in Idaho. He helped Chuck after I left.

Well, I have to get on my homework again.

Don't forget to write again.

Love, Bob

XXXXXXXXX

Monday, May 31, 1943

Dear Folks,

It seems funny to be writing you from below the equator but that is what I am doing. The trip so far has been grand and we are seeing a lot of country.

---

[150] Dan and Jack Lynch were first cousins to the Biner children. They were the sons of Kendall & Grace Sullivan Lynch.

The enclosed bill is worth twenty-five cents. A pocket full of nickels down here is a lot of folding money. I was going to send you a bill from Trinidad but I lost it someplace.

Got a big kick out of flying over Devil's Island[151], but it doesn't look so fierce from the air. We went out of our way to see it and to get some pictures. Things are awfully cheap down here but it would take me a long time to get used to the food.

Good weather is plentiful and we all bought what are called "short-snorter"[152] boots. They are about twelve inches high and made out of very soft leather in brown and it seems that everyone in the air corps down here wears them. I bought a Swiss watch today for you, Dad and now I have to find some way to mail it. It's a Trissot[153] and would cost around $55 in the U.S. I got it for $27 here in the P.X. Our boots cost $4.50. That gives you some idea of the prices here. The natives working

---

[151] Devil's Island, off the coast of French Guyana in northeast South America, was a notorious French penal colony from 1852-1952. *Papillon*, an autobiographical novel by Henri Charriere, describes an escape from the island.

[152] A short snorter, according to the Random House Dictionary, is a member of an informal club of pilots, crewmen and passengers who have made a transoceanic flight.

[153] Trissot has been manufacturing quality watches in Switzerland since 1853. In today's market Trissot models sell in a range from $200 to $1,000.

on the field get 35 cents a day. Straw bosses[154] get $1.00.

We buy bananas, watermelons and coconuts from the natives for a song and I am getting a "banana belly." The beer is very heavy and all the bottles smell moldy so I stick to scotch or gin when I want a drink at the club.

This "touriste" life is about over and I can't say where I am or where I am going but you'll hear from me soon again. Put airmail stamps on V-mail[155] and you get high priorities.

No more for now – Love to all, Bill

P.S. Tell Uncle Paul that I liked his last picture of Bob & Bing.[156]

---

[154] An assistant foreman; or member of a work crew who acts as the boss.

[155] V-Mail stood for "Victory mail" and originated in England. It was the process of censoring and microfilming soldier's letters to send them to America where they would be reprinted at 60% of original size and delivered. According to the National Postal Museum, it would take 37 mail bags weighing 2,575 pounds to transport 150,000 one-page letters from Europe to America. V-mail could deliver the same amount in a single bag weighing just 45 pounds. Many of the letters from Bill and Bob Biner were in V-mail format.

[156] "Road to Morocco" starring Bob Hope and Bing Crosby, and produced by Bill's uncle, Paul Jones, was released in November, 1942. It is likely that the men

June 4, 1943
Cedar City, Utah
Dear Mom, Dad, and Fritz,

*Well I finally got time to write. I'm on C.Q.[157]
again today. Last nite we had a fire drill. They
waited until we all got asleep, and they started a
fire in a waste basket. They put the fire right next
to my bunk, so naturally I was the one to give the
alarm. The only trouble was they had to wake me
up. The Sergeant shook me, pointed at the fire
and said what are you going to do mister? I lay
back down and started to sleep again. They finally
got me up and the alarm was given.*

*I received a nice letter from Bill the other nite. He
said that would be his last nite in this country for
some time, so I guess he is enjoying summer
someplace else. You don't want to start worrying
about him. He can certainly look out for himself.*

*They haven't posted last month's deficiency report
yet, but I think I made it.*

*I supposed Fritz will be home for the summer now.
You're going to have to limit her to a ton of shells a
day, or you won't have room to move around. Find*

---

chose to watch this film since they were on their way to
Morocco.

[157] C.Q. stands for Charge of Quarters. This is the
person in charge of quarters where military personnel
are billeted – in other words Bob had to wake the other
men up. Not a popular or coveted position.

out if Molly sent a letter will you? I've received none.

The time is now 3:15am, and I'm getting damn sleepy. By the way, I'm the guy that gets the bugler up. I got some more pictures developed, but I left them at the hotel.

That's all for now. Write soon.

Love, Bob

June 6, 1943
Cedar City, Utah
Dear Bet,

I got your package yesterday. You are too nice to me. I want you to know we really appreciate everything. I'm sorry I didn't answer your last letter yet. They are really putting the pressure on us now.

They have been shipping the boys out of here ahead of schedule. We expect to leave here at least a month ahead of time. From what we hear the physical at Santa Ana is really rugged. Don't let up on those prayers because I'm really going to need some help.

I missed getting on the deficiency list by a hair. The math and physics get harder every day. I am finally getting so I enjoy this town. The swimming pool is really nice, and I managed to find a Mormon that isn't too Mormon.

By the way, tell Betty Pao she better hurry up and write or I won't date her the next time I'm around. They are even trying to cut out our Saturday nights. Mom tells me you might go to work in Seattle. You must be nuts. The only reason I'd even go back to Seattle is it's near Port Orchard, and the Burg.

I sure got a nice letter from Bill before he left. I almost feel like not trying. Well, I have to write a few more letters tonight. Keep those letters coming they really help out

Love Bob

Bill Biner arrived in Morocco on June 5, 1943, during a major Allied offensive against Italian forces on the island of Pantelleria located in the Strait of Sicily. Following seven days of heavy aerial bombardment Allied ground troops landed at Pantelleria. 11,000 Italian soldiers quickly surrendered, which cleared the way for the island to become a critical air base for operations against Sicily and the rest of Italy. Dubbed *Operation Corkscrew*, it was a significant victory, and it can be assumed that esprit de corps was high at the Allied bases in North Africa when Bill arrived.

French Morocco[158]
June 14, 1943[159]
Dear Mother & Dad,

I can tell you I am in Morocco but I can't say where or for how long because of restrictions. You should have the watch and stockings I sent from Brazil by now and I hope they got there in good shape. I sent a pair to Julia and Helen also. Do they fit? We are living in tents here and conveniences are scarce but we make out alright. Everyone dreams of large bottles of cold American beer and they would sell for unheard of sums if obtainable. Cold beer and ice cream are about all the men crave for – outside of getting back to the U.S.

The towns and cities here are very much Frenchified, and if it weren't for the natives you could imagine yourself in France very easily. Sidewalk bistros, and all things French, but give me Ellensburg, or Port Orchard, any day.

Europeans seem to have a fetish against anything cold and bright lights. Just the opposite from what I like. And there is only one temperature in their wash basin taps – cold, or rather, luke-warm.

---

[158] France controlled Morocco as a "French Protectorate" from 1912 through 1956.
[159] At the time of this letter King George VI of England was visiting troops in North Africa. If Bill saw the king, he doesn't mention it.

I'll have to tell you about their toilets in person. You won't believe it.

I've seen some strange sights in different parts of Africa – even snow – but if anyone wants to know what we are fighting for, all they have to do is come over here for a while. No wonder they call America the "New World."

Saw Jerry Patenaude[160] again, in Brazil this time. He is with the Ferry Command. Also have run across a few men who were at Williams Field with me.

Now that Fritzy is out of school you shouldn't be so lonely. I'll bet she has a whale of a time at the beach this summer. I wouldn't mind being there myself. Right now I could use a good swim. I can't seem to get clean around here. How is Bob coming along with his flying? Or has he started any yet?[161] Give me all the news and here's hoping I get to see some of the games in Seattle this fall.

Love to all, Bill

---

[160] The Patenaude family lived in Ellensburg. Jerry and Mary Patenaude had four sons, Ludgar, James, Joseph and Louis, who was closest in age to Bill and Bob Biner. Jerry Sr. was dead prior to WW II, but perhaps Louis was also known as Jerry.

[161] Bob was in Cedar City, Utah at the time of this letter. He had finished his basic training on March 23rd and was taking some college courses at Utah State Agricultural Branch prior to his preflight training.

June 15, 1943

Dear Mom, Dad and Fritz,

Well I just got through phoning Dad. It's sure a shame you couldn't hear me. I could hear you swell. It makes me feel a lot better just hearing your voice. I hope you didn't wait around long after five. I would have phoned again only I couldn't get enough quarters. We have a payphone here.

I'm on C.Q. today and I thought you could tell Mom Happy Birthday for me. It makes me mad.

As I said before, I probably won't leave for Santa Ana for a couple of months or six weeks. We only have three squadrons left, so I'm drawing plenty of K. P. & C.Q. lately. The thing I don't like about it is I miss out on my class, and it's harder than heck to make the stuff up.

That's all for now.

Love, Bob

June 21, 1943
Cedar City, Utah
Dear Mom, Dad, and Fritz,

Well, today is the longest day of the year, and I mean long. I was on K.P. I got up before the sun and got back after it. K.P. is really rugged now.

Your letter arrived today. That's sure tuff about that phone call. Where is Betty going to stay when she gets to Seattle? I hope she doesn't have to go all the way out to 57th.

Jim Driscoll's sister and girlfriend arrived last week. We went to the dance Saturday nite. Either these Cedar City girls are spoiling me, or she doesn't know how to dance. I stepped all over her feet. They took some pictures Sunday. The next time you're in Seattle go up and see them. She can tell you all about this dump. Squadron 5 is really going places. We won the yellow ribbon for marching and discipline for two weeks straight. If we win it this week, we get an all-night pass.

I haven't taken out insurance yet. The Capt. was supposed to arrange a time for us to get it, but he didn't. However, I will have it inside of two weeks.

When are Poolers going to move to Cal? Do they know where they are going to live? I'll want their address. Personally, I'd rather look them up than a bunch of strange relatives I can't even remember. Of course that doesn't include George Biner and Grandmaw.

If I write to Bill, will I have to write it on V-mail? Well, it's time for taps, and I'm really tired.

Love, Bob

p.s. I got your letter last week Fritz, I'll write as soon as I get time Hun. XxxxxMom xxxxxFritz

June 24, 1943
Cedar City, Utah
Dear Mom, Dad, Fritz,

Your letter arrived the other day and boy what a surprise. I thought you were going to tell me all about it. When are you leaving? I don't think Pocatello is so far from here. If you ever come down here, make sure it's on a weekend. I couldn't get out of a class on a week day for hell or high water, and we only have two free hours in the evening. We can't even get out for a phone call.

The old town is really busy. They are filming another picture here. It will be "Old Oklahoma", starring John Wayne. They were 'shooting' today right across from our barracks at the train depot. They had it fixed up so you wouldn't even recognize it.

Well, Monday was the longest day of the year, and take it from me, it was long. I was on K. P. every second of the day. Well, squadron five has done it. We got an all nite pass, and we were complimented by the captain personally. He said we were the best squadron he has ever had. He said our boys were really making a name for themselves at Santa Ana.

I don't know whether I told you this or not, but I am not deficient this month. It was a lot closer this time though. We will probably be flying in a couple of weeks now.

When is Betty moving to Seattle, and when are Poolers moving to Cal?

Write soon.

Love, Bob

An extract from the Office of the Group Commander, 97th Bombardment Group, dated June 25, 1943, lists the following men as members of the 342nd Bombardment Squadron:

1st Lt. Frank W. Cranz, pilot (Glendale, CA); 2nd Lt. Edward J. Hart, co-pilot (Little Rock, Ark); 2nd Lt. Winfield S. Bascom, navigator (Knox, Indiana) ; 2nd Lt. William D. Biner, bombardier; Sgt. Fred Neufeld, engineer (Dallas, Oregon); Sgt. Leonard R. Hardy, assistant engineer (Salt Lake City); Sgt. Stanley E. Gonsier, radio operator (Suffield, CT); Sgt. George G. Wright, assistant radio operator (Chicago); Sgt. Roy E. Henthorn, Jr, gunner (Easton, PA); and Sgt. Hoyt W. Rogers, assistant gunner (Concord, NC).

(Editor's note – The following letter and several future letters were in envelopes that included the notation "Censored by Lt. Wm. D. Biner 0-733517." The envelope for this particular letter also featured a small bomber with the saying "Keep 'Em Flying")

Algeria[162]

June 26, 1943

Dear Mother & Dad & Fritzy,

Just a few lines to keep you posted as to my whereabouts. We have finally settled down to business in a regular squadron[163] now and it's a lot better than when we were in Rabat.[164]

Jake Schell[165] and Frank McBreen[166] are here and we had quite a get together. Jake played guard and Frank was a fullback at Gonzaga, 'less your memory fails.

The nights are cold as the devil here but it makes sleeping well. The days are hot but you don't perspire much and it's good for suntan. Conveniences just aren't and the same goes for the Vienna sausages, but we all have home and home cooking staring us in the face when our missions are over and we get to go home.

---

[162] At the time the 97th Bombardment Group was stationed at Chateaudun-du-Rhumel, Algeria
[163] 342nd squadron.
[164] Rabat is the capital of Morocco and was first settled in the 3rd century B.C.E.
[165] Jake Schell (1918-2009) was the son of John & Catherina Schell. He joined the U.S. Air Corps on Jan. 19, 1942.
[166] 1st Lt. Francis J. McBreen (1919-1989) was a friend from Spokane. He joined the U.S. Air Corps on Nov. 3, 1941.

We have a navigator in the tent now that has finished and is awaiting orders to leave. We figure we have a good chance on being home for Christmas. Well, must buzz off now. Read about us in the papers.

Love to all,

Bill

July 8, 1943

Dear Mother, Dad, Freddy & All,

Still looking for mail every day and never getting any. Haven't heard from any of you since that one letter in Rabat.

Well, how did you spend your Fourth of July? Ours was exciting, but not as exciting as the day after. We really had a lot of fun trying to inaugurate our national holiday on the Italians. But then, you follow our doings in the paper and know as much about that as I do.

By the way, we have a lot of time on our hands between missions and reading is a pleasant pastime, so could you send the "Coronet"[167] and

---

[167] The Coronet was a general interest magazine, owned by Esquire and published from 1936 through 1971.

maybe the Sunday P.I. or Times?[168] It would be appreciated.

We have an old quarry near the field that a creek runs into and which we use as a swimming hole on these hot afternoons. There is a wind here that blows off the desert and is called a sirocco.[169] It is about the hottest air outside a blast furnace I have ever felt. The wind has shifted now, but during the sirocco siege the temp stayed around 107° all the time. If I ever needed a cold beer, it was then.

We are in the oldest and most famous group in the present war and they have a hard time remembering the last time they lost a ship. Even then the crew was saved and interned in Germany. So don't fret too much. This is the safest plane in the world, and the most feared by the pursuit.

I have yet to get a shot at any plane – they usually stay out of range and stunt for us. Especially the Italian pilots. The Germans will get reckless occasionally, but they don't last long with a bunch of 17's. Thirty-five out of fifty were shot down Tuesday for being too daring.

---

[168] The Post-Intelligencer and the Times were the two major Seattle newspapers.
[169] Random House Dictionary describes sirocco as "a hot, dry, dust-laden wind blowing from northern Africa and affecting parts of southern Europe."

Here's hoping I get mail soon. You can send regular mail if you want to write more.

Love to all,

Bill

During the first few days of July Allied Forces in North Africa were engaged in Operation Husky, the invasion of Sicily. Diversionary operations to Sardinia and Greece kept the Germans off-guard. The Allied air forces launched 3700 aircraft to soften up the German and Italian defenders of Sicily before General George Patton led his Seventh Army ashore on July 10, 1943. After five weeks of fighting, during which Bill participated in further bombings of the strategic island, Sicily fell to the Allied forces. Unfortunately, most of the German troops, under the command of Hermann Goering, escaped across the Messina Strait to the Italian mainland. However, 100,000 Italians were taken prisoner and over 10,000 Axis troops were killed.

July 13, 1943

Cedar City, Utah

Dear Mom, Dad and Fritz,

I got your second letter today. I'm glad to hear you've heard from Bill. I hope he does get back next fall.

Well, I'm still flying, but that's all. Frankly, I'm not doing too well. I just can't seem to do the right things at the right time. But that doesn't worry me too much, since I still want to be bombardier. Keep praying for me. I hear they are really cracking down on them at Santa Ana. If I do make it, I'll probably be there only a few weeks.

I got two letters from Bob Perkins[170]. I answered the first one, but I haven't had time to answer the last one yet. They are really keeping us busy here. I'm way behind on my letters.

We had another field meet today. Squadron five won just about every event. Also an open pass night. How does Fritz like Pocatello? Has she made a bunch of new friends? Tell her not to date any of those cadets.

Love, Bob

July 15, 1943

Still no mail, but guess it will catch up one of these days. Would sure like to get some soon, though. They are keeping us pretty busy as you can tell by the papers. I would like to read some of the accounts in our glorified "journals."

Have had a birds-eye-view of the whole thing and it has been quite exciting. The most exciting part

---

[170] Bob Perkins was Bob's first cousin, the son of his aunt, Mary Cecelia Biner Perkins.

was my own participation in the affair. We have really done a great deal of damage in our own way and everyone has come back without a scratch.

After my sixth mission yesterday[171] they took my name and (Seattle) address for the Seattle papers. Don't know what it will be, but more than likely "bunk." McBreen and Schell are almost through with their missions; five to go I believe, and ready to go back to Spokane. They don't seem any too sorry about it. They are both going to get married – the sad characters.

How is Freddy getting along at the beach?[172] I bet she isn't as tanned as I am at that.

There isn't any news, really. All I do is read detective books between missions – my first venture in that line – and that is all.

More later, Bill

---

[171] Bill's first six missions were all over the island of Sicily. His plane, the Berlin Sleeper, dropped 300 and 500 pounds on railroad lines and air bases near the towns of Sciacca, Gerbini, Catania and Messina. Softened up by the constant bombardment, Sicily would fall to U.S. and British ground troops on August 17, 1943.

[172] Bill's little sister was not frolicking at the beach on Puget Sound. By now their dad had accepted the job as brewmaster at the East Idaho Brewing Co. and the family had moved to Pocatello, Idaho. Bill did not know. He was still addressing his letters c/o Silver Springs Brewery in Port Orchard, Washington.

July 17, 1943

Cedar City, Utah

Dear Mom, Dad and Fritz,

I'm writing this at the airport. I had my 5 hr. check the other day. I didn't do too well, but I think I'm improving now. Yesterday and today I did spins and stalls. You have no idea what it feels like to drop 500 feet in about two seconds. My instructor said if I could do the easier stuff like my spins and stalls, I would be O.K.

Just because I said I may leave anytime, it doesn't mean you can't write. Even if I leave they forward the letters. However, there may be one today. Our detachment is putting on a program to raise funds. One seat costs 18.75. We're all sold out, and have over 10,000 all ready.

We had open pass last night for winning the track meet. I guess the girls around here will all miss me. I was just getting to enjoy this town.

Well, Santa Ana isn't far off. In about 3 weeks you'll find out if I'm a wash-out or officer material.

Well, what is Ignats[173] doing with herself these days?

Write soon. Love, Bob

---

[173] Yet another nickname for his little sister.

P.S. Falstaff on Fred Allen's program[174] entertained us the other night. He was really good. Well the mail came, but no letter. I expect to leave somewhere around the first of next week.

Three days later Bob Biner was on a train destined for Santa Ana, California. The following is a form letter that Bob was required to send home after his arrival in Santa Ana. The only thing in his handwriting is what follows the address at the bottom of the letter.

July 22, 1943

Santa Ana Army Air Base

Dear Mom and Dad,

I'm sending this from the Classification Center here at the Santa Ana Army Air Base, where I arrived today. I was met at the train and am now here with the rest of the future Army Air Crews.

I've been registered and assigned to Squadron 5, where I shall remain for about two weeks. During that time, I will have my physical examinations and test which will determine whether I become a

---

[174] Fred Allen (1894-1956) was a radio celebrity and comedian who hosted *Texaco Star Theater* from 1940 through 1944. The variety/comedy show featured a host of humorous characters including the pompous poet Falstaff Openshaw, played by the voice actor Alan Reed (1907-1977), who later became the original voice of Fred Flintstone.

pilot, Bombardier, or Navigator. After being classified, I will be assigned to another squadron here on this post, and then my actual preflight training begins. That preflight training will last for about nine weeks and then I will be sent to one of the flying schools to start my flying training.

You will, no doubt, think it strange receiving this type of letter from me instead of a personal note, but here is why: Our Commanding Officer knows that during the next few days, some of us will be apt to forget to write to the folks at home.[175] This is his way of letting you know where I am and that I am well. It's just one of the many indications that I shall be well taken care of in the Army Air Forces. Another is my protection by National Service Life Insurance which is granted me free of charge all through my training period.

I know I'll have more nice things to tell you when I write a real letter. In the meantime, please let me hear from you. My address is:

Squadron 5, Army Air Base, Santa Ana, Calif.

Arrived last night. I'll write again as soon as I get time.

Love, Bob

---

[175] Not likely with Bob Biner, who seemed to write several times per week.

P.S. We couldn't leave the platform at L.A. so no one knows I'm here. I didn't have Grandmaws phone number anyhow.

July 23, 1943

Santa Ana, Cal

Dear Mom, Dad, Fritz,

Well, here I am in Santa Ana. It goes without saying of course. I don't like it. I never tasted such rotten water in all my life. We haven't done anything so far except stand in inspection. They were really nice to us before we left Cedar City. Some of us went on a picnic before we left. We went to Cedar City. We went to Cedar Brooks. It's a canyon. You certainly don't have to leave the U.S. to see beautiful sights. We also had some fried chicken. Boy it was just like home.

We left Cedar City Tuesday night and arrived here Wednesday evening. We laid over in Los Angeles about an hour, but none of us could leave the platform.

After Monday, we start our tests. It will take us about two weeks to get classified or "wash-out". We will be quarantined for two weeks and then we can see visitors. After six weeks we can get off the post. The food is O.K., but you have to eat fast and reach faster. The inspections are really rigid, and you have to be on your toes all the time.

The sun here really burns, but it isn't too hot. The nights are cool.

Did you get my box yet? We go to the P.X. one hr. a week, so we don't enjoy many luxuries. There is a church here on the post, so maybe I can get to church next Sunday.

The talk around here is very discouraging, but I'm still hoping and praying. I'll know in about two weeks if I make it or not. All for now....Love, Bob

---

July 25, 1943[176]

Dear Freddy,

I should have written you sooner but I know you will not hold it against me. We have been pretty busy and letter writing is pretty tame. I'll bet you are having a swell time there in Port Orchard this summer swimming in the Sound. When I get back I'll have to tell you about the places I've been swimming since I left. Once we went swimming off a tiny island right in the middle of the ocean. It was really swell and we didn't know the little fish swimming around us would attack and eat us if we stayed still long enough.

I will try and send you something for your birthday if I can ever get to a town where there is

---

[176] This endearing letter to his 11 year-old sister did not reach Pocatello until August 12th. But mail to the troops was even slower. Bill did not yet know that his family has moved to Idaho.

something to buy. It will probably be late though, so don't expect anything until it gets there. Happy Birthday! [177]

Tell Mother there is a chaplain in a camp near here whose name is Lynch and comes from the east someplace. I have never met him so don't know if he is any relation, but it is a common name. She will like that.

I still haven't received any mail this month but expect a pile of it one of these days. Have Mother send my glasses and some candy bars if she can. The glasses are in one of the bags at Grandpa's. (The candy is in a store.) (Not rock candy)

Take good care of yourself and I'll pop in one of these days and surprise you.

Love and kisses, Bill

P.S. Are you going into the eighth grade this fall, or high school?

Note – On the very day that Bill wrote this innocent letter to his little sister, U.S. troops were engaged in close combat with German and Italian forces in northern Sicily. Much of the island was now under the control of Allied forces, thanks in no small part to the precision bombing of the U.S.

---

[177] Fritzy's 12th birthday was on August 26th.

Air Corps and the Royal Air Force. Because of the crisis Italian Prime Minister Benito Mussolini received a vote of no confidence from his own Grand Council of Fascism. On July 25th he was relieved of his duties by King Victor Emmanuel III and placed under arrest. He escaped two months later and was put under the protection of Adolf Hitler. But his power, health and influence over the Italian public had seriously weakened. He was executed by a mob on April 28, 1945, two days before Hitler committed suicide.

July 28, 1943

Santa Ana, Cal.

Dear Mom, Dad, and Fritz,

I got your letter today. It really came at the right time. I've been feeling pretty blue lately. Yesterday I was gigged for a loose bed. Today I spent a half hr. on it, and he gigged me again and gave a tour. I wouldn't feel so bad if I didn't try so hard.

We've been taking tests for the last two days. I don't know how I did, but I think I passed the mental O.K. I'm in nice condition for the physical. I got the piles again. I hope they don't find out about it. They can wash me out for that.

I saw Bill Andrews, my pal from Fresno. He has been classified as a pilot. Bevo is still my bunk mate. I got a letter from Bob Perkins and one from

Auntie Rie yesterday. Bob is sure a cute kid. He has written me three letters so far. That's as many as Fritzi has written.

Tomorrow we get our personal interviews and Friday we get our physicals. I'm going to try to phone some of the relatives as soon as I get a chance. Well, it's almost time for me to walk off my tour. Love, Bob

July 31, 1943
Santa Ana, Cal.
Dear Mater, Pater, and Sister,

I received the last letter you sent to Cedar City yesterday. Well, we finished our tests yesterday.

---5:30p.m.

I just got back from retreat and your letter was here. I'm sure glad to hear Bill is doing well. I'm going to write him again tonight.

I also have some bad news. I don't think I'll make bombardier. The Lt. called me in yesterday and told me my aptitude rating showed I was not likely to make good as a pilot. I'm so disgusted I don't know what to do. I told him I would take pilot if the board decided against my being bombardier. I doubt if I'll ever make the grade though. My heart just isn't in it. Of course I don't know if I'll make anything until the results of the physical come out. I'm pretty sure I didn't wash on my eyes. They were 20-20. My depth perception was 3, which is practically perfect. Three means I was 3 millimeters off, and we are allowed 30. A lot of the boys from Cedar City have already washed out. Most of them on eyes, color blindness, (?), and personal interview.

We had two Catholic Chaplains around talking to us today. They heard confessions and are saying mass at 6:00 tonight. They sure are swell guys.

After that I'll be walking another tour. Our C.O., the worst in the place, told us yesterday we would have no inspection today. I was lying on my bunk with my tie off when in he popped. He gave me a tour for being out of uniform and said we should be ready for inspection at all times.

Our squadron is composed of Sqd. Five from Cedar City and 150 guys from Grand Forks. We took 3rd place in retreat last Sunday, our first time here. It's some sort of a record.

Sunday, August 1.

Well, I'll finish this letter yet. Today is free. The only thing we have to do is make mess formations and march in the parade today. If we get first place, we'll go to the beach someday. We only have to beat about 35 other squadrons.

We should be classified about the end of next week. It sure is hot here. The boys just said to tell you hello, and we'll all be up for a chicken dinner and about a barrel of beer in about 9 months.

Jim Kelly[178] is now a Lte. and is stationed at Moses Lake. Love, Bob

---

Meanwhile, back in North Africa, Bob's older brother was receiving a decoration for his first missions. On August 4, 1943, Lt. William D. Biner was awarded the bronze Oak Leaf Cluster for the Air Medal, "for meritorious achievement while participating in five sorties against the enemy."

Aug. 7, 1943
Santa Ana, Cal
Dear Mom, Dad and Fritz,

I got your letter the day before yesterday. This will be the last one from me for a week. We are going on a bivouac for a week, starting tomorrow.

Well, we were classified today. I'm not a bit satisfied. I'm a pilot. I'm the only one that requested bombardier training that didn't get it. All my other pals got pilot, so I guess that will make it a little better.

I got a letter from Uncle George the other day. He said he was expecting me this weekend. When I said I was confined to the base for six weeks, I mean I don't leave it. I also got a letter from John

---

[178] James J. Kelly was from Ellensburg. He was born in 1921.

Pooler. He is coming down with his folks. He could come out to the post to see me, but I'll be away on bivouac. I'm sure getting disgusted with this air corps.

The mail just came in. I got a letter from Aunt Julia telling me to come out when I get into town.

Even though I'm classified, I won't be a "cadet" until I move to pre-flight school here in Santa Ana.

Love, Bob

August 16, 1943

Dear Mom, Dad, and Fritz,

We got back from bivouac today. We had to walk all the way back. It was only 14 miles, but my feet are really sore.

We slept in the open along with scorpions and tarantulas. Only one kid was bitten, but we killed plenty. We went on two hikes. One seven miles with half packs, and one 12 miles with full packs. We went to lectures and a bunch of other stuff. We didn't have to shave all week. The worst part about it was the flies. There were millions of them all over the place. It wasn't too bad, but we all appreciate the barracks now. Boy, were we dirty.

We have freedom of the post now. I went to the service club tonight. Boy you ought to see it. It's really swanky. Deep chairs all over the place. Oil paintings all over the walls, also two huge murals. A big soda fountain and a library full of the latest books and magazines. Ping-Pong tables. Study tables with typewriters. Everything is strictly modern, and it's plenty big.

We got our mail at the bivouac area. I received your last letter and the candy today. The candy is really good, and if you don't believe me, just ask the guys around my bunk. That was really a swell letter from Bill. I told Uncle George I wouldn't be able to make it.

Jim Driscoll was classified bombardier. He wanted pilot. I wish I could trade with him. Only about ten guys from sqd. 5 in Cedar "washed". We should go into pre-flight in about a week or so. Then we have to start studying again. We got gypped out of our cadet uniforms. They quit issuing them the week we came. Now the only way you can tell us from the regulars is by the collar insignia. We should be getting in to L.A. in about two weeks.

P-38s[179] are flying over the base all the time. They sure look neat. This is all for tonight.

Love, Bob

August 18, 1943

---

[179] The American-made Lockheed P-38 Lightning was a long-range fighter-bomber that could carry 1000 pounds of bombs and reach speeds of nearly 400 mph.

Dear Folks,

I'm sorry to be late writing but conditions beyond my control prevented me from doing so sooner.

We had a big celebration yesterday – barbecue – movies –after our raid, celebrating the 97th's 152nd raid and a year of bombing.[180] The oldest outfit in the business.[181]

Sunday we had a pleasant surprise when Bob Hope[182], Frances Langford[183] and troupe gave a show for us. It was the best thing I have seen since arriving in this hell-hole. After the show I introduced myself and I wrote a note to Paul which he will give him on his return. He said Paul was making his (Hope's) next picture[184] and that "Dixie"[185] was quite a success.

---

[180] The 97th Bombardment Group flew its first mission out of England as part of the 8th Air Force on August 17, 1942. They bombed a German marshalling area near Rouen, France.

[181] The men might not have realized it yet, but there was an additional reason to celebrate. Allied ground forces won the battle for Sicily on that very day.

[182] Bob Hope (1903-2003), the legendary comedian and actor, entertained American troops with his USO show for nearly half a century. He and his wife Dorothy were good friends of Paul & Julia Biner Jones. Paul Jones produced six of Hope's movies.

[183] Frances Langford (1913-2005) was an American singer and actress.

[184]The production of "Road to Utopia," starring Hope, Bing Crosby and Dorothy Lamour, and produced by

Spent Sunday night in Tunis and was eaten alive by bed bugs in one of the <u>better</u> hotels. Got about an hours sleep all night and my buddy got two. I still have big red welts all over my body. Some fun!

I received a letter from you yesterday-my first-and it was mailed July 24. Today I got a V-mail that was postmarked July 8th. As far as I am concerned you can stop all V-mail writing. You can't put as much in them and I can't see where they get here any faster. Also got a letter from Helen and George that was very enjoyable.

Got by my thirteenth raid[186] yesterday in a very easy manner although we wreaked a great deal of damage on the enemy. Only have thirty-seven to go now and I can go back to the land of cold beer and air-conditioning. Still don't know if the watch and stockings reached you and just what goes on. From your letter you are now in Pocatello but that's all I know. Do you have a nice place to live?

The picture of Bob was good but did he <u>have</u> to stand under a malted milk sign? That's what I

Jones, began on Dec. 3, 1943. It was not released until March 1946.

[185] "Dixie" opened on July 30, 1943 and starred Bing Crosby and Dorothy Lamour. Produced by Paul Jones.

[186] Following the attacks on Sicily, Bill dropped 500 pound bombs on marshalling yards in Naples, San Giovanni, Foggia, Rome and Terni, Italy. On his 13th mission he dropped fragmentation bombs on an air base on Salon, France.

call subtle torture. Well, no more for now. Keep on writing. If you send me any magazines I think they have to come through subscriptions, direct.

Love to all, Bill

August 23, 1943

Dear Mom, Dad and Fritz,

I got your second letter today, Mom. I know I've been lax in my letter writing lately, but I just haven't been writing.

Well, I had a nice visit with the Bass family over the weekend.[187] They came out Sat night and Sunday afternoon. Sunday Mr. & Mrs. Strutzle[188] came with them. Their Grandma came too. She sure is cute. They also brought a letter from Aunt Julia. She sent me five dollars and asked me to write her. It sure made me feel foolish. I'm sure in a fix. How am I going to spend my first night

---

[187] Alton Bass and his wife Nellie Eichelberger Bass were old friends of the Biners. They lived in Spokane before moving to Los Angeles. Their son Tom was in the Air Corps.

[188] Joseph Strutzel (1875-1955) and his wife Mary Punch (1883-1971) were old family friends of the Biners and the Lynches. They were married in Phoenix, British Columbia, the mining town where Theophil Biner built a brewery. They moved to Calexico, California with the Biners when they opened a brewery in Mexicali, Mexico. This would suggest that Joseph Strutzel had a job at the brewery.

with Julia, Bass's, Geo Biner and Poolers? They all expect me.

We paraded for the Governor last Sunday.[189]   If they show it in the newsreels, look for me at the end of the squadrons.   Tomorrow I have to go down and get my wisdom teeth pulled out.   They are doing it to a lot of the group.

What a nice piece of praise. Did Betty make it up?

Taps always cuts me short.

Love, Bob

August 24, 1943

Dear Grandma and Gramps,

Well, here I am months behind again. I'm all through with my classification tests and everything. I have been classified a pilot. I was the only one who requested bombardier that didn't get it, but maybe they know best.

They are really giving us an education, but most of it seems to be for an infantry soldier. I just came back from a week of bivouac. On that we do everything a food soldier does. We sleep in the

---

[189] The governor of California at the time was Earl Warren. Warren went on to become the Chief Justice of the U.S. Supreme Court. The Warren Court ended legalized racial segregation in the United States through several landmark decisions.

open, along with the tarantulas and scorpions. We eat "k" rations all done up in a little box. We take extended hikes, with a full pack. We crawl on our belly and capture imaginary positions. It doesn't resemble the Air Corps very much, but it's all in a day's work. We still have K. P. and all the other details.

Today I have to get both my wisdom teeth pulled out. Some fun. In ten days we get our first day off the post.

I hear you had another fall Grandma. You shouldn't try walking when there isn't anyone around. I saw a friend of Grandpa's the other day. Mr. Strutzle. How long did Grandma Biner stay with you? Can you imagine her flying like that?[190]

Well, I have to start cleaning the windows.

Love, Bob

August 24, 1943

Dear Mom, Dad and Fritz,

I just got through writing to Uncle Fred and Grandma. I haven't anything to say that you haven't heard before tho.

---

[190] Juliana Biner flew to Seattle to visit family and friends and stayed with Dan & Mate Lynch. Juliana was 82 at the time.

I went to a show last night. We have three theatres on the post. I'm going to send some records home. Danny Gaunt[191], one of my roommates at Cedar composed all the songs. I won't get them for a couple of weeks yet.

We will probably move into Pre-flight sometime next week. There the discipline will be stiffer. It gets worse the farther we get along. I sure hope you can find some way of getting down here Mom. You could visit the relatives and the Poolers during the week and me on the weekends. If you two can't get enough gas, I may be able to put enough aside to finance a trip when they start paying me $75.00 a month.

I wish you would send me that letter of Bills, about flying the Berlin Sleeper. The first one he sent me is in that pile I sent home. Did you read those student regulations I sent home? Last Sat. we went to a radio broadcast in town. It's called "Hi Mom", and they broadcast about three days a week. It's in the morning. It's put on by the Air Forces.

---

[191] This could be a Daniel Gaunt, who was born in Indiana in 1917 and died in California in 1962. Danny Gaunt is mentioned in a gossip column in the March 13, 1943 issue of Billboard Magazine. "Off the Cuff," which reported on the latest news concerning various artists informs readers that, "Danny Gaunt, piano-voice, (has gone) into the air force." On Feb. 20, 1941, Danny Gaunt, who listed his home as Indianapolis, took out a copyright on a song. It was called *Go 'Way Now.*

Love, Bob

North Africa
August 24, 1943
Dear Mother, Dad, Freddy;

Just a few lines to ask a few questions. I haven't had any more mail other than the two I answered. Funny thing: the first one I got was mailed July 24th and the second one was mailed July 8th. If you don't have a letter in the mail now with this information, I wish you would write and give it to me.

Did you receive the stockings and wrist watch from Brazil? Did you receive my request to send a picture to Maxine Gray [192]– 311 E. Sinto? Have you paid George and Julia what I owe them and looked into the income tax problem? I don't think I have to pay anything now since some bill has been passed.

Can't understand why you haven't received more than two letters. I didn't know you had moved and was addressing all of them to Port Orchard. I guess you know all this moving necessitates red tape over here on my part. No offence intended. Only hope you are settled for good now.

---

[192] Maxine Dorothy Gray was a young woman who lived on the same street as the boarding house in Spokane. Bill met her while a student at Gonzaga. With Jeanne now out of the picture Maxine would become the object of Bill's affection.

I've been through Pocatello but didn't stop long enough to remember it. I would like to get back and learn to love it though. Another 36 missions[193] now and I can.

No more for now.

Love to all,

Bill

P.S. Enclosed are some postcards I picked up in Tunis on a visit.

August 25, 1943

Dear Mother, Dad & Freddy;

Just got back from a very successful raid to find two letters from you. One dated July 30th, the other August 9th. I was pretty darn tired and my nerves edgy, but the letters were a better pick-me-up than a shot of Rye. (Which we don't have anyway.) Now that we have the correct addresses there shouldn't be any hitch in the mail service.

A couple of us went on a little jaunt across the country the other day for gravel to put on our tent floor and we happened on one of the roads the Germans used for their retreat. There were wrecked tanks and trucks and unused ammunition all over creation and neat little rows

---

[193] On his 14th mission Bill dropped fragmentation bombs on a depot in Tortorella, Italy.

of iron-crossed graves with names like Gruber and Vogel and Schultz lettered in gold. The majority had been in their late teens and early twenties.[194] On one crossroad a large French tank had received a direct hit and the crews of two Frenchmen were buried right beside the tank. One of the treads was used as a border for the graves and the French farmers keep fresh flowers on it at all times.

It's so darn peaceful here now that it's hard to imagine what a hell it was at one time. We have flown low over the famed Hill 609 many times and it certainly is a sight. That was some battle![195] The entire country is dotted with wrecked German planes and an occasional Spitfire.[196]

Saw a beautiful dogfight[197] this afternoon over the target with our P-38's coming off winners. One

---

[194] All German graves in Algeria from WW I and WW II have been relocated to the German War Cemetery in Deli Ibrahim, Algeria.

[195] On April 22, 1943 the U.S. II Corps, under the command of General Omar Bradley, successfully battled German troops to gain control of strategic Hill 609 in Tunisia. As U.S. forces moved from the west, and British forces under Field Marshall Bernard Montgomery moved from the east, the Germans were dealt a major strategic defeat and were forced to retreat from North Africa.

[196] The Spitfire was a fighter used by the RAF (Royal Air Force) of Great Britain.

[197] A dogfight is a military term for an engagement at close quarters between small and highly maneuverable planes. The big bombers like the B-17 had fighter

Fritz came so close to us I could see the pilot. He wasn't looking for trouble; just trying to get out of the way.

Only thirty-five[198] more now and then the homecoming. Only hope the rainy season holds off.

Write often. Love to all. Bill

N. Africa

August 27, 1943

Dear Betty,

Mother informs me that you are mad at me for not writing, when actually I have written two letters that have never been answered. One was from Florida and the other from Morocco. In fact, if it wasn't for the G. Biners and the P. Jones' I would have hardly any mail at all.

From what I gather, you are coming up in the world and your new base is in Seattle. Is that right? Also, what is this business about continuity

escorts to protect them en route to their targets. Consequently, the bomber crews witnessed many dogfights.

[198] Bill's 15th mission dropped 500 pounds on the town of Foggia, Italy.

writing?[199]   Mother is always so vague about everything.

It's hotter than h___ in this damnable country and the flies drive a person crazy. This would be no country for a squeamish stomach like yours.

Bob Hope and Frances Langford gave us a show a couple of Sundays back, and I had a talk with him afterwards. He is going to give Paul a message when he returns.

In case you are still under the allusion if you were, the famous French gentleman is quite extinct as far as I am concerned. He always sits down first etc. and the woman is definitely in second place. And you will find much better-looking girls on a Kansas farm than these French "babes."

How about dropping me a line?

Love, Bill

August 30, 1943

Dear Mom, Dad and Fritz,

---

[199] Bill's sister dreamed of being a writer. Perhaps she thought she could "get her foot in the door" as a continuity girl. According to Random House Dictionary a continuity girl is a motion picture term for a "secretary whose records of the details of each take are of special use in determining or directing the process of editing a film."

I haven't heard from you yet, but I'm writing anyway. I might get one today. Tomorrow we move into pre-flight, and then the work will begin. Pre-flight is a lot tougher than classification,

but the food is a lot better. I was on M.M.[200]. twice last week. Starting tomorrow I will be known as aviation cadet.

They pulled one of my wisdom teeth last Tuesday. That was the most painful procedure I've ever been through. Only a small part of the tooth was out of the gum, so he had to cut the gum away. Then he used a small screw driver to separate the gums. It bled for two days straight. I couldn't swallow or chew. Tomorrow he takes one out on the other side. Happy Day.

Next weekend we get open post. All my pals are making big plans. Do you suppose Julia & George would care if I took a couple of my pals with me? I don't want to go up there alone, and I don't want to crowd them.

Squadron five is still making records. We won the award for squadron of the week. For that we get to go to the beach today. The only trouble is we have to walk, and is a good 12 miles there and back. Last Sat. we won a track meet between all the squadrons in classification. We are really a pretty good bunch of boys.

---

[200] Bob remembers M.M. as Meal Management, a private's more dignified term for K.P.

Have you heard anything more from Bill? Don't forget to send me that letter. I'll send it back. Do you have my electric razor? If so, please send it down. I'm getting pretty anxious to get into town.

I suppose Bumps is back in school by now. It seems like I should be going back myself. Of course pre-flight is all school. When is Betty going to move to Seattle? Is she going out with anyone in particular now? If you can't come see me now, you'll have to save up and come down for my graduation. If I go all the way, I probably won't graduate until 11 months.

I wrote a cutting letter to the Fred Lynches so I'll probably get an answer pretty soon. You better start writing sooner too. Love, Bob

August 31, 1943

Dear Mom, Dad, and Fritz,

Received your letter yesterday. Poor Bet, she sure has her troubles. Who is this Chuck?[201]

Today we moved into pre-flight. As I expected, it's going to be plenty tough. We must have our barracks and ourselves ready for inspection any time during the day. We no sooner got there and

---

[201] "Chuck" might be Charlton Fulton, Betty's boss in Pasco. However, he usually went by the name Pat. There were other men trying to woo her at the time, and her relationship with the Mormon ensign was apparently still going on.

started packing when they called us out and lined us up for a personal inspection. Of course none of us were ready. Just to give you an idea how rigid the inspections are, they use a white handkerchief to look for dust. Even the soles of our shoes must be shined. (The ones we put under the bunks.) It does have its advantages though, namely $75.00 a month and better food. We also have the use of the service club.

I had my other wisdom tooth pulled today. I always bleed like a stuck pig. I'm glad it's the last one.

Tell Ignats I'm expecting a letter from her. Don't forget to send me that letter from Bill. I have an idea I'll be pretty rushed from now on so don't expect too much.

Love, Bob

A/C R. Biner, Sqd. 33

North Africa
August 31, 1943
Dear Grandma and Grandpa,

Hope you will forgive me for being so tardy with this letter and not think I am an ungrateful grandchild. And before I forget – thanks for sending that check when I was in Salina.

If I know you both you are right up on the latest war news, so you know what I have been doing over here. I have seventeen missions[202] to my credit now, and they have been very successful ones.

We bombed Sicily before and during the invasion, and now Italy. I was on the first Rome raid when Doolittle led it, and we really had a field day. I don't think there were two feet of railroad left in one piece in all their great yards. However, we had two engines shot out that day, and just made it back on the other two.[203]

One of my first missions, over Messina, (now in our hands) we had a nose shot off the ship by anti-aircraft, (German) but only got a scratched thumb and finger to show for it. (This is not for publication with Mother & Dad.)

We all live in tents and keep one hand free for brushing off flies and eat Spam and Vienna sausage every day – otherwise it isn't bad here. I still find it hard to drink coffee without sugar, though.

I've been over some of the old battlefields in my spare time – notably Hill 609 and the lines of retreat the Germans used – and it is quite a sight. There are German graves all over the country in

---

[202] Missions #16 and #17 dropped fragmented bombs and 500 pounders respectively on Foggia and Terni, Italy.
[203] The B-17 Flying Fortress was a four-engine low-wing monoplane bomber.

little groups. They all have black iron-crosses with gold lettering and most of the occupants were pretty young when knocked off according to the dates on the crosses.

Noticed one large French tank that was hit at an intersection of two highways and left there. The two Frenchmen were buried right beside it, and the farmers keep flowers on it and care for it pretty well, in a colorful, old-country way.

This letter is for Mollie & Fred and Ken & Grace[204] also, so I get three birds with one stone. I would just have to repeat myself anyway.

Don't drink all the beer in the country, because I know a lot of thirsty men who are just waiting to get back for a crack at it – with me at the head of the line! Love to all, Bill

---

North Africa
August 31, 1943
Dear Mother, Dad & Freddy,

Just finished tabulating my mail and I find that since I left the U.S. I have received only five letters from you. Heard recently that there was a fire in one of the main A.P.O.'s and maybe some of my mail was burned, but it isn't likely. I'm not

---

[204] Grace Sullivan was the wife of Kendall Lynch, Bill's uncle and the son of his grandparents, Dan & Mate Kendall Lynch. Fred Lynch, the other sibling of Bill's mother, was married to Molly Wiittanen.

really keeping track, but Frank[205] and the rest get mail almost daily and it is discouraging.

Is that box of candy and my glasses on the way? If you need a request to send them there is one in the letter I sent asking for them. The letter itself is all you need, and don't let some clerk tell you differently!

When the post office rush is over I am going to send a forty-dollar money order. Give ten of it to Freddy and put thirty in my account. I haven't been able to get her anything here yet, so maybe there is something she would like to buy at home. Have her get a chocolate malted for me while she is shopping.

I wrote Betty the other day, and have yet to get my first letter from her – also Bob. Food and mail have become an obsession with me.

Went to Tunis on my last day off and ate something that didn't agree with me. Was sick all night and had to miss a mission. The boys knocked over the Leaning Tower of Pisa and I'm sorry I couldn't have helped.[206]

---

[205] Probably Frank William Cranz, the pilot of Bill's bomber.

[206] On August 31, 1943 about 150 B-17s destroyed bridges and marshalling yards in Pisa, Italy. But Bill's crewmates must have been teasing him about the Leaning Tower. Although the Germans, in a typical sign of arrogance, endangered the tower by using it as

No more for now.   Did the pictures of our crew arrive yet?

Love to all, Bill

North Africa
Sept. 3, 1943
Dear Mother, Dad & Freddy,

Just received two V-mails from you dated August 12th & 18th and was glad to get them.   As you probably noticed in my preceding letter I was getting "browned-off"[207] on this mail deal.   Still would like to know where my June and July mail is.

I'm looking forward to getting my glasses and the magazines and would you send me some candy?   If there was a perpetual dry-ice I would have you send me ice cream!

You asked me why we have a different ship – I thought I explained it but if you had ever been in the army you would understand.   We just had it taken away because it was new and the person who wanted it outranked us.   Simple isn't it?

Coming back from a very successful raid on Bologna, old Sweet Betty tacked on to our formation.   It was the first time I had seen it in three months.

---

an observation post, the Allied forces were ordered to spare this magnificent and historic structure.
[207] An old expression that means "getting annoyed."

Its sweltering hot today and we are just sitting around sweating, swatting flies and thinking of old swimming holes and cold drinks we know back in the states. By the way, what does my bank balance look like now? I want to finish college in style when this war is over.

So Bob is disappointed over his classification? Well, I think he is more suited for a pilot anyway. I think he will enjoy it when he leaves Santa Ana.[208] How about sending his address?

Will write again when I send the money order and don't get so out of breath when you write a V-mail, Mother. And how is Willie's broken hand coming along?[209]

Love to all, Bill

North Africa
Sept. 10, 1943
Dear Mother, Dad & Fritzy,

Well, I guess all of you are pretty excited over the Italian set-up right now, but by the time you get this it will have worn off. Actually, it hasn't made

---

[208] Bob Biner finished up his classes in Utah in August and started preflight training in Santa Ana on September 23, 1943.
[209] This was an expression the family used when someone was negligent about writing. Since Bill prefaced it to "Willie" he is talking about his father, William.

any difference in our lives; we just go on bombing the Germans and wait for the real Armistice.

I think I have all my mail now. Got about 16 June and July letters yesterday, birthday cards and all. Also got a letter back that I had mailed in June to you and where I asked to have a picture sent to Maxine Gray. The censor took till now to return it. Also returned the letter I wrote to Betty last June, so no wonder she didn't hear from me.

Received four letters and a greeting from Helen and George and one from Julia – also one from B. Webster – so I had an orgy of letter reading for a while.

Glad to hear the watch and stockings arrived safely. It had me worried for a while. However, I still don't know whether you have paid off Julia, Helen & George. If you haven't I wish you would right away.

Have been bothered with a sore throat and have missed some missions so I only have twenty at this present time.[210] Thirty to go and I don't expect to be home by Christmas. But who knows, maybe the big Armistice will be signed by then. I wish I could say more but this will have to do for now.

---

[210] Missions #18 and 19 dropped 500 lb. bombs on air bases and marshalling yards in Bologna and Viturba, Italy. Bill's twentieth mission was to drop fragmentation bombs on Foggia.

Love to all, Bill

Sept. 12, 1943

Dear Mom, Dad and Fritz,

Well, today is the end of an interesting weekend. I rode in with Tom Bass yesterday. Aunt Julia and family were waiting for me at his place. They took Bill Andrews and me out to their place. The George Biners were there and then my three cousins came out. They are three good looking gals. They had fried chicken and lemon pie. Boy did I ever eat.

We spent a considerable part of the night around his bar. Aunt Julia had a little gal out there. She is majoring in art in high school. I think she was trying to fix things up for me. She was a nice gal and everything, but you know me, I'm very fussy.

Say Mom, this is important so don't forget about it. Do you still have my ration book? If so, please send it. I only need stamp 18, but they have to tear it out.[211]

I'm still trying to save some money. I'm determined that at least someone in my family comes down to see me. You probably wouldn't

---

[211] War ration stamps were issued for many items during WW II in order to save as much material as possible for the war effort. Stamp #18 allowed the holder to purchase one pair of shoes between Jun. 16th and Oct. 31st, 1943.

even recognize me. I broke the earpiece on my glasses. I lost the set out of my ring, and I lost my watch in Cedar. I'm sure hard on material.

Tell Fritz I'm still waiting for a letter.

Love, Bob

North Africa
Sept. 17, 1943
Dear Mother, Dad & Freddy,

Just received your grand box of eatables and it was the object of much apt attention. It was carried in style to my tent by two men with the largest tapeworms in our camp and I suddenly became quite popular with everyone.

You know me better than to think I got the short end of the deal – in fact, I have a good share left at this writing – but you were blessed a hundred times by one and all for the taste of home. Everything got here in good shape and it really tasted like a million dollars. You certainly haven't lost the old knack, Mother.

I'm writing this with one eye out of the tent watching a herd of cows. If the Arab cowboy lets them come any closer I'll bet we have fresh meat in the chow, for once, tonight.

I have a picture taken of us after our record raid but it is too large for the envelope. I'll try and get it home some other way. I'm sending a memento of that raid – I don't think the censor will take it out – and Dad can sport it in his office for visitors.[212] Gives you a fertile field to work on Pappy! Also enclosed is the money order. Don't forget; ten dollars goes to Freddy for whatever she wants. Give her fifteen if you like.

No more for now, sweethearts, hope I hear from you soon.

Love to all, Bill

Allied forces received some unexpected assistance in their attack on German forces in Italy by Italian résistance fighters. During late September 1943, the people of Naples put up a spirited fight against German troops. Hitler had ordered Naples to be destroyed before it fell into Allied hands, but the good people of Naples would not let that happen. The four-day battle became known as "Four Days of Naples". Hundreds of citizens died before Allied troops arrived on October 1st and the Germans retreated.

---

[212] The memento Bill sent to his father was a bomb pin from the 100th mission of The Berlin Sleeper, the first B-17 to complete 100 missions. It was Bill's 21st mission and his first drop of 1000 lbs, which destroyed a bridge in Capua, Italy. The pin is now in the safekeeping of James Bernazani, the son of Bill's sister Fritzi.

The crew of the legendary B-17 Berlin Sleeper, in Depienne, Tunisia, after the completion of its 100th mission. Bill Biner is third from the left in the back row. The super-sized bomb logo marks the 100th mission. Back row (left to right): Roy Henthorn, tail gunner; Ed Hart, co-pilot; Bill Biner, bombardier; Frank Cranz, pilot; Scott Bascom, navigator; George Wright, radio/ball turret gunner. Front row (left to right): Stan Gonsier, radio/waist gunner; Hoyt Rogers, waist gunner; Leonard Hardy, 2nd engineer; Fred Neufield, 1st engineer/top gunner.

Sept. 20, 1943

Dear Mom, Dad and Fritz,

This is just a short note. There isn't much to talk about. I went into L.A. again last Sat. It took me 2 ½ hours to go the 30 miles from Santa Ana.

I looked up the Poolers. They sure seemed glad to see me. So was I. Loretta[213] and I went to the Coconut Grove[214]. Freddy Martin[215] and orchestra was there, also Shirley Temple[216]. She is a cute looking little gal. The floor was really packed. The place is nice, but rather expensive. I had more luck with Taxies this time.

I bought a cap in Santa Ana. It is a regular officer's cap with the cadet band on top of the officers. I don't know if I'll get to go out this week or not. I already have 5 demerits for this week, and I still have 3 more days to go.

The work is getting harder all along. I don't know how I'm even going to learn code. The other guys are way ahead of me all ready.

I got my pictures, but I don't know when I'm going to get time to mail them. They are only two inches

---

[213] Loretta Pooler, sister of John & Betty Pooler, was another friend from the Ellensburg days. She married G.J. Mittleman.

[214] The Coconut Grove was a nightclub in L.A.'s Ambassador Hotel.

[215] Freddy Martin (1906-1983) was a bandleader from Cleveland, Ohio.

[216] Shirley Temple, born in 1925, was an enormously popular child movie star.

square, but they cost plenty. How about my stamp book?

Love, Bob

Sept. 24, 1943

Dear Mother, Dad & Freddy,

Received your V-mail telling me about the Idaho Senator, so I guess you hadn't received the letter I sent saying that all my mail had caught up. Something like that would do more harm than good.[217]

I have a picture of the crew taken in front of our famous ship, but I am afraid to send them until I find out that they won't be "lifted" en route. Incidentally, our ship is going back to the states on a bond-selling tour, but a crew from another outfit

---

[217] Bill's father had complained about Bill not receiving their mail and his boss at the East Idaho Brewing Co., Laurence M. Parish, took it upon himself to contact Democratic U.S. Senator D. Worth Clark. Senator Clark in turn contacted Adjutant General James Alexander Ulio, who looked into the matter. General Ulio , who was a native of Walla Walla, reported the reasons for the delay to Senator Clark and revealed that Lt. Biner had since received all of his missing mail and that service to North Africa was now "particularly good." Senator Clark wrote to Mr. Parish to convey the good news. But needless to say, the slow mail delivery continued.

is flying it. If we were through we would be the lucky ones, but we aren't.

I picked up some little purses in Tunis the other day, but I am going to wait until I pick up more souvenirs and then send them all at once. If you people get any snapshots taken from time to time, how about sending them along? I would like to see what the new place looks like.

We have an armament officer here whose father is the brewmaster at Salt Lake. His name is Rubisch[218] and he says his Dad went to Hantke's.[219] I believe he said he did also. Also knows John Winkler in St. Paul. Do you know him?

The food has improved 100% here, and I have regained a little weight. Also got two-fifths of Scotch from a boy who picked up a supply in Cairo and Alexandria. He says nothing is rationed there at all. Can rent new Buicks for 50 cents an hour.

No more for now. Love, Bill

Sept. 25, 1943

---

[218] The soldier was Kurt Otto Rubisch (1917-2011), and like his father Otto Rubisch, he was a brewmaster. On June 25, 1943, 2nd Lt. Rubisch was relieved from the 340th Bombardment Squadron H and reassigned to the 342nd.

[219] Bill's father, along with his uncle, Gus Biner, attended Hantke's Brewery School in Milwaukee, Wisconsin from 1910-11.

Dear Mom, Dad and Fritz,

I suppose you think it's about time I wrote. We have really been busy the last week. We had a test in one thing or another almost every day. It is now Sat night, and I am now at the base. The whole post was confined this week. They are having a bus strike down here, so we couldn't go anyplace anyhow.

I should be here about four more weeks, Mom. (last of Oct) You will never see a picture of me in my cadet uniform. The main reason is we don't have any. They quit issuing those two weeks before we were classified. The picture is small, but even they are expensive down here.

What did Bill have to say in his last letter? Does he need anything? I can get any kind of candy or stuff he wants. We can get any kind of candy cheap and there is plenty of it.

I hope this strike clears up pretty soon. I think Weaver and Allen are coming down on a vacation. Tonight is only the third time I have been to the Service Club since I've been in Pre-flight; I have been to one show, which might give you an idea of how lucky I am. We never have quite enough time.

Love, Bob

The following is a "Spiritual Bouquet" that Bob prepared for his parents at the Easterbrook Chapel. It was a form that he filled out and includes a rather antiquated and now humorous offering. It is followed by a poem that was given to Bob by the Chapel's priest.

●●●

SPIRITUAL REQUEST FOR LOVED ONES

Dear *Mom & Dad*

I offer this gift as proof of my love for you. It has been purchased with my own efforts. It will bless you who received it and I am better for having prepared it.

Masses	*(4)*
Communions	*(2)*
Rosaries	*(4)*
Ejaculations[220]	*(10)*
Other Prayers	*(Every night)*

Signed Bob

SOLDIERS OF CHRIST:

We offer the following without comments. God Bless You, Father Clasby.[221]

---

[220] Bob was not being forced by the church to reveal anything embarrassing to his parents. An ejaculation was a short prayer or exclamation of faith. The term is no longer used for the obvious reason.

THE PILOT

By Joan Helen Mangan[222]

A thunderous drone from out the skies
And I look up to see
The flashing wings of man-made birds,
Flaunt with Eternity.
Dashing, diving in and out
The endless skies of blue,
As if to seek the Face of God
Hidden from our view.
I stand spell-bound, in silent prayer
And know that it may be,
My own dear boy at the controls
In Heaven's boundless sea.
And tho he be not mine, dear God,
He's still some mother's boy.
Whose every hour is filled with prayer
To guard her pride and joy.
Dear God, keep strong his brave young heart
And guide his skillful hand
You are the Master Pilot, Lord
Keep him in your command.

Bob was sent to Oxnard, California in October, 1943 for a month of primary training. The following letter was on special stationary with a picture of a B-17 dropping bombs and a letterhead

[221] Father William J. Clasby (1912-1986) was a colonel in the U.S. Army Air Corps and became a Monsignor of the Catholic Church in 1962.
[222] Joan Helen Magnon published her wartime poems in 1946 under the title Silver Wings.

that read: United States Air Force "Somewhere in Africa" 97ᵗʰ Bomb Group

Oct. 1, 1943

Dear Mother, Dad & Freddy,

Maybe this letter will break the spell. The first correspondence I have had in quite some time was a letter from Betty yesterday which was written in July. If you people have been writing I would certainly like to know where they are. The mail service gets worse all the time.

This is a red-letter day otherwise. Received official notice of my promotion today and am sporting silver bars.[223] It was effective on the 23ʳᵈ of last month but I didn't hear about it until today.

We had some men go on a trip to Cairo last week and they brought back a stack of Scotch. I managed to get three bottles of Old Parr[224] so I guess there will be some celebrating tonight. Also

---

[223] Bill was promoted to the rank of 1ˢᵗ Lieutenant.
[224] Old Parr is a blended Scotch Whiskey named in honor of Old Tom Parr, and Englishman who was purported to have reached the age of 152. An autopsy suggested his age to be less than half the claim but he remained a celebrity even in death.

have reached the half-way mark in missions, so that will be another excuse.[225]

Had a day in Tunis last week and the Red Cross have just opened a club there where, wonders, we can get a dish of ice cream! I sweated out a line for an hour for my dish and you could taste the condensed milk quite strongly, but it was a wonderful treat.

How about sending me some snapshots of yourselves and the new place? I would like to see what I'm over here for.

Keep writing and maybe some will leak through.

All my love, Bill

A/C Robert J. Biner 19194940
44-E Sqd 7, 7th A.A.F.F.T.D.
Oxnard, Cal.
Oct. 3, 1943

Dear Mom, Dad, Fritz,

Pinch me, I must be dreaming, this can't be the army.

We arrived here about nine last night. We drew our bedding, and were assigned our bungalows. Boy, what a deal. We sleep four men in a cabin,

---

[225] Bill's 22nd through 25th missions were over Benevento, Torre del Crecco, Eboli and Bologna, Italy. He dropped 100 lbs on Eboli; 500 lbs on the others.

with all the luxuries of home. We eat in a big mess hall, and have women waiters.

Today, we went to lectures, and drew our flying equipment. We drew gabardine flying tags, leather jackets, sweater, goggles and stuff. Tomorrow we get parachutes, and probably start flying Friday. This place is really modern and I have a hunch there is a catch someplace.

After our two weeks' confinement, we get every 6th day off. That means we will have to fly on some Sundays. We are flying Stimpsons.[226] They are really rugged little ships. The field has a record for the least amount of accidents of any on the coast.

We will probably be plenty busy here, just like Santa Ana.

I'll write again as soon as I get time.....Love, Bob

On October 5, 1943, General Charles Franklin Born (1903-1979), a member of Major General James Doolittle's staff, joined the 97th Bombardment Group on a mission. A copy of his letter regarding the mission, written on October 8th, was saved by Bill Biner. General Born wrote

---

[226] Bob must be referring to a Stinson. The Stinson Aircraft Company developed several models during World War II. The Stinson B-5 series was used extensively in support roles such as aerial reconnaissance and medical evacuation.

to Lt. Col. Leroy A. Rainey, Commanding Officer, that the 97th Group "kept close together and did very good bombing despite very accurate, moderately heavy flak. The conduct of the Group on the breakway was an excellent execution of a carefully prepared plan." He went on to say that "The performance of your Group on this mission impressed me deeply. The attention devoted to the planning was matched by the splendid execution of well trained and thoroughly indoctrinated combat crews. You have every right to be proud to command such efficient group of officers and men. It is my desire to commend you on the combat efficiency of your organization, its esprit de corps, morale and aggressiveness. I extend my congratulations on a job well done."

Born forwarded a copy of his letter to Major General James Doolittle. On the bottom of the copies that Rainey sent to his men, including Biner, the proud Lt. Colonel predicted that when his men "look back on your service with this organization you will be able to say with truthfulness, "I was in the 97th –the best Bomb Group of 'em all!"

Oct. 6, 1943

Dear Mom, Dad, and Fritz,

Did you get my wonderful typewritten letter? As I said before, I spent last Saturday at Balboa Beach. I had H.P. Sunday, so I didn't have time to go all the way into L.A. I had a lot of fun there, but the season is over.

I went to a dance and met Harold Owens. He is in the navy. He enlisted with Tom and Whipple[227] and Driver[228] and Richardson.[229] They are all on the same ship except Tom. He said he and Whipple would try and come out here. Ollie is the kid I used to go skiing with all the time.

I have had everyone in the barracks buying candy for me to send to Bill. We can only buy three bars at a time. I now have ten large bars, ten packages of gum and seven small bars.

We went to the pistol range today. I didn't get too good a score, but they don't keep track of them anyhow.

Is Betty still there? Tell her I have a picture for her too.

We are through with math, gunnery, ground forces, and medical aid, but we now have a flock of different subjects. We have a test in physics tomorrow. I'm still flunking in code. I just can't take it fast enough. I still have a few weeks to bring up my grade.

---

[227] Bob Wippel of Ellensburg enlisted in the Air Corps on Sept. 25, 1942.

[228] Jack Driver graduated from Ellensburg High School in 1941.

[229] Jim Richardson graduated from Ellensburg High School in 1940.

Well, I have to get busy on my physics. Write as often as you can.

Love, Bob

Oct. 7, 1943

Dear Mom, Dad, and Fritz,

I supposed you have received my last letter by now. I imagine Dad is happy now that he's got his little wife back. You're sure greedy Pop. I saw her three times in 8 months, and you only missed her for 3 weeks. They haven't forwarded any of my mail from Santa Ana yet, so I'm getting kinda anxious.

I still haven't been off the ground. Everyone has been grounded for the last 3 days. The wind has been blowing at about 70mph. They have quite a program mapped out for us. We are going to be just as busy as we were at Satan Ana. We have plenty of studying to do, and they don't give us a second chance here.

Mom, I have to have a watch. I just need something to keep track of the time while I am up. I will send you a money order for it as soon as I can, but don't wait. It doesn't have to be expensive. Today is Sunday, and it sure feels funny to be going to classes and everything. They will have a mass for us tonight. L.A. isn't out of bounds, but there is no way of getting in, except by hitch-hiking.

Gotta go to class.

Love, Bob

Oct. 10, 1943

Dear Mom, Dad and Fritz,

I received your letters Thursday. I've been going to phone you for a long time, but I haven't been able to find the time.

I'll try to get to the Jones' as soon as possible, if I get out. I already have five demerits for this week. That mean I'll have to go 4 days with not more than 3 demerits. It is practically impossible here, but I'll put out a super human effort.

I went to the Jones' last night. I really had a lot of fun. Paul is a kick in the pants, no kiddin. When are you folks coming down? Don't forget to bring my bag with you if and when you do.

I'm really in a tough spot now. I flunked my physics exam. I have two chances to bring my average up. If I don't, I'll be confined here for 4 weeks after my squadron leaves and I'll be shipped someplace else. Don't expect too much mail. I'm really cramming.

Have you heard from Bill? I still didn't get his letter about the "Berlin Sleeper".

Gotta hone up on Physics. Love, Bob

Sometime after this letter was written, Bob's mother, Harriet Lynch Biner, came down from Seattle to visit her son and other family members.

Oct. 12, 1943

Dear Folks,

Just received two letters from you, one from you Dad and I'm glad your hand is better. Really enjoyed both very much as mail has been as slim as usual. You can write V-mail if you want, Mother, but type it so that you can get something in it.

I'm sending a picture of our crew and our famous ship that someone else has flown home and selling bonds with now. Pretty poor picture of me isn't it? The pictures I'm sending have been published back there. Have you seen or read anything yet?

Aunt Helen wrote and told me the news and they want me there for the Christening.[230] Here's hoping I can make it.

This war seems to be going into its final stages. I've seen all I want of France, Italy and the Balkans and it can end anytime now. Should have thirty missions but only have twenty-eight.[231]

---

[230] George and Helen were expecting their third child in April.

[231] Bill's 26th, 27th & 28th missions dropped 1000 pounds on Brenner Pass near Bolzano, Italy and 500 pounds on Bologna.

However, it shouldn't take too long. After Christmas though, I'm afraid. Bad weather is beginning to rear its ugly head.

Never mind about sending any subscriptions now, I'd never get them, but send me all the eats you can. Fruit cake is obtainable and candy bars, etc. No nuts. We get them over here, unless they are cashews.

Here's hoping you get that deer, Dad, and I was thinking about buying your car myself. How about it? I have a $500 bonus coming next month, payable after the war and my allotment will continue to build up for some time yet.

No more for now. Love to all,

Bill

Undated Letter from Bob Biner (Could be out of order. Might have been written before Oct. 10th letter)

Dear Mom, Dad and Fritz,

Danny is playing the piano while I am writing this letter. I am writing this from the U.S.C. in Balboa Beach. I am having a good time.

I didn't go into L.A. this weekend, because I am on K.P. tomorrow. When are you coming down? I will try to be an extra good boy that week so I won't be confined.

Our squadron is doing pretty good these days. We have been winning quite a few awards lately. We have been taking most of the retreat parades. We also won the award for squadron area.

Is Betty still home? How did you like the pictures? They were the best I could get under the circumstances.

This is the first time I have touched a typewriter in two years. I got a letter from Bill the other day. He has twenty-two missions completed. I have to cut this short.

Love, Bob

Oct. 17, 1943

Dear Mother, Dan & Freddy,

Well, the days continue to roll by, but I haven't been making much progress this month. Our weather is getting worse all the time and I wouldn't be surprised to see spring in Africa.

Just got two letters from you, both mailed in August and a V-letter from Julia mailed Sept. 30th. I really am through trying to figure this mail situation.

This is wonderful country. Right now we have a plague of little red bugs that look like ticks, but aren't. There are literally millions of them all over the tent and our belongings. I only have a few inside my mosquito net, but a few can be uncomfortable in bed. Speaking of beds, I have an air mattress and a sleeping bag now so my nights have become something to look forward to. It's cold enough for a sleeping bag, too!

I hope Fred addressed the P.I. to this address, otherwise he had better get it changed or I doubt if I will ever get them. I am sending a small money order and you can use it up in L.A. Mother, if you haven't already been there. If I had known sooner, I could have been more prompt and it would have been larger.

Am sending another snapshot, and I hope you get this one. They took this one for the squadron records, and I think it is pretty good. Any news on the Berlin Sleeper II yet?

No more news for a while.

Love to all, Bill

Oct. 19, 1943

Dear Mother, Dad & Freddy,

Just received your letter with one from Bob enclosed and I'm glad to get another one soon. It's too late now to stop that investigation, and maybe it will be a good thing, if I don't get in trouble over it. I think they are doing the best they can and things can't be helped.

Glad to hear you received the pictures OK and I am sending some souvenir money for your scrapbook. I believe a lira is worth one cent right now.

You all might as well make up your minds to the fact that I won't be home this winter, as I mentioned in my last letter. In fact, I wouldn't be surprised if I was here to see the end of the war, and it might not be so bad at that, if it doesn't last too long.

In the meantime, I am getting thinner and could use something to eat. How about sending me a box of candy bars? Those bars you sent last time were good, but they didn't last long! Any kind at all will do, as we don't get anything but a little hard candy now and then. Use this letter for the post office requirements. If you have any room you could fill up the space with cashew nuts.

No, I haven't received any of the magazines or the P.I. Hope they turn up one of these days. We, the four in our tent, are buying a radio in Tunis for $110. It would cost about $30 in the states. Supply and demand and the pecunious French.

No more for now. Take care of yourself.

Love & Kisses, Bill

Oct. 22, 1943

Dear Dad and Fritz,

I guess I kinda neglected you since Mom arrived, but I've really been busy these past few weeks. I flunked my first physics test, but I made it up last exam. I got a 90. I'm still flunking my code. I have one more chance. If I don't pass it then, I'll have to stay 4 weeks longer while my squadron leaves without me.

Our squadron won the red flag this week. That makes us the top sqd for the week in pilot school.

I saw Mom Saturday night. I drove into town with Al Bass.[232] I ate supper at the Bass' and they took me out to the Jones'. It was sure swell to see Mom. I wish you and Fritz could have made it. I'll be up there some day though, and you better have a whole keg for me.

Dad, this Santa Ana is the roughest thing I've ever seen. We get gigged for the smallest thing. At times I get so mad I feel like taking a private rating and giving my nerves a chance to get back to normal. I hear life at primary is pretty soft, so I guess I'll be able to stick it out for the rest of my time here.

---

[232] Alton Bass, husband of Nellie and father of Tom Bass.

We have our naval test tomorrow, so I guess I'll have to start boning up.

Love, Bob

Oct. 27, 1943
Santa Ana
Dear Bett,

I know it's been a long time, but I've really been busy lately. We had all our tests last week and this. I finally passed code and physics. They were both plenty tough, and I just got through. We are just killing time now until we ship out, which will probably be sometime next week.

We are second from the top in pilot school, so we get our second choice of primaries. We are trying to get one close to L.A. All primary schools are heaven compared to Santa Ana.

Well, I've seen Mom for two weekends. She sure looks great. The first weekend I was supposed to be confined with tours, but my pal, Bevo got me out of it. Last weekend I was supposed to be on fire guard, Bevo got me out of that too. So far as I know, I don't have anything to hold me back this week.

Weezy and Allen came down last week. Weezy was out with her cadet, so Peg and Lorretta came out to the house. They didn't get there til after midnight, so we talked till 3 am. They slept there for the night.

Mom is leaving next Monday. I phoned Dad last Saturday night, it was sure swell hearing his and Fritz's voice. Fritz was half asleep. Well, I'm sending the picture. I only got two of them and Mom has the one.

Give my love to Grandma, and Gramps.

Love, Bob

Oct. 28, 1943

Dear Mother, Dad, & Freddy,

This is the first time I have been able to sit down and write since I received your last letter four days ago. I was called by the post-office on the same day concerning the investigation. There wasn't much I could do, as I have received most of my mail and I didn't get much satisfaction out of the deal. Maybe they will do something about forwarding mail a little faster from B.T.C. now, though.

I'm still waiting for the packages, but they are slower than mail. Could use some of those cookies and date-loaf now. Got a couple more bottles of Scotch from Cairo and it helps the morale to no end. Someday I would like to take a trip to that town. Nothing is rationed – including shoes.

In answer to your question, Mother, I now have thirty missions behind me[233] and am on the downhill run. With the weather like it is though, it will take me a long time to get the last twenty. Spent a couple of unexpected days in Sicily last week but as I didn't have any money or time, I didn't get any souvenirs. Next time I won't get caught short. They say there is some beautiful lace-work to be had for next to nothing. I will try to get some for you, Mother.

I forgot to tell you before, but I have the Air Medal now, have had it for a couple of weeks. Most everyone on a combat crew gets one sooner or later.

We almost got washed away last night during a rain storm, but it has cleared up today and we have dug a huge drainage ditch around the tent for future storms. They are really terrific.

Keep writing. Love to all, Bill

United States Air Force
"Somewhere in Africa"
97th Bomb Group
Oct. 30, 1943

Dear Mother, Dad & Freddy,

By the time you receive this the L.A. trip will be over and Dad and Freddy will probably start to

---

[233] Bill's 29th & 30th missions dropped 500 lbs on a depot in Larissa, Greece and fragmentation bombs on Rome.

regain their lost pounds. Hope you had a nice time, Mother, and how about all of us taking another trip next year?

Bob must be in primary by now and I would appreciate a letter with his address. It's raining again today and cold as the devil. I really wouldn't be surprised to see it snow. There never is a happy medium around here.

I only have 19 more to go[234], and I hope November isn't as lean a month as October was. However, I can't see how I can make it for Christmas.

Some of the stores in Tunis had imported American cloth for sale the last time I was there and the women of town were wild. They were letting the customers in the door one at a time and I actually expected to see some women seriously hurt. I guess it has been a long time since the last cloth went on sale. More stores are opening again every day, but I don't see why. They don't have a darn thing to sell.

Cigarettes are scarce down here. We nearly didn't get our allotted four packages this week, so if you can send a carton or a box of cigars I would appreciate it, also some candy if you can get it.

Love to all, Bill

---

[234] Mission #31 was a drop of 500 pounds over Weiner Nuenstadt, Austria.

United States Air Force
"Somewhere in Africa"
97th Bomb Group
Oct. 30, 1943
Dear Bette,

Received your letter from Pokey[235] with the change of address and I am glad to hear Mother still sets a good table. I would give anything to be there now.

Looking forward to the day your package gets here. You needn't send any more sugar, as we have plenty now for our coffee. However, four packages of cigarettes a week is our quota and if you have any extras lying around I would appreciate them very much.

Bought my Christmas cards today, they aren't bad considering the fact that they were made in Tunis (What a poor excuse for a city!) The cards were made with the 97th insignia embossed on cardboard. C'est la guerre![236]

I'll keep on the lookout for some of that perfume. Who knows, maybe I can find some Chanel for you. They had a lot of it in South America.

I only have nineteen to go now but expect to be here until the end of January, anyway; and this African winter is not something to look forward to.

---

[235] Pocatello.
[236] Such is war.

It's really wet and cold. And living in a damp (underscore) tent is not what I would call the American Way of Life. We have four separate families of mice living under our four cots (you would appreciate that) and they hold jubilees every night. What fun!

Well, old girl, thanks for the picture and Maxine does write – quite often.

Love, Bill

(V-Mail, early November, 1943)

Dear Mother, Dad & Freddy,

Still getting mail quite regularly from you but the packages are still among the missing. Some of the men said that last year their Christmas packages didn't arrive until March. Hope mine don't take that long.

Well, Willie is coming up in the world. Am doing a little leading now and Scotty, our navigator, has a chance of becoming the new Group navigator. That would mean a Captaincy for him. Our leading a squadron means a Captaincy for Frank, the pilot.

I have thirty-three missions now and I hope I have over forty by the end of the month.[237] Maybe I will if the weather gets better.

Have a few odds and ends of souvenirs that I will try to get home by Christmas if I can find a box for them. Anything really nice actually costs over $100 in Tunis so you can see I haven't done much shopping in the higher brackets. No more space so I'll close for now.

Love, Bill

Nov. 13, 1943

Dear Mom, Dad, and Fritz,

I got your letter the other day, but this is the first chance I've had to answer it. There isn't much to talk about. I now have 4 hours flying time. I must solo between 8 & 12 hrs. Twelve hours sounds like a lot of time to be in the air, but when you figure there are a hundred things to learn, and your life depends upon it, you really have to learn fast.

I want to set you folks straight right now. There is no need to worry. We have the best instructors in the world. All of them have at least 1000 flying hrs. We are check by two different pilots before we are allowed to solo. With the traffic pattern

---

[237] On mission #32 Bill dropped 1000 lbs on factories in Genoa, Italy. On #33 he dropped the same amount on a bridge in Recco, Italy.

here, the flying regulation, it is impossible to have an accident.

My instructor is a little shrimp like me. We both use 3 cushions to reach the controls. He really knows his stuff, and if I ever "wash out" it won't be his fault. It's really tragic to see the kids leave that have been washed out, but it's for their own good.

Robert Cummings[238] and Patric Knowles[239] are both instructors here. I'll send you a bunch of pictures of the place. You can get a good idea of our "County Club".

How do you like this, we fly and have classes as usual on Thanksgiving and Christmas. Tough luck eh?

Gotta write to Bill.

Love, Bob

N. Africa
Nov. 13, 1943
Dear Mother, Dad & Freddy,

---

[238] Robert "Bob" Cummings (1910-1990) was an American TV and screen actor. He was also the first certified instructor for the Army Air Corps in WW II.
[239] Patric Knowles (1911-1995) was a British actor who starred with Bob Hope in *Monsieur Beaucaire*, a Paul Jones movie.

Received your fruitcake the day after I sent my last letter. It was pretty dry and crumbled when cut, but that didn't stop us from gobbling it up in about half an hour. Thanks ever so much. I also received a Sunday edition of the P.I. on the same day.

The labels are for you Dad. I got them off bottles in a wrecked hangar on Corsica where the Germans made one of their last stands. The orange one looks like a take-off on Coca Cola. Apparently it's some type of soft drink or chocolate milk.

I have thirty-five now and am beginning to feel like a veteran.[240] Almost got a Me 109[241] on my last trip but my shooting was a little off. It scared him a bit though, as he didn't come in again.

We built a tunnel and door for our tent and put in a stove. Things are cozy as the devil now, but for a while we darn near froze. Our $110 radio is working pretty well and if we could get a few more cigarettes in our rations everything would be bright. Four packages a week doesn't stretch very far.[242]

---

[240] 1000 lbs was dropped on Montalto de Castro on mission #34 and he dropped incendiaries on a factory in Turin during his 35th mission.

[241] The Messerschmitt 109 was the main German single-engine fighter plane.

[242] Bill's constant search for more cigarettes shows how the tobacco industries' "patriotic" contribution of

You ought to see the Alps now, Dad, they are really beautiful, but it makes one shiver just to see them.[243]   No more for now.   There is a movie tonight and that is one occasion I can't miss.

Love to all, Bill

P.S. I got Betty some perfume.

(V-mail, mid-November, 1943)

Dear Mother, Dad & Freddy,

It's colder than anything right now, but our fire is going pretty good and I can see through the smoke well enough to jot down a letter.

The books and your letter with Betty's note arrived day before yesterday. We had a large parcel call today but I drew a blank- maybe tomorrow. All mail doesn't get here though. We still lose a few ships on the Atlantic now and then.

The clipping you sent of Lt. Bowen[244] hit it right on the head.   He was in our squadron and flew back on the Berlin Sleeper.   I suppose they will

cigarettes to the soldiers was having its intended result. Hundreds of thousands of U.S. soldiers would become addicted to tobacco and lifetime customers for the industry following the war.

[243] The Biner family came from Zermatt and Randa, Switzerland, in one of the most beautiful regions in the Alps. The famous Matterhorn towers over Zermatt.

[244] Lt. David Quinton Bowen (1918-1991) is buried in the Morris Hill Cemetery, Boise, Idaho.

have him publicized as the Sleeper's regular crew member like some of the new releases of the gunners that got a ride back on it. C'est la Guerre!

Also received your breathless note from L.A., Mother, and am waiting to hear a more lucid account. And where is Bob now?

Thirty-six now.[245] Fourteen more.

Love to all, Bill

Nov. 24, 1943

Dear Mom and Dad,

I'm sorry I waited so long to write, but I've been waiting to see how things would turn out. I told you last week how I was flying, but it's worse than that. I might as well tell you, tomorrow I go up for my last elimination ride. I know it's going to hurt you Dad, but I hope you don't think I'm just quitting. I've tried everything I know, but the fact still remains, I just can't fly. I hope you folks will understand I feel so miserable I don't know what I'm doing.

I'll probably be sent back to Santa Ana, which is the headquarters of the West Coast. You can continue to send my mail here. I didn't go any

---

[245] Bill's 36th mission dropped incendiaries on Bolzano, Italy.

place last weekend. I was going to see Allen and Weezy, but now I'm glad I didn't go. I phoned the next day. It cost me 40 cents to find they left for Wash the week before.

Now for some second hand news. Betty Webster was married last week. Nancy Robertson is engaged. Ellensburg has a P-38 base, and an artillery range. I'm sure glad to hear Bill got a medal. He sure deserves one. He's really going places.

Tomorrow is Thanksgiving. They are ready to be good to us. We won't have to go to study hall.

I've had several letters from Bevo. He is really doing fine. He was the first one to solo in his class at Cal Ana. Butch has also soloed. Boy I'm really going to hate to leave this place. It's almost time for me to go to study hall.

Love, Bob

(V-mail, Thanksgiving Day, Nov. 1943)

Dear Folks,

Just received two more packages. One was the fudge and hard candy with the small tree. The other was the cake and diary with the large tree. Thank you very much. Seems funny to get Christmas packages on Thanksgiving. Incidentally, we had a very good meal today – turkey with all the fixings. Last year at this time I was in Salt Lake and feeling very important. Wonder where I'll eat my turkey next year?

Frank and Scotty have acquired a German jeep now and we have transportation anytime we want it. It is a Volkeswagon (?) or Folk Wagon – the car of the People that the Nazi's were going to have in every garage.[246] I'm afraid they won't be doing any driving for a long time – especially in Berlin!

I have thirty-seven now, Mother.[247] Led the squadron the last time and I did a very good job if I say so myself. Received a few pats on the back. Get a good batch brewed for some time in January, Pappy, I've acquired a great thirst. No more for now.

Love, Bill

Bill sent at least two other V-mails around this time, one to his sister Betty and one to his parents, but they are completely faded and unreadable. One of them was also censored. And so there is a gap in his correspondence. At some point during this time the 97th Group was moved from North Africa to Italy and that is where we next hear from Bill in December, 1943.

---

[246] The Volkswagen, or "People's Car" was first produced in 1937. It was introduced to U.S. markets in 1949.

[247] On mission #37 Bill drop fragmentation bombs on a German air base in Estres Le Tube, France.

Nov. 30, 1943
Dear Folks,

I can't think of anything new since I phoned this noon. I spent the weekend in town with the Poolers and George Biners. I slept at Poolers Sat night, and went to the show Sunday afternoon with Geo Biner.

Tomorrow morning I leave for Denver. I will be taking armament. I don't know how long the course will last. After that I will take flexible gunnery.

Tomorrow I will revert back to the title of Pvt with the usual 50 bucks. I have decided to keep my $10,000 insurance policy at my own expense. It is pretty cheap.

The money order is for safe-keeping. I won't need it for some time, and I don't trust myself on the train. You can use the other money I sent to pay for the phone bill. I tried hard for a furlough, but it fell through. I've only been in the army 9 months. Most drafters get them after a few weeks.

Love, Bob

Dec. 4, 1943
Pvt. Robt. J. Biner 19194940
Lowry Field, Denver, Colorado

(Postcard- Braynard Lake and the Arapahoe Peaks are in the boulder Glacier district, the

southernmost Glacier in the Rock Mountain district)

Dear Folks,

Just arrived this morning. Didn't see much on the train. We were lucky and got Pullman.

Will report to the field this morning.

Love, Bob

P.S. Don't have an address yet.

Dec. 5, 1943
(V-mail)
Dear Mother, Dad & Freddy,

Well, I'm one of the old-timers now and in the forty & over club.[248] Only ten to go now so don't uncross your fingers yet. If only I had got here a month earlier I would be home for Christmas.

Received your box with the two types of pistachio and the fudge, which was very welcome. Also received two letters and one from you Dad. Yes, Maxine has received the picture and thanks for sending it.

Our mail service may be interrupted soon, but not for long I hope. Anyway, by the time you receive

---

[248] #38- Toulon, France (1000 lbs.); #39 – Ciampano, Italy (500 lbs.); #40 – Turin, Italy, ball bearing factory (1000 lbs).

this I hope I am near the end of the line. If we get awfully busy it shouldn't take over a month. I don't want to go home until the winter is over anyway. Besides, I would like to stay around until we take Rome and visit the place. No more for now. Love to all, Bill

---

Dec. 6, 1943
U.S. Army Air Forces
Lowry Field, Colorado
Dear Mom, Dad and Fritz,

Well Folks, here I am, a G.I. again after 10 months. We arrived here Sat, and they welcomed us by picking out a detail for K. P. I missed it because my fatigues weren't here yet.

We won't start school until the 20th, so in the meantime, I'll be in a guard sqdn. It's a great life, guard duty every day. The let-down in discipline is terrific. I haven't done a thing since I've been here.

It is really cold here. Everyone seems to have a cold here. This armament course will last 12 weeks. I may not even get a chance at gunnery. They are cutting down now, because they have too many gunners. As a result, they are not giving gunner's sergeant ratings any more.

There are plenty of "wash outs" here. Just about every second guy was a cadet at one time or other. I have never felt so free in all the time I've been in the army. Maybe it's because I don't worry about

being washed out anymore. My barracks is located in a nice spot. We are right next to both the P.X and the service club. The Catholic chapel is just across the street.

Did you get the money order? The chow here is strictly G.I., but it isn't bad. They say Denver is a swell soldier's town, so I think I'll enjoy this life. I'm not too far from Pocatello now. We have to go out to the rifle range this afternoon, so I guess I better get ready.

Write soon. Love, Bob

Dec. 9, 1943

Dear Mom, Dad and Fritz,

I'm finally settled for a short time. I've moved three times since I've been here. I am now living in the guard house. Officially, I'm a guard, but I wonder where they draw the line. We sleep behind barbed wire, and go everyplace the prisoners go.

The prisoners shovel coal, dump garbage and ashes and shovel snow. I follow a few steps, with a 12 gauge shot gun in my arms. It looks good if officers are looking, but it wouldn't be too hard for them to get away. For 16 hrs. a day, I guard prisoners. They aren't bad guys. Most of them are in for A.W.O.L. I have 3 prisoners and right now we are on the ash run. I get so dirty you can hardly tell me from the other prisoners.

I wouldn't mind it so bad if it weren't so cold. We had a regular blizzard last night. At the present I am wearing an undershirt, sweatshirt, woolen O.D. shirt, coveralls and a mackinaw. I get so cold; I march my prisoners into some nice warm engine room and spend half the day there. I feel like an old G.I. all ready. I'm learning a lot of little tricks on how to miss out on details. Now I'm really getting lazy.

What do you hear from Bill? I haven't received any letters yet, but I should get one in a day or so. I never did get the package. What did you send me?

Love, Bob

Dec.10, 1943

Dear Mom, Dad and Fritz,

I got your letter, cards, pictures and packages today. It almost seemed like Christmas, but I might be able to make it next year.

I'm wearing the slippers right now. My old ones were really shot. Thanks honey. The food is swell, and there is plenty of it. I used my head and waited until after supper to open it. For some reason or other, the boys weren't too hungry.

Your letter was the first one since I've been here. Dad, I don't feel so bad about "washing out" any more, but those bars sure would have been nice.

Dad, I really enjoy your letters, so write again when you have time.

That rosary card is the best present I've ever had. You won't have to worry about me losing the faith. It has really meant a lot to me since I've been in the army. The pictures are fine. Fritz is getting bigger every day. She's probably got a lot of beaus by now. The glamour boy, as Fritz calls him, looks fine.

I haven't been in town yet, and I don't know when I'll be able to make it. I guess my shopping will be a little late, and probably not on time. I'll probably be here until about the middle of March. This prison chasing is a little slow, and I haven't had a day off yet, including Sundays.

I've got a lot more letters to write, so good night.

Love, Bob

Dec. 18, 1943

Dear Mom, Dad and Fritz,

I'm out of ink, so please excuse the pencil. This is Sat. night, and I'm still spending it on the post. I hope I at least get one pass for Christmas Eve. I got your big box tonight. I'll try not to open it till Xmas. I'll have to hide it tho. I'm not living with cadets any more, and not everyone can be trusted.

Now I'll try to answer your questions. In the first place, you cannot transfer from the Air Corps, so that lets quarter MC out. Second- there is no commission in armament, not even a Pvt, 1st class. Third- O.C.S. is closed and they won't start drawing on their waiting list until 6 months. Fourth- and this will break your heart, as soon as we finish this course they many send us directly to gunnery. But don't worry, because I have plans that may keep me on this side for a long time.

Sauve[249] is someplace in Okla, learning Aircraft maintenance, and when he finishes, he will probably take gunnery also.

Kelleher and Johnson both played for U of Kansas this year. Scotty missed 1 ft. off making a touchdown. I'm still chasing prisoners, but I'm supposed to start school Monday. I don't know if I will or not tho. I'm listening to truth or consequences right now, and it's really good.

Love, Bob

Dec. 20, 1943

Dear Mother, Dad & Freddy,

---

[249] Bill Sauve was Bob Biner's best friend from Ellensburg. He served in the Navy and later moved to Wenatchee, Washington. The two men continued to stay in touch with one another in the years following the war.

Well, I think our A.P.O. service has started again so maybe you will get this in a couple of weeks. I can tell you for now that we are in Italy and feeling pretty damp about it. It's wet as anything around here all the time, and since you know what the Gulch in Trail[250] was like you can have a pretty good idea of how dirty the towns are around here.

Well, I have 46 now – four to go.[251] When I pull my last one I will send you one of our prepared wires. When you get it you will know I am all through. I hope that will be before you get this! These last four will seem like an eternity. They get rougher all the time. I've lost so much hair I'll look like your twin when I get back, Dad.

Received a box of candy, some cards and poker chips from Ken & Grace, and a letter from Bob and one from Raymond Biner[252] since we moved. Also got a Christmas package from Betty that was very nice.

---

[250] The historic Gulch was on the edge of Trail, B.C. where Bill's dad was the brewmaster from 1929-36. The Gulch was populated by Italian immigrants at the time.

[251] Bill really extended his range on missions 41 though 46, and perhaps that is part of the reason they moved into Italy. He hit German air bases and marshalling yards in Marseilles, France; Athens, Greece (twice) and Innsbruck, Austria (twice) with 500 pound bombs.

[252] Raymond Joseph Biner (1923-2004) was Bill's cousin and the son of Gus and Florence Biner.

We are pretty well restricted on what we can say so I will have to wait until I get more particulars on it. I would like to describe this country but I know it is forbidden. All I can say is that everything is green and the towns are almost as dirty as those in Africa. Also, I don't see where these people have suffered so much, even if *Life* thinks differently. And I don't like their attitude, like I didn't like the French's.

Well, no more for now. Hope you get the telegram before this letter.

Merry Christmas! Love, Bill

Sunday, Dec. 26, 1943

Dear Mom, Dad and Fritz,

Well, Xmas is all over, and I sure wish I had been home for it. I went into town last night, for the first time. Everything was closed because of Xmas. I'm writing this with my new pen. It sure comes in handy. All the presents were swell. I was out of soap, and I was borrowing the other boys sewing kits. All the presents were perfect and I couldn't have picked them better myself. I went right up and got the money order after I phoned you. Now I don't feel so lost.

They still have me casing prisoners, and I don't know when I'm going to start school now. I got a second box of cookies today. Did you send it to me by mistake? I hope you folks had a nice Xmas. You'll probably get my present sometime in Jan.

Can't concentrate on the letter. I'm listening to the Bear- Redskins game.[253] Ray Hares' doing all right.

Gotta go to church. Love, Bob

Italy
Dec. 27, 1943
Dear Betty,

You're very welcome and appreciated Christmas box arrived just before Christmas for which I thank you ever so much. By the heading you can see where we are in a general way and as much as I didn't like Africa, this isn't any better. It is probably alright during the summer, but right now it's wet all the time and cold, very cold! It's a continual battle, keeping warm and dry.

By the grace of God, I'll be out of here before long. Only have two more to go at this writing and they can't come too fast for me.[254] It may be my imagination, but they seem to get tougher all the time.

---

[253] The Chicago Bears beat the Washington Redskins 41-21 in the NFL Championship Game on Dec. 26, 1943.
[254] Bill's 47th mission was to hit docks in Toulon, France. #48 was on Bolzano, Italy.

What I have seen of Italy I can realize why so many Italians leave for America. (Poor sentence). Really, the towns are filthy, and so are the people. There doesn't seem to be a lack of soap and water, either. Barbering is the national occupation and for a nation that has produced such great artists, they love the most garish colors. Some of the houses look like a dipso's dream.[255]

(Most of the next sentence in this letter, which said something about a Christmas Day mission, was cut out by the censors.)

....mission on Christmas Day so you can see what kind of a holiday it was. Had a good turkey dinner when we got back though, so it ended well enough. I would trade this mud for a little snow though. The worst part is that my galoshes are still on the way over. Also my heavy jacket.

Received a new pair of shoes from Julia today and I really needed them. I won't have to go home barefooted now. Bought a nice tray for Mother here, but I am still trying to figure out how to send my stuff home. I'll bring your perfume with me.

Give my love to the Lynch's. Hope to see you soon.

Love, Bill

Italy
Dec. 27, 1943

---

[255] Dipso is a slang term for a drunk.

Dear Mother, Dad & Freddy,

Received your card today, Fritz, thanks a million, and I hope you had a good Christmas.

Got a pair of snappy shoes from Julia today and I really needed them. They fit fine. Also a book from Dan & Rose and some candy from Fred & Mollie. It seems I have a lot of friends. Hope all my mail gets here before I <u>leave</u>! Only have two more to go, Mother.

(The next sentence was partially censored but it also referred to what happened on Christmas day.)

...Christmas Day and helped the Germans celebrate the day their way.

We had a swell dinner (turkey) after we got back and that night an Englishman came to the tent with a bottle of Seagram's and shared it with us. These Limey's are good boys and they really have the Christmas spirit. This particular one has been overseas since 1940 without a break. Started in Egypt with Wavell![256]

Sorry to hear about Bob, but I really don't have any regrets.[257] Wish he would follow something like John Pooler's line. Tell him if he doesn't care what he is doing now, to get grounded and apply

---

[256] Field Marshall Sir Archibald Wavell (1883-1950).
[257] Bob Biner washed out of pilot training in November, 1943, and was sent to armament training at Lowery Air Field in Denver, Colorado.

for some ground job. I know he must feel pretty low, but when I get home I'll visit him and we'll take in the town. Maybe I can fix him up with something.

Don't make any more bets, Dad. I fail to see your optimism. I guess they haven't told the Germans the war is supposed to be over. If they have, they aren't paying any attention to it.

No more for now. Love to all, Bill

P.S. Happy New Year

Buckley Field, Colorado
Dec. 30, 1943
Dear Mom, Dad, and Fritz,

If you noticed the address, you'll see I have been shipped again. This time it was only 8 miles. I am now stationed at Buckley Field. It's another armament school. I suppose there will be another delay before I start school.

They took me off the prison chasing yesterday and told me to pack. Then they shipped me over here today. I think the field will be a lot nicer than Lowry, even though the barracks aren't as good. We had a hot air furnace in our other barracks. In these we have 3 coal stoves. I'm sure glad to get off prison chasing. I hope I start school pretty soon.

I finally got your Thanksgiving box. A few cookies were still intact, but I almost broke a tooth on the candy. I'll write again when I have more time.

Love, Bob

P.S. Today is New Years, and I'm at the U.S.O in Denver.

Harriet Lynch Biner as a young woman, circa 1910. She was the mother of Betty, Bill, Bob & Fritzi Biner, and wife of the brewer Billy Biner.

The Christmas card that Bill and his crew made for Christmas, 1943.

Part Three: 1944

Jan. 3, 1944

Dear Bet,

You probably think I'm an ungrateful snot, but the time is way ahead of me. The presents were really swell, and of course the bracelet is what I have been wanting for a long time. Honest Bet, you spoil me. My shopping was postponed before I even started it. Someone lifted my bill fold, with all my Xmas money. Dad wired me some money, so when I get a day off, I'm going to get you folks sumthin nice.

I've been moved again, but this time it was only 8 miles. I'm now at Buckley Field, and it's a lot better than Lowry. Besides, I don't have to chase prisoners. I really got a boot out of those prisoners tho. One of them celebrated Xmas on a bottle of Bay Rum he found in a trash can. He was dead out for 3 days. They're all a bunch of radicals, and they're all trying to get mental discharges.

I spent a very quiet New Year's Eve. Went to half a day: shows and had a dozen beers, but I missed the old crowd. I sure missed Ellensburg that nite. How's the cold? Hope it didn't interfere with your holidays. Heard the Rose Bowl Game. Wash. sure stunk.[258]

Say Bet, that book is sure a honey. It's gonna help a lot. I got another pleasant gift 3 days after Xmas. It was the box of cookies and candy Mom sent a week before Thanksgiving. Did you ever eat a box of crumbs? It came in very useful tho. They're just the thing to sprinkle between sheets. And the candy was excellent for cracking nuts, or putting in a sock, which makes a nice blackjack.

It's really cold here. The boys have finally convinced me it isn't Siberia, but they still can't explain the igloos. Does Gramps have any more old long handles lying around?[259] How do you like your new job? Sounds like a little place to me.

Write soon.

Love, Bob

January 10, 1944

Dear Mom, Dad and Fritz,

---

[258] USC beat the University of Washington 29-0 in the Rose Bowl.
[259] Long handles were one-piece long johns. Bob said his Grandpa Lynch wore them in the winter and summer.

I got your letter this evening. Don't start worrying about Bill, I know he's O.K. He's probably just a little sick, or maybe he wants to surprise you. He sure is doing swell. I hope I get to see him when he gets back.

As I was saying, furloughs are a thing of the past. I can't quite make up my mind what to do. As long as I keep going to technical school, I won't get a furlough. But, on the other hand, as soon as I stop, they'll ship me over. They are sending a lot of the guys over from here as soon as they finish school. So, as long as I go to technical schools, I am comparatively safe. Even that isn't too safe. They pulled some of the boys out of school today. They're heading for the port of embarkation.

Betty forwarded a letter from Louie Dagnon to me yesterday. He is overseas, and I think he is in England. He couldn't say, but that's what it sounded like. He is in the Signal Corps. I also got a letter from the Poolers. They are sure lucky John and Bet were both home for Xmas. John had to leave the next day though.

I just heard from my roommate in Oxnard, that one of the boys from our Sqd. in Santa Ana was killed in a crash. He spun in at Hemet Field in Cal. All the boys at Oxnard did O.K. They just left for Basic. I sure wish I was with them.

Bevo and Batch are both doing O.K. They are going to take basic at the same field, (Ontario,

Cal), from the same instructors. My pal Bill Andrews is getting his basic out in the middle of Arizona.

We started school today, it wasn't bad but it's going to be awful boring. Did you see the show Old Oklahoma?[260] That's the one they filmed at Cedar City.

Well, I have to do my homework. Don't worry about Bill. Everything will turn out O.K.

Write again.

Love, Bob

January 12, 1944

Dear Mother, Dad & Freddy,

Just got back from a tour of Italy and a week at the Air Force rest camp where I got used to a bed and clean sheets again. If you read Time Magazine you will know what I mean. I thought I would be on my way home by now but there is some hold-up and no telling when I'll get my orders.

I'm not flying anymore and after all the excitement things seem pretty dull, but it's a grand feeling to be through for a while. I'm a very lucky guy! Frank is finished also and Scotty has

---

[260] *In Old Oklahoma* was a 1943 film starring John Wayne.

one more to go. Only one enlisted man is still flying – he has two more to go. So we will probably all go home together. After my leave at home I believe I will be sent to Salt Lake for two weeks for rest and reclassification. That will be pretty handy for Pocatello, won't it?

Don't know if I told you before, but I received the bracelet and books and soap and thanks very much. Also received some slippers from George & Helen. The letters with the pictures and novena arrived O.K. Both were appreciated very much. Freddy, you certainly have grown, but your Mother and Old Man look like they miss their T-bone steaks.

No, I haven't heard from Bob since he went to Denver. If he is still there when I get home I'm going down to spend some time with him.

Maybe I'll spend my honeymoon there![261]

We don't know when or how we are going back, but hold on for a while and I hope it will be soon. I'll write as soon as I know anything definite, which should be around the fifteenth. No more for now.

Love to all, Bill

---

[261] Bill intends to marry is girlfriend, Maxine Gray, from Spokane. It is unclear whether or not he has proposed.

Jan. 13, 1944

Dear Bet and All,

I got your letter today along with the pictures, and I can't tell you when I've enjoyed a letter so much. Do that again. The snapshots were almost as good as a furlough. Take some more. I have my favorite pinned just about my head. I call it "Smiling Buddha with Dancing Girls". Rodge looks like the pouting sailor, and Hurbert in Colliers. Of course the first thing I notice were my clothes, and second the bags in your stockings. Hattie looks natural. I'd like to be sitting in her lap right now. I've decided not to get married til I find someone who will baby me the way she does, and who can cook at least half as good. That should give me plenty of time. Ignats of course, is really getting to be a beauty. A girl that looks like that can afford to keep the boys guessing, but I must say she didn't give the lad much hope. I can't see Pat too well in the picture, but he looks like he's happy about something. I hope I get to meet him when I get back. I guess that covers everything except of course that you're as cute as ever.

We haven't been doing much the past few days. Just sitting around reading and sleeping and such. The mail is coming through pretty well now that everyone has my permanent address. Now that I'm thinking of it, will you inquire in a magazine store or something if it would be possible for me to get a subscription to a magazine to be shipped directly to me? Post or Colliers or Digest or anything. Also while I'm at it I want to thank you for the dough. It was really swell of you; only next time use it for yourself. I know you have plenty of uses for it.

The chow over here is really improving. We've had steak twice in about a week. I still miss the milk tho. I sure hope Bill is home by the time this letter arrives. This time I hope he stays. I don't know how long I'll be here, but I hope I'll be there before the summer is over. Don't forget to write again.

Love, Bob

Jan. 19, 1944 (V-mail)

Dear Bob,

I received your letter from Oxnard right after we got to Italy and in the middle of another move. (I've moved so much in this theatre that I feel like a gypsy). Then Mother's letter came telling me that you were in Denver and feeling pretty low.

It's tough little old man and I know how you feel, but I actually wasn't sorry to see it happen. One of us flying is enough for Mother & Dad; and it's a helluva life at times. I've lost too many good friends over here to have any great love for this game anymore. So don't feel bad about it, Bob.

How about developing a thirst and when I get to Denver we'll have a time. I know a cashier in the Brown Palace[262] who wanted me to stay there an extra day once, and maybe she has a friend.

I think I'll buy Dad's car – maybe, and get married – maybe! Anyway will be seeing you soon. I finished up Dec. 29th and should leave the end of this month. It can't come any too soon. So long for a while.

Love,

Bill

Jan. 21, 1944

Dear Folks,

There's not much to talk about. It sure was nice hearing your voices last night. Fritz talked so fast I could only understand that she was going to another dance. Is it going to be a formal? If so, does she have one of those little purses? I don't know what to get the kid.

I'm going to look up the DeLougharys' Sunday, if I don't get my pass pulled. I wised off to the wrong

---

[262] The Brown Palace is an historic hotel in Denver. It opened in 1892 as the Grand Salon and is still in operation today.

buck Pvt[263] the other day. It turned out he had a little authority, and he is trying to pull my pass.

I hope you're not worrying about Bill now. He is probably on his way home now. There is no telling when he'll get there, so don't worry.

Let me know ahead of time when you are coming. This town is fairly busy, but I can reserve you a room or so. Write again.

Love, Bob

P.S. I'm getting the paint already Dad

On January 22, 1944, Major Charles R. Renick wrote a letter of recommendation for Bill Biner, who decided that he might be interested in serving as a bombardier instructor upon his return to the states. This is what Major Renick had to say about Lt. Bill Biner:

To Whom It May Concern:

1. It is my desire to recommend that 1st Lt. William D. Biner, 0-735517, be favorably considered for assignment to a School for Bombardiers, to serve in the capacity of instructor and lecturer.

---

[263] A buck private is an enlisted man of the lowest rank, so this particular private probably had some connections on the base.

2. Lt. Biner has served under my command for the past six months, and his service in this organization has been highly satisfactory. He has performed the duties of a Bombardier on a Flying Fortress, and has successfully completed his tour of combat duty, having flown on fifty daylight bombing missions. On many occasions, he has flown as Lead Bombardier for his Squadron, and at all times he has shown outstanding skill and ability as such.

3. The character of Lt. Biner is unquestionable. He is competent and efficient in carrying out the assignments given him. He has shown considerable willingness and determination in both training and combat. His devotion to duty has been paramount, and his great leadership has played an important part in the success of this organization.

4. It is with great pleasure that I recommend Lt. Biner. I feel that he possesses all of the characteristics desired in an Instructor in the School for Bombardiers, and that his experiences in combat will render him highly valuable for this position.

Charles R. Renick, Major, Air Corps, Commanding

Jan. 24, 1944

Dear Mom, Dad, and Fritz,

I got your letter today. I must say, you don't sound very cheery. I certainly don't see anything to get nervous about. Bill will get there as soon as he can, but on the other hand he may be delayed for some time, so there's no use expecting him till he gets there. So there.

I went out to the DeLougharys yesterday. Doc took the day off, and got an early start. He's a real Irishman, and funnier than a crutch. They drove me all over the mountains. They took me out to the open air amphitheater.[264] It was carved out right in the mountains. Then they took me out to Buffalo Bills grave.[265] We went past Coors Brewery, and it's really a honey. I wish Dad had it.

I didn't say I wanted to get out of the Air Corps, and besides, I couldn't if I wanted to. I hope Bill gets here before I have to make any decisions.

Write sooner.

Love, Bob

---

[264] The Red Rocks Park Amphitheatre is located on Dinosaur Ridge west of Denver. It remains a popular and breathtaking venue for entertainment.

[265] Buffalo Bill Cody (1846-1917) is buried on Lookout Mountain a few miles west of Denver. His grave remains a popular tourist attraction. Ironically, Bob would later marry a great-niece of Buffalo Bill.

P.S. Peggy Allen was married to a Sgt. from Spokane.   Also Les Hoadley[266] to Betty Hurt. Some stuff!

Buckley Field, Colorado

Jan. 28, 1944

Dear Fritz, Mom and Dad,

I got your letter yesterday Bumps, and you're quite a card. Where did you learn all those moron jokes? I'm sorry to hear Mom isn't feeling so well, but if she doesn't stop worrying, she'll never feel any better.

Tomorrow will be the end of my 3rd week of school. Time is going pretty fast around here. We had 8 inches of snow the other night. The first in two weeks of nice warm weather. Will you send me Betty's address? I can't seem to find it. Tough luck about her Ensign getting sent away. How does she like her job now? I hit the jack-pot today with 5 letters. I was beginning to think I'd lost all my friends.

Don't spend too much time on your dancing, Ignats, or the first thing we know you'll be killing all the boys.

---

[266] Les Hoadley was a 1941 graduate of Ellensburg High School.

Write again.

Love, Bob

Jan. 31, 1944

Dear Mom, Dad and Fritz,

Well, today I am a man. Darn it, I feel like an old man. I wish I was sixteen again. I got all your wonderful presents last Sat. They were all swell, but you shouldn't have done it. The ring and wallet are sure neat. The cake was appreciated by all. I feel guilty getting all these things.

Yesterday, (Sun) I went down to the K.C. hall.[267] They have a nice U.S.O there. We had free chow, and a dance. They had plenty of good looking dolls there. Some of the numbers tried to talk me into going into the 4th degree.[268] They're offering it at bargain rates and everything, but I don't know.

Have you heard anything from Bill? It's a relief to hear he has completed his missions anyhow.

Denver is a nice place, but I still haven't been able to get into town before the stores close. I wish I could be home for this birthday, but maybe I'll be there next year.

---

[267] Knights of Columbus, a Catholic service and fraternal organization.
[268] A higher ranking in the Order of the Knights of Columbus.

Love, Bob

This is an undated V-mail letter, probably from early February, 1944.

Dear Folks,

Just have a few minutes to catch a train to the port we are shipping from and I dread the train and boat trip. They will both be long and tiresome. The boat will probably be a Liberty ship[269] and they take twenty-one days to cross. Not much to look forward to but there will be an end sometime and I'll be home.

Pappy is with me again.[270] He got on the orders and came down from Germany so we are going back together. His brother wants to give him one of his bars, so Pappy's wife wants to move to California. Reminds me of you, Mother. No more until I phone or wire. Love to all. See you soon.

Bill

If the military records are correct, they show that Bill Biner departed on February 10, 1944 and arrived in the United States on February 19th. Certainly less than the 21 day crossing he expected. He enjoyed a leave and his family

---

[269] Liberty ships were giant cargo ships that transported goods, and in some cases, troops, during World War II. Thousands of them were made.
[270] Pappy Heinz, Bill's old friend from the training schools.

visited him in Denver before he was sent to Santa Ana Army Air Base to await reclassification. His sister Fritzy clearly remembers the day her brother came home and shares the touching memory that follows.

"By the time he got home he was a wreck, having seen a lot of B17s go down by then, and one of his best friends bail out of another plane without a chute! Not long after he came home a good part of the 15th Air Force had been shot down over the Ploesti oil fields in Romania. His first night home he and Dad were up all night while Bill let it all pour out and wept and wept."

Bill reported to the Santa Ana Base in March, 1944, and it gave him the opportunity to visit the Biner relatives he had so much fun with during his training days. Two letters, both undated, remain from his month at Santa Ana and will follow the February, 1944 letters from his brother Bob.

Feb. 7, 1944

Dear Bet,

I got your card Sat. It was a cutey. The ring is sure swell. It was a little large, but I'm getting that fixed. How do you like your new set-up? What kind of place is Auburn?

The weather around here is really swell most of the time. The other Sunday I visited the

DeLougharys. Bill is quite a character. He's a real Irishman, and full of the devil. He's a railroad man, and is always embarrassing his wife with his stories.

Denver is a pretty nice place. The K.C.'s have a nice U.S.O. with a lot of good lookin gals. The only trouble is most of them are taller than me. I think more gals ought to be your size.

What do you want for your birthday Bet? I cleaned up in poker last week, so I'm flush.

Write again please, and don't take so long.

Love, Bob

Feb. 7, 1944

Dear Mom, Dad, Fritz,

Pardon the delay. I got your letter Sat. night, but I went out, so this is the first chance. There isn't much news around here. I went to the show and a U.S.O. dance. I spent about 5 hrs. walking around town trying to find a steak. We never found one, but we sure saw the town.

I got a few charms for Fritz. Tell her I'll get her something better. If I ever get into town before the stores close. What size does she take in a sweater or skirt? Bets birthday is coming. What is the exact date?

This is my fifth week of school. We take the 20 mm. cannon and 30 cal. machine gun this week. Last week we had the cal. 50. The kind they use in the forts.

Have you heard anything new from Bill? I hope he gets here soon.

I'll write again tomorrow. Love, Bob

P.S. Mom, the cake was in pretty good condition.

Feb. 8, 1944

Dear Folks,

Well, I'm back to the old grind again, and I don't like it. Did you have any trouble getting home? I hope Fritz didn't miss out on too much school work. I really felt homesick Sun afternoon. It seemed like I just left home. We're hearing a lot of rumors that this will be our last week here, but it's probably like all the other rumors.

I guess you left at just the right time. We've been having rotten weather the last few days. The wind is really blowing, and it's as cold as ice.

Don't forget to have Bill wash the car while he's home. It looks terrible.

Write when you get time. I can't tell you any news. I'm sure glad you all got to come.

Love, Bob

Feb.9, 1944

Dear Mom, Dad & Fritz,

I've been waiting for a letter from you folks, but I won't put it off any longer. I got a letter from Bill last night, also one from Auntie Rie. Bill said he expected to leave about the end of Jan. I hope he decides to come down here with you folks. He's going to have to help me get a pass. There pretty strict around here. We only get a pass on weekends.

Did you get the trinkets? I'm really going to get you something better, but there was only one store open last week when I got in. Mom, will you send me a couple of snap-shots of myself? I got another letter from Louie the other day and he wants one. (Army uniform)

School is still rolling along and it gets more boring by the day. We're on 20 mm cannon today. The weather around here is sure funny. Warm one day and freezing the next.

Write. Love, Bob

Feb. 11, 1944

Dear Mom, Dad and Fritz,

This letter is going to be short and not too sweet. Frankly, I'm disappointed with you. No letter in more than a week. You have more time than I have.

Right now, I have a pretty bad cold. If it's not better by the morning, I'm going to the hospital. This is a helluva place. They won't let you in the hospital unless you have a fever and if you aren't in the hospital, you have to work as usual. The weather around here is really cold.

If you come down here with Bill, don't try to surprise me. Send me something in writing so I can produce it. Then I might get a few hrs. extension to my ordinary pass. We have a new C.O. now, and he's really a stinker. We have to keep our windows wide open during the day. When we come back from school, it's like an ice box. Write.

Love, Bob

Feb. 14, 1944

Dear Mom, Dad & Fritz,

I got your letter Saturday, so I feel OK again. I stayed in bed Sat. night, and most of Sunday morning. It broke up my cold; so now I'm well on my way to recovering.

Yesterday afternoon, I went out to the DeLougharys. They are sure swell to me. Doc gave me the key to the house and told me to make myself at home anytime. I felt like it.

It's really cold around here. I heard it snowed as late as June here one year, so I guess we've got plenty of winter left yet.

Happy Valentine's Day Dad – Mom –Fritz (drew a heart). Write again soon.

Love, Bob

Feb. 17, 1944

Dear Mom, Dad & Fritz,

I got your letter today. It came in the nick of time. I was just getting ready to write another scorcher.

There isn't any news around here. Yes, I get every week-end off, from Sat. evening to 1 a.m. Mon. It isn't much time and I usually go back to the post Sat. night & go out again Sunday. I usually go to a few shows on 'Sat. and to the K.Cs on Sunday.

I don't know where Louie is, but I think he's in England or Newfoundland. He mentions York soldiers around, so it could be either place.

I got Fritz valentine. I hope she gets some good out of the poster contest, even if she doesn't win.

Write again

Love, Bob

Feb 17, 1944

Dear Dad,

I got the letter to-day. I'm enclosing Bills letter I don't think there is anything in it Mom shouldn't see, so I'll leave it up to you. It's been quite a while, but he may be coming by ship. However, I got a letter from Aunt Helen yesterday and she said Bill told her his orders were held up, so that may mean he hasn't left yet. He's finished all his missions, so there's nothing to worry about.

I've got quite a problem myself; I'll show you how things are with me. If I go to gunnery, I'll have a good chance of getting a rating and of course flying pay. With all that, I could probably go to coll. the way I want. On the other hand, if I go as armorer, I'll probably stay a buck private, but I'll keep my butt on the ground.

I just about decided to take armorer, when I heard they are pulling the guys out of school and sending them to gunnery if they want to or not. One kid was "washed out" of cadets because of air sickness, but they sent him to gunnery anyhow. I can refuse gunnery, and if they send me I can still wash myself out. Two "wash outs" on my service record may not look so good tho.

I took an overseas physical today & passed it. That also qualifies me as gunner. I passed it.

If, when I graduate from here, & if I don't go to gunnery I'll probably get a fifteen-day delay in route. If they send me to gunnery, I won't get one till I graduate or "wash out", but I can't tell about that. If I stay on armorer, I may go overseas pretty soon. Gunnery assures me of at least six weeks longer.

Well, that's the facts as I get them. Don't think I'm too eager to get overseas or behind a gun, but it's a gamble. I don't mind the gamble, but I realize, like Bill says, it's harder on Mom & you. I guess the last two years have been pretty hard on Mom & I don't want to be the one to ruin her health.

I wish I could talk to you about this, but maybe I'll get to see you and Bill before I have to make any decisions. It's nothing to worry about tho, and I'm not losing any sleep over it. See you soon I hope.

Love, Bob

Feb. 18, 1944

Dear Mom, Dad and Fritz,

I got your letter to-day. I was just sore because I wasn't getting any mail. I haven't heard from Sauve or anyone for a long time. I think Sauve has been moved.

My cold is almost gone, but the weather isn't any better. We never get a lot of snow, but it's really cold. Tomorrow is Sat. and the end of another week. I'll be glad when I get out of this school. This place is getting worse every day. Our C.O. used to have a cadet sqdn. And he thinks we should get the same.

That's too bad about Jim Eccles. This war is really getting me down. The news is getting a little better though.

You'd better quit expecting Bill. There's no telling how long he may be delayed. How did Fritz make out in her poster contest? You don't have to bring me anything to eat, just make sure that you all get here. I'm sure getting homesick.

Write soon.

Love, Bob

Feb. 21, 1944

Dear Bet,

I got your letter to-day and I'm going to answer it right away. Happy birthday kid. As soon as I can get into town again, I'm going to get you something for it. Let's see – your 23 now aren't you? What are a few years more or less? I'm even feeling older. Can you buy a drink yet?

What are your chances of getting off when Bill comes? You could all come down to Denver, and we could all get drunk. I want to get Mom feeling good again. I give her hell about worrying every time I write, but she expects Bill every day.

I'm doing OK in school. It isn't hard. A moron could pass the tests they give. I've got six more weeks to go. I took a physical the other day for overseas replacement, and passed it. I think I got at least six months over here tho.

Who is this Pat? What's he do and what is he like?

Write me again soon.

Love, Bob

Feb 22, 1944

Dear Mom, Dad, and Fritz,

I got your letter yesterday. Not much going on around here today. I went to the DeLougherys again last week-end. I slept there Sat. nite, and spent the Sunday with them. We had chicken for dinner and it was really good. They had a friend of theirs there. An old gal who used to live by Buffalo Bill. He was really an old sport. There is another cousin here. His name is Bill Corbett, and

273 | Brewmaster's Bombardier & Belly Gunner

he's supposed to be a third or fourth cousin or something.[271]

Who is this Pat that Bet is talking about? I didn't take the 4th degree. I've got plenty of time, and I don't want to change councils again.

By the way, what is happening to my K.C. insurance? Is Dad getting the bill? I don't want to let it drop.

I've got a lot of letters to write tonight, besides Fiffie is on now.

Love, Bob

Feb. 25, 1944

Dear Mom, Dad & Fritz,

Got Dad's letter today. That's the best news I've heard in a long time. Now maybe you will be able to get some sleep. I'm sure glad Bill's back. I hope you folks will be able to get down here soon. If you can't get gas, come by train or bus. It wouldn't cost too much. I'm going to phone next Wednesday if I can.

---

[271] Bill Corbett (1917-1993) was Bob's 2nd cousin. His father, William Harris Corbett, was a 1st cousin to Bob's maternal grandfather Dan Lynch and to Doc DeLoughary. The mothers of William (Anna), Dan (Bridget) and Doc (Katherine) were sisters.

Let me know long enough ahead of time, so I can reserve some rooms. I might even need Bill to help me get out. Our C.O. is only a 1st Louie, so Bill has as much rank as he.

Nothing new around here. We're studying synchronizing this week. It's the toughest course in school.

Sat. 26, I'll be in the army a year. It sure seems longer than that. I hope this war is over before I see another year. Write me right back and let me know what to expect. Love, Bob

---

Between this letter and his next Bob enjoyed a reunion in Denver with his parents and his siblings, including Bill.

Santa Ana

Dear Mother, Dad and all —

Well, I'm still here and from the looks of things we may be here next week at this time but by then we'll be confined to the post. Right now we aren't doing much and spend most of the time in town, but I can't get off long enough to get to Pocatello.

Besides, I have an infected gum over my last remaining wisdom tooth and I have been going to the dentist every morning for treatment. When he gets rid of the poison he is going to pull it. For a while I thought I was getting the mumps and it had me scared, because I heard there were some cases in the camp.

There are plenty of rumors in the camp but no one knows when or where we are going so I guess your curiosity will have to smother like mine.

Pappy and I have been making the Aviation Club and the Allied Officer's Club our headquarters here and I think we have paid up their overhead for the month. We sit around throwing the bull at each other until the place closes. Then we go have tamales smothered with chili. It has become sort of a routine. He really has a lot of stories to tell about his experiences in England.

And then there is that sport where we get new men going over and we give them a "snow" job.

Say Pappy[272] - how about sending me fifty or seventy-five dollars? I am not going to put in a pay voucher this month and I'll need a little if we go to New York, say. I can't cash a check here (transient officer) and you can either write a check on Sam Houston now and send me the dough, or write one later and pay yourself back. I guess a money order would be best, or you could wire it. Will you do that?

I waited too long to write this but my resolutions are still good. Till later then –

---

[272] Bill called both his friend and his father Pappy.

All my love, Bill

Santa Monica
Wednesday

Yes, I'm a bad boy, but I've been going at such a terrific pace that I've even been lax in writing to Maxine, and she is mad! However, everything is smoothed over now.

As far as I know, Mother, she is supposed to write you first. You can always look it up in your *Home Journal* or *Good Housekeeping.* And please, put a capital after a period or question mark when you write.

I've been out to the studio twice now. If I didn't tell you about it the first time, here goes. There was a reception for Speaker Rayburn[273] (stumping for vice-president) and all the movie big-wigs from all the studios were there. Paul took me and we sat with Victor Moore[274] and William Demarest[275]

---

[273] Sam Rayburn (1882-1961), D-Texas, was one of the most powerful politicians in American history and the longest serving Speaker of the House of Representatives. He did not become Franklin D. Roosevelt's final running mate in 1944. That honor went to Senator Harry Truman of Missouri.
[274] Victor Moore (1876-1962), American actor, comedian, writer and director.
[275] William Demarest (1892-1983), American actor, most famous to Baby Boomers as "Uncle Charley" in the TV series *My Three Sons.*

(Miracle of Morgan's Creek)[276]. I had my picture taken with Paul and Moore and Margy Reynolds.[277] Haven't seen it yet but hope to get it someday. Also met Betty Hutton[278] and Buddy De Sylva.[279] Not to mention numerous directors and producers. Almost forgot, also met Miss Paxinu,[280] the For Whom the Bells Toll [281]gal. You remember her – she was the chief's wife.

Went around again yesterday with my roommate and Paul showed us around the lot. Have more fun though sitting in his office and listening to him make phone calls. It's better than a movie.

Played golf with Tommy[282] and Paul last Saturday at Lakeside[283] and had a wonderful time. Got a little sunburned and a few stiff muscles, but the golf bug has bitten me again. Think I'll invest in some clubs when I get situated.

---

[276] A comedy written and directed by Preston Sturges.
[277] Marjorie Reynolds (1917-1997) was an American actress. Among her 70 films was an anti-Nazi drama, *Enemy Agent* (1940).
[278] Betty Hutton (1921-2007), American actress, singer and comedienne.
[279] Buddy DeSylva (1895-1950), songwriter, film producer and a founder of Capital Records.
[280] Katina Paxinou (1900-1973), Greek actress.
[281] 1943 film starring Gary Cooper and based on Hemingway's novel about the Spanish Civil War.
[282] Possibly his sixteen-year-old cousin Tommy Biner, son of George and Helen.
[283] The Lakeside golf course is located on Toluca Lake in Burbank, California. The area was and still is the home of many movie stars.

Saw the Gus Biners last night and am going to see the Lynch's tonight. [284] Tomorrow I leave for Midland, Texas to an instructor's school. Don't know how long I will be there, but it will be good to get back to a steady schedule again.

Glad you like the tray. You can send Julia and Helen one of the little wallets if you want. Outside of that, you and Freddy and Betty can split up the junk between you. I don't want the toilet kit, but you can send the clothes when I get settled.

No more for now. Write again when I get the new address.

Love to all, Bill

March 13, 1944

Dear Folks,

I'm sorry to have kept you waiting so long, but I was in town for the weekend, so I didn't get around to it. I've only got two more weeks to go after this.

I applied for instructor, to-day, but I don't know if I'll get it or not. I heard they were only taking guys who couldn't pass their overseas physical.

---

[284] Cornelius Francis Lynch (1879-1956) was Bill's great uncle, the older brother of his maternal grandfather Dan Lynch. Uncle Con and his wife, Jenny "Jane" McKenna (1879-1948), lived in Los Angeles at the time.

There's no harm in trying tho. Is Bill still home? Is he finding enough to do to make him happy?

To-morrow, I'm going to the dental clinic. My eye tooth has been keeping me awake for the last two nights. I know they'll pull it tho, and they don't give peg teeth anymore.

Bill Corbett came about 10 minutes after you left. We just fooled around for the rest of the day. He's a drip. It's snowing to-night. I'll write again soon.

Love, Bob

March 15, 1944

Dear Mom, Dad, Fritz & Willie,

I didn't get a letter from you to-day, so I'll write one myself.

Guess I'll start off by telling you my troubles. I went to the dentist yesterday. They took X-rays and found I had a couple of abscessed teeth. Both of them are in the front. They pulled one and if the other one doesn't feel any better, they're going to pull it too. It doesn't. (Bob drew a picture of his mouth and teeth with an arrow to the offending tooth.)

I got a letter from Auntie Rie yesterday and she doesn't even know Bill is home, so tell him to write to her.

Kay Kyser[285] is on now, and I can't concentrate.

It's still snowing around here. I guess they'll ship us out when the weather gets good. This is our last week of turrets. The next two weeks we spend on the line. Then we pull K.P. till they ship us out.

I haven't heard from Sauve yet. I'm getting worried about him. I can't think of anything.

Write soon. Love, Bob

P.S. I sat on my pen, so that explains the writing.

March 20, 1944

Dear Mom, Dad & Fritz,

Well, I suppose Bill is on his way by now. I hope he had a good time while he was home. It was probably a little dull, but I'd do anything to get home.

We have two weeks of school left now. I'm sure going to hate leaving Denver. I really like it here.

This week-end I went to town with a couple of the boys. We took in a couple of basketball games and shows. I saw Paul's show, "Standing Room

---

[285] James "Kay" Kyser (1905-1985) was a bandleader and radio personality.

Only".[286] It was a pretty good show. I had to wait in line 40 minutes.

They have finished all my teeth now, except for my bridge. I won't get that for a couple of weeks. I smile with my mouth closed now.

My mail has been catching up with me now. I still haven't heard from Sauve yet.   Bevo is in advanced now.   He'll be sporting those bars in a few weeks now. I'm sorry I waited so long to answer your letter.

Love, Bob

April 4, 1944

Dear Mom, Dad & Fritz,

Well, I'm still here, but now it makes me mad. Just about all my pals shipped to-day. Most of them went to gunnery school at Las Vegas or Harligino, Texas. I'd have left with them, but they held me back because of my bridge. My tooth is in now, and it looks pretty good, but I don't like it as well as my other one.

Well, I graduated last Sat. and I am now an armorer, and qualified for any type of K.P. Which reminds me; I had K.P. to-day. It was a long day. From 0300 a.m. this morning until 8 to-night.

---

[286] *Standing Room Only* (1944) was produced by Paul Jones and starred Fred MacMurray and Paulette Goodard.

Boy, it was really rough. I'd rather go to the dentist all day than do K.P. As long as I'm here, I'll get it every second day.

I spent last Sunday with the DeLoughary's! They are really swell people.

What is Bill's present status and how long is he going to stay at Santa Monica? I sure hope he sees the Poolers while he's there. Please answer soon. If I leave before your reply arrives – they'll forward it.

Love, Bob

P.S. I got another box of candy from Auntie Rie

April 8, 1944

Dear Mom, Dad, Fritz,

Could you use a good housemaid? I'm an expert at all types of housework from cleaning toilet bowls to cutting meat. My only drawbacks are dishpan hands, and housemaid knees. You have probably guessed by now that I've been given a few minor details. K.P. again yesterday and latrine the day before that. I wonder why they sent me to armament school.

I got your box Thursday, Mom and as usual it hit the spot. Everything is OK and Fritz did a good job on those eggs. Did she get the box yet? I hope you all have a nice Easter. I'm going to receive communion for you to-morrow.

What do you hear from Bill? Are they going to keep him as an instructor or what? What is Betty doing? How is Grandma?

We're having nice spring weather here now and I hate more than ever to leave the place. I imagine I'll leave sometime next week, but keep sending your mail here until I tell you.

Love, Bob

April 10, 1944

Dear Mom, Dad & Fritz,

I'm in the orderly room again to-night as a runner, so I'll tell you about Easter.

Now you know I'm a guy with a lot of patience. I've taken these Denver snow storms and blizzards all winter long and most of spring. But, yesterday it rained all day long and snowed all last night and most of to-day. Most of the roads were blocked and none of the civilians were able to get out to the post. It took me two hours to get in this morning.

Where are your letters? I still want to know what they are going to do with Bill. I don't see any furlough for me for quite a while. I hear they aren't giving delays from gunnery any more. But,

I'm not worrying, because I'll go A.W.O.L. before they ship me over. This Air Corps is getting on my nerves. [287]

I'll write from gunnery.

Love, Bob

The following letters, from the spring of 1944, were written by Bill while he was training to be an instructor in Midland, Texas. Some of the letters are dated but others are not. He arrived in Midland on April 8, 1944. The editor has done his best to determine the correct order of the letters. Interspersed are letters written at the same time by his brother Bob.

Midland Army Air Field,
World's Largest Bombardier School,
Midland, Texas
April 14, 1944
Dear Folks,

Have been going to school for five days now and am still in a daze. We have three weeks and ninety-hours of nothing but navigation for the first three weeks and then six to nine weeks of flying navigation missions and dropping bombs and going to bombardier ground school. It's really a tough schedule and I don't have much free time

---

[287] A clearly exasperated Bob Biner, who had no intention of going A.W.O.L., left for Nellis Air Field in Las Vegas for Gunnery Training after this letter.

but I don't mind it much. It's not like Tunis or any of the other places.

Midland is a rich oil town-about twenty-four millionaires – but not much to do. Odessa, the oil worker's town, is ten miles on the other side of the field and is called Sinton. Midland is very hoity-toity.

It's been old home week here for me. All the boys left out of our class from Hobbs with a few exceptions are here. A baker's dozen. And some of the men I knew overseas. My buddy from the 342nd is here with his new bride. Something that surprised me; but she is a pretty nice girl. Pappy Heinz is here, too but he wants to go back to England.

However, our C.O. told us that we couldn't go back to combat unless it was as a staff officer, and there won't be any bombardiers going back in a position like that.

When we graduate from here we will be navigator-bombardiers and qualified for cadet instructors. Most of the men will be going to cadet schools to replace the present instructors. You can see how popular we are around here with the present instructors. I don't blame them any, but we had to go to combat, and the worst is about over, so they are not so badly off.

Have you sold the car yet? And before I forget it, thanks a lot for the Easter card, Freddy. Send me Bob's new address if he has moved or the old one if he hasn't.

Love to all, Bill

April 15, 1944

Dear Mom, Dad & Fritz,

Well, here we are at last. The wind is blowing so bad we can't even leave the barracks.

All in all, this post isn't too bad. We have nice big barracks just like Santa Ana. With inside plumbing. The chow is the only drawback, but they have plenty to eat at the P.X. We arrived Friday, and started our processing yesterday.

We start school next week, and this stuff ought to be kinda easy after armament school.

The discipline around here is kinda strict. A lot tougher than Buckley, but after Santa Ana, nothing they pull could surprise me. Were only a few hundred miles from L.A. but no one gets enough time off to go.

We will get about one day off in the seven weeks we are here. I guess they are afraid we will lose all our money in town. Which reminds me, I'm flat broke. All the time off in Denver didn't do my bank account much good. I would like about 10 in a money order. They won't cash personal checks around here. I don't know when we'll get paid around here.

I'll write again, as soon as I get situated in a permanent squadron.

Love, Bob

P.S. Maybe they'll send Bill here.

April 15, 1944

Dear Mom, Dad & Fritz,

Excuse the pencil, but I'm all out of ink.

Well, I'm back where the sun shines every day, and I kinda like it. We started wearing sun tans Sunday.

We're going through the same old stuff you get at every new post. Same old lectures, (?) and gas chambers. They're trying to scare us with all the strict regulations here. It's too much like Santa Ana for my money. The thing that gets me most of all is the rising hour. We get up at 5 am and stand reveille. At Buckley we got up at 8 and there they had to drag us out.

We only get one pass all the time were here.

I'm still up against the same old problem, but I haven't got guts enough to make a decision. I think I'll ask Bill. By the way, what is his address?

I got a card from my pal, Bill Andrews today. He's a 2ⁿᵈ Louie now, and I'm really jealous. I still think I'd make a good officer.

Send DeLoughary's address too please. Did you get my S.O.S.?

Write soon.

Love, Bob

April 19, 1944

Dear Mom, Dad & Fritzi,

Well, here it is, another day and I miss Denver more and more each day.

Here's the deal here. This is a six-week gunnery course, when we graduate we are gunners, and we may get a corporal rating, and we may not. They promise one before we go overseas tho. However, I can't see where it's worth it. The increase in pay would come in handy all right, but if I can't wear bars up there, I don't think it's worth it.

To-morrow we'll have a chance to state our preference, & I'm going to say "no gunnery."

It will probably mean doing K.P. around here for a month or so. If I do a lot of crying and moaning in my letters, don't pay any attention to it. It's just a way of getting it off my chest, and then I always feel better.

I was vaccinated for small pox last week, so now I have a nice big scab on my arm. The weather around here is really nice, except where the wind blows like it's doing to-night.

No, I haven't heard from Sauve or Lambert. I guess Sauve is overseas.

I'm hoping for a delay enroute when I leave here.

It doesn't make any difference how long I've been in the army; no one can get a furlough if he is going to a tech school or is unassigned. This is a tech school, and so was Buckley.

Love, Bob

P.S. Didn't you get my letter thanking you for the Easter box? –P.S. I almost forgot, happy birthday, Dad. We'll celebrate when I get home.

April 21, 1944

Dear Mom, Dad & Fritz,

I got your letter to-day, Wed, and it was manna from heaven. I've been bumming cigarettes and pinching butts all week. I don't know when we'll ever get paid here. We haven't even signed the payroll yet.

Nothing new around here. I had to take the pressure chamber test again. Yesterday we went up to 20,000 for fifteen minutes without oxygen. I nearly passed out.

I finally got a letter from Sauve. He's some place in Cal. Going to a gunnery school. He's a 1ˢᵗ class seaman now. I don't know if they will send me to school or not. I should know as soon as they check the statistic blanks.

Gonna hit the sack. Thanks for the assistance.

Love, Bob

April 24, 1944

Dear Mom, Dad & Fritz,

I'll see if I can get this short one off before lights out. I got your second letter to-day.

I guess that was just a rumor about Bill being grounded. I don't see where he'll have a long job. All C.T.D.s have been stopped and also cadet enlistment.

Not much going on around here. We started school today. We get two weeks on the cal. 50 machine gun, and we know as much about them as the instructors do. We signed the pay roll to-day, but we won't get paid till about the middle of next month. I think I could use another five, just so I won't be short.

I really feel sorry for you about the snow. It gets pretty warm here. Guess I'll have to write and congratulate the Geo. Biners. I got a letter from Mrs. Pooler before I left Buckley and she told me Bill & George came over.

It's all for now.

Love, Bob

Tuesday April 25/44
Midland (Deep in the Heart of)
Dear Mother, Dad & Freddy,

It's about time I was hearing from you. Do you realize I have had only three letters from you since I left? I'm still interested you know! Seriously, I'm sorry if you are sore at me and I wish I had known about Dad's birthday before this. I'll have to do something about that.

I don't know who started the rumor, but I am sound as a rock physically, and in full flying status. I wouldn't be here if I wasn't. Scotty is in a hospital for his nerves. The doctors said he was on the verge of a breakdown.

I saw all the Lynch's and Aunt Jane is home and doesn't look too bad. Con certainly was thin though. Howard[288] is fat and a little worried about

---

[288] Howard Patrick Lynch (1903-1978) was the son of Con and Jane Lynch.

diabetics – at least they have him on a no-sugar diet. And I saw all the Poolers.

The winds blow sand and dust all the time and I'm going back to 17's as an instructor if I can to get out of this country and away from these little planes. I like four engines under me.

I don't think the studio wanted to release that picture because Paul was trying to get one for me. Apparently, it doesn't flatter Reynolds.[289] Don't you think I would have sent you one if I could have gotten it?

I'm going nuts over this concentrated navigation and try to play golf every chance I get, which isn't often with this wind and our schedule.

No more for now. Love to all,

Bill

Wednesday
"Deep in the Heart of"
Dear Mother, Dad & Fritzy,

Late again and I'm sorry, but if you saw my schedule you wouldn't mind so much. This place is worse than cadet training was. Some days, when we fly navigation missions, we go up to midnight. The days we don't are just as bad.

---

[289] Bill is probably talking about the still controversial film *Dixie*, produced by Paul Jones and starring Bing Crosby, Dorothy Lamour and Marjorie Reynolds.

Hope your present got there in time Mother. I had to buy it at the P.X. because I never get to town on weekdays. They wouldn't wrap it so I didn't send it off in a very good manner. The lighter is for your birthday, Roger.[290] If you'll notice, the Swiss had something to do with it.

Received a grand new picture of Maxine today. If she goes to Pocatello, maybe you can talk her out of one. She was afraid to go without you inviting her, but I think I have talked her out of that by now, so you will probably hear from her soon.

Heard from Bob yesterday and he seems to enjoy gunnery pretty well. I'm glad he does because he'll have a pretty good time once he leaves there and gets on a crew. If he tries to wash-out they make it tough now. If I tried it here, they can discharge me and my draft board would put me in the infantry as a private. He has a better chance and a better life where he is than the infantry so I wouldn't feel bad about it if I were you. If he has to go over, there is one consolation, the gunner's usually get out where the officer's don't and I'm not just handing a line either.

Fritzy would like this school. One of our instructors tells us a moron story every day before class.

---

[290] "Roger" was one of many nicknames that Bill had for his father. This one came from answering his dad's orders with "Roger."

No more for now. All my love,

Bill

___

Midland
April 27, 1944
Dear Folks,

Nothing new of any note has happened since I wrote last, but I have something to pass on to you. Maxine may be down in Pocatello in a week or two. If she can get away she will write and tell you when to expect her. So wear your teeth Roger.

I forgot to mention that I received the telegram announcing Michael William's arrival. I guess you have heard all about it too. Am anxious to hear from them by letter now, and get all the particulars.[291]

Saturday we take our final in-classroom navigation and I might just make it. If I don't, it

---

[291] Michael William Biner was born on April 15, 1944. He was the youngest child of George and Helen Biner. In fact, he was 12 years younger than his nearest sibling and his father was 47 at the time of his birth. Bill became Michael's Godfather, but could not make it to his baptism. Sadly, and ironically, it would be Bill that identified the body of his young cousin 25 years later when Mike Biner was killed in a car accident on July 5, 1969. Mike Biner's widow, Maureen Kane, would have her "15 minutes of fame" a few years later as the "mysterious blonde beauty" who was then married to presidential lawyer John Dean, the primary whistleblower in the Watergate scandal.

will mean another three weeks of the same thing, something I don't want. I'm half batty with figures now.

We never get to bed before midnight and one or two days of golf a week is all the recreation I get. Let me know when you hear from Maxine and my love to all of you –

Bill

April 28, 1944

Dear Mom, Dad & Fritz,

I got your letter to-day, also two you sent to Buckley. One Fritz mailed on the 10th and one you mailed on the 18th. Good service eh?

I was sure surprised to hear the Jones' were here. I haven't been in town since I've been here, so it must have been someone else. Besides, if I'd been that close, I would have seen her myself. I don't doubt that they could have shown me a good time.

I got a letter from Sauve to-day, with all the latest bad news. Marie Ford[292] died, but he doesn't know just what was wrong with her. Jim Kelly and Leonard Deranould (?) are both prisoners of war.

We finished our first week of school to-day. Just five more weeks to go, so I'm afraid I won't be here

---

[292] Marie Catherine Ford (1925-1944) is buried in the IOOF Cemetery in Ellensburg, Washington.

next summer Bumps. I hope you're over your hay
fever. What did the Doctor mean when he said he
never saw a face like yours? Write soon.

Love, Bob

P.S. I enjoy your letters Dad. Keep them coming

Midland Army Air Base
Thursday
Dear Mother, Dad & Freddy,

Well, the big visit is over and how did it come off?
I got a kick out of your drawing Roger. I didn't
know you had such a big mouth. I suppose
Maxine was duly impressed with the swank office
and no doubt she was introduced to "all the boys."
I don't think she likes beer very well though.

I had a letter from Scotty the other day and he is
having quite a time of it. After he got out of the
nerve hospital he ruptured a cushion in his spine
and for the past three weeks he has been lying on
a board in a Florida hospital. I guess an operation
is forthcoming and things would be pretty bad for
him except that he has fallen in love with his
nurse. It takes quite a bit to get Scotty down.

Some more men have arrived from our outfit and
they tell me that some of our groups were wiped
out after I left. It never reached the papers like
the 8th Air Force, but the losses were up in the
forties a few times. Looks like the final death kick

for the Luftwaffe.[293] I can't see how they can hold out much longer.

I'll be through here on the 10th or 30th of June, depending on whether I am to instruct cadets or pilots. If I instruct pilots, I can get back into a real airplane again and out of this dreary state of Texas.

I'll see what I can do about those post-cards Fritzy, but watch who you call stinky after this!

No more for now. Glad you both liked your presents.

Love, Bill

May 1, 1944

Dear Mom, Dad & Fritz,

I got your letter today, and it came in the nick of time. We have a few expenses here. We are wearing sun tans and the laundry takes too long. It's been 10 days now and mine isn't back yet. So I send my shirts and pants to the cleaners. It's also nice to get a few P.X. beers after a hot day. Yesterday and to-day were really hot. The wind really blows here, and the sand stings like buck-shot.

School right now is pretty dull. We're still in the cal. 50, and I knew it inside out before I ever got

---

[293] The German Air Corps.

here. The next few weeks will be a lot better because we'll be on the range most of the time. We really get to do a lot of shooting here, including skeet.

You really got a good deal on the car. I guess a little walking won't hurt either of you. You will have to wear sensible shoes, Mom.

Monday mass is for you two. I didn't get to go last night because of school, but I'll go next week.

Love, Bob

May 5, 1944

Dear Mom, Dad & Fritz,

I got your letter yesterday. They are keeping us pretty busy even on our time off, so I don't get to write enough letters.

Now that we're over machine guns, we are having a pretty good time. I detailed, stripped and assembled the 50 cal. in 20 min., blindfolded, so you can see we know our guns pretty well.

This place is just like a penny arcade now. It's really a lot of fun when we go to the range. We do a lot of skeet shooting which is really a lot of fun. I tied for the highest score in my group to-day. We also shoot at the "pigeons" from a truck going about 30 MPH. It's really a lot of fun. I fired 100 rounds to-day, and my shoulder is really sore.

We also track projected images in the turrets. We shoot at them with an electric ray and it tallies our score.

Well, it looks like everything is "really a lot of fun", to-night, so I better get out of this rut.

Love, Bob

P.S. Boy is it hot here.

May 10, 1944

Dear Bet,

I got a letter from Dad to-day, and he asked me if I ever wrote to you. I'll admit I've been pretty bad about writing, but you're not so good yourself.

Well, it looks like I'm heading for a career as a gunner, and there isn't much I can do about it. If I wash myself out I'd be letting myself in for about 3 months of K.P. and maybe a transfer to the infantry, which would be plain hell. However, after I leave here I have a 50-50 chance of not making it.

It's really hot here, but it cools down at night. I haven't been into town yet. It's wide open, and every second place is a gambling joint. Guess the army is afraid they'll take our dollar away from us.

Is Betty Poo there? Is she with you? If so, give her my love. After this week, I'll have 3 more to go till I get my wings. It's getting hotter every day, so I'll be glad to leave.

It's kind of short, but I'm too weak to write more. Write soon.

Love, Bob

May 18, 1944

Dear Mom, Dad & Fritz,

A little late huh? Now don't be mad, I can explain. I just got out of the hospital to-day. I've been there since Mon. I don't know where they came from, but I had a case of acute tonsillitis.

I couldn't eat for two days, and I had a slight fever, and all my joints were aching, so I decided I would go on sick-call. They fixed me up in a hurry, but I'll have to spend another week on this damn desert.

I washed back a class, and have lost all my buddies I left Buckley with. I'd like to get just one good break out of this army. Got a letter from Aunt Helen, also one from Bet, Bill Sauve, Bevo and Doc.

Bevo had some trouble with his instrument flying. He almost washed out, but they washed him back a class. It's gonna be tough on him watching the old gang graduate this month. They graduate on the 23rd.

Aunt Helen says Mike looks like me. She said he was really going to be spoiled. She's really good about answering my letters. J.J. never answers any of my letters.[294]

I don't think we'll get a delay from here. They stopped that just before I got here. But cheer up Kids; they always give a guy at least 10 days of home before they ship him overseas. It's rumored we may all go to Florida when we graduate. I'd hate to get a delay from there. It would take all my time traveling.

What do you hear from Bill? How much more school does he take?

Please send Bill Lamberts address. I owe him a letter. Write.

Love, Bob

P.S. If there is a pen around, please send it. The tip of this one is really gone.

May 20, 1944

Dear Mom, Dad & Fritz,

I got your letter to-day Mom, I've just been laying around to-day, trying to keep out of work. I start school again Monday.

---

[294] Possibly referring to his aunt, Julia Biner Jones.

Last Sat. night our whole Sqd. went to town. I was feeling kinda bum there so I didn't stay very long. It's quite a place tho. The jewelry stores are the only ones that don't have slot machines. Even the drug stores have them. The whole town does nothing but gamble. Everything there is expensive. A pt. of Acme beer[295] costs 65 cents.

I didn't try any of the games because I was too low, but most of the guys that tried went broke. The town is nice and green tho, and it was really good just to see some green grass again.

This whole Sqd. is filled with kids just from Basic training, and are they eager. I don't know anything new about the instructor deal.

Love, Bob

May 24, 1944

Dear Mom, Dad & Fritz,

I got your letter to-day. It's been a long time since I've had a letter. Sqd 7 is at another field for a week, and they get all their mail sent directly to them. We go next week as soon as they come back. It's our last week of firing, and then we just have one week after that.

---

[295] Acme Beer was made in San Francisco. The brewery was a branch of Leopold Schmidt's Olympia Brewing Co. Bob's grandfather, Theophil Biner, was a friend of Schmidt and helped build the Olympia Brewery in Tumwater, Washington.

I should graduate about the 10th. After that I'll go to Lincoln or Tampa, Fla. I should get a delay from either place.

I guess I'm not the only one around here who can get sick. The whole sqd has been struck by an epidemic. About 20 guys out of my barracks are in the hospital. The hospital is so crowded they have them in the aisles. The "meat wagon" has been running back and forth all day. The only reason I washed back was because I missed out on too much range work when I was in the hospital.

I'm running out of paper so I'll write later.

Love, Bob

May 27, 1944

Dear Mom, Dad & Fritz,

I've only received your one letter, but I'll write anyhow. We've been quarantined to our barracks since Thursday. We couldn't go any place and it got kinda tiresome. They just lifted it to-night.

To-morrow we go to Indian Springs.[296] It's a place about 40 miles from here. We take our ground to air firing there. We will stay all week. Sqd 7 was there this week.

---

[296] Indian Springs, Nevada was the location of the Indian Springs Air Force Auxiliary Field, now Creech Air Force Base.

I'm broke again, and it's the end of the month. If I was still in Sqd. 7 I would get paid on the line, but now I don't know when I'll get it. Just tuck a couple of bucks inside an air mail letter, and they'll send it up to the springs. Most of my mail was sent up to the springs I guess, and I don't know when I'll get it.

How did Maxine like the town? Did you find any way to entertain her?

Only two weeks to go now! I'm hoping I'll get home about the middle of June.

Love, Bob

May 31, 1944

Dear Fritzy,

I just got your letter to-day honey; I finally got my mail from Sqd. 7. I also had one from Bill.

I had my first ride in a B-17 yesterday. Boy, it's really a nice ship. I got an idea of the size of the desert around here. There isn't a thing growing as far as the eye can see. I also got a chance to fire one of the waist guns. We were shooting at targets on the ground.

Mom tells me you were elected pres of the music club. Keep up the good work but don't neglect your art. We should have at least two artists in the family.

Well, Ignats, how do you like your sister-in-law?[297]
I suppose you were all excited.

The boys are getting paid to-night, but I'll have to wait a few more days. I've been borrowing so many cigarettes, stationary, and ink off the boys, I'm beginning to feel like a bum, but everyone else is doing the same.

Write again Bumps,

Xxxx   oooo   Love, Bob

Midland Army Air Base
Wednesday
Dear Mother, Dad & Freddy,

Received your welcome news about the visit the same time I got one from Maxine. It looks like everyone was pleased so things must be alright. Maxine said Roger had all his teeth in so I guess he was on his best behavior. Still don't like the movies, though, do you Roger?

What's the business about the baby pictures? I don't care much for that. I suppose she knows about the dresses too? Just strip me bare and unveil my entire past. I'll be over in a B-29 one of these days and wipe youse off the map.

---

[297] Bob is jumping the gun a bit. Maxine Gray, Bill's new girlfriend, had visited the Biner family in Pocatello, but the two would not marry until October, 1945.

When are you leaving for Seattle, Mother? I can hear Dad moaning from here. However, the diet ought to do him some good. I still haven't written to Betty but intend to do so before the week is up. Our schedule is relaxing a little now and I have more time.

Before I forget it, if the motion picture "Memphis Belle"[298] gets to Pocatello be sure and see it. It is an actual bombing mission from start to finish and no fake. Be on the lookout for it. I guarantee you'll sit on the edge of your seats, or maybe it was because it was so real to me.

Ralph Bockmier,[299] one of our tackles on my high school team, is missing in the Italian theatre. He was pilot on a B-24. No more for now. Glad you liked Maxine and had a nice visit.

All my love, Bill

June 2, 1944

Dear Mom, Dad & Fritz,

I didn't have a chance to go to mail call to-night, but I'll write anyhow.

---

[298] A 1944 documentary film about a B-17 Flying Fortress named the Memphis Belle.
[299] Ralph Brockmier was a classmate of Bill's at Gonzaga Prep. Brockmier survived the war. He died in Spokane, Washington in 1984.

I heard some news to-day that sounded pretty good if it's true. The general rule around the place is we will get delay enroutes from Las Vegas. I hope it's true, but don't count on it too much. If I do go from here, it shouldn't take me more than two days.

I went up in a B-17 again to-day. I really got air-sick. It was a 4 hr. ride, and I was ready to come down after the first fifteen minutes.

Well, I finally got paid. It should be enough to pay for my train fare, but if you get a telegram, don't wait. We go back to Las Vegas Sunday, and it won't be too soon to please me. We are still quarantined and we have to go every place in formation. It's a wonder we don't go to the latrine in formation. Sqd. 7 will be graduating this Sat. All my old buddies will be leaving, but that's the army for you. You meet a lot of swell guys, but you can't stay with them long enough.

I suppose Ignats will be graduating any day now. Is she going to be the first in her class? Write soon.

Love, Bob

Bob was transferred to Lincoln, Nebraska in late June. The following is his first letter written from Nebraska.

July 5, 1944

Dear Dad,

I suppose you got that typed form by now.

I don't quite remember what it said, but from the looks of things I'll probably be here at least two more weeks. The bad part about it is we pull details all the time we're waiting for an assignment.

I'll either meet my crew here, or go as a replacement for a crew that has already been formed. The replacements are for guys who washed out in operational training. Usually from air sickness.

We got paid yesterday so I'm sending back the 20. I know it isn't all mine. We don't do any flying here, so I probably won't get the pay this month.

If I leave here with a crew, we should have about 8 weeks of training on this side, and then some on the other side.

The trip down wasn't too hot. I sat in that smoking car all the way to Denver and no sleep. I was really dog tired when I got here, but I got a good night sleep in a hotel before I came to the field.

I phoned Hilma[300] in Denver but she wasn't home. What's the latest news from Bill?

---

[300] Hilma Johnson DeLoughary was the wife of Doc DeLoughary. Perhaps Doc was away at the time.

Love, Bob

July 7, 1944

Dear Mom, Dad, Fritz, Grandma & Gramp,

This is going to be short, because I'm too damn hot to sit around very long. There is nothing new here; I'm still waiting to get on a crew. There isn't much chance of going west for my training. Boise is the only one in the West and that is for B-24s. I've had all my training on a B-17, so I'll probably stay here in the mid-west.

I got a letter from John Pooler the other day. He mailed it to Buckley field in May. I don't think he minds it there too much, because the only thing he had to crab about was the water they put in the wine.[301]

I'll be here at least another week, and maybe longer. In the meantime, they find plenty of work for us to do. Is Fritz enjoying herself?

Don't forget to see Dan Drew, and give my love to the K.O. and Fred Lynches.

Love, Bob

July 11, 1944

Dear Dad,

---

[301] Pooler was in Italy at the time.

Well, I'm finally on a shipping list and I don't know if I like it or not. I'm beginning to like Lincoln and I've been pretty good at getting out of the hard details.

However, here's the latrine rumors as I get them. The rumor is we are headed for Mountain Home, Idaho. I don't know how far from home it is, or if I'll ever get time to get home.[302] The thing I don't like about it is it will probably mean I'll be on a B-24. Of course the 24 is as safe as a 17, but I'm prejudiced towards the 17s.

I'll probably meet my crew here.

I should leave here no later than Sat. If we go by train we may pass through Pocatello. Of course as I say it's just a latrine rumor so you can take it for what it's worth.

Love, Bob

Mountain Home, Idaho

July 16, 1944

Dear Dad,

---

[302] Mountain Home, Idaho is located 190 miles west of Pocatello, by way of Interstate 86/84. However, this was before the interstate freeways and the trip on the old state highways was about 30 miles longer and more rugged.

Well, I just got in to-day, and I just got through calling you. We left Lincoln Fri. nite.

I met all the enlisted men in my crew in Lincoln. I also met the co-pilot. The pilot came up by car, and I don't think the navigator and bombardier will join us till later.

I doubt if I'll get in my flying time this month, but I sure could use the flying pay. If everything goes according to schedule we should be here about 3 months. This is without a doubt the crumbiest field I have ever been on, but the chow is not too bad, and no details. We also get a class A pass when we finish processing.

What's the matter with the brewery? They are selling L.A. Eastside beer here at the P.X.

We fly B-24's. I'll let you know more about the set-up when I find out.   Love, Bob

---

July 18, 1944

Dear Pop,

I should have written a letter to Mom, but she wouldn't receive it in time.

I went through a processing again to-day. We had a clothing check, and were issued our flying equipment, took a physical and got two new shots. (Cholera and Typhus)

We have to report to the flight line at 0400 in the morning, but I don't think the gunners will fly for a while yet. The pilots and engineers are the only ones that fly at first.

So far I think we have a pretty fair crew. Some of the boys are a little young, but everyone seems to be on the ball. Our pilot and co-pilot are 21. Two career gunners are 26 & 23. The engineer is 19 and so is the radio operator. Our other career gun is 20. The bombardier and navigator will join us later on.

We should be here from 10 – 11 weeks. Besides flying we have plenty of classes and work on the firing line. We don't have any details, the chow is good, and I get plenty of sack time. The only thing wrong is we are too far from anything. But, I'm sure going to try to get home.

I took out an allotment to-day. Forty bucks a month and its effective Aug. 1. Write the bank in Seattle and ask them to send you a monthly statement. I'll write soon.

Love, Bob

July 24, 1944

Dear Mom, Dad, Bet & Fritz,

I didn't mean to make you wait so long for a letter, but this isn't the way I had things planned.

I started hitch-hiking for home last sat. afternoon. I got as far as Twin Falls, but I couldn't get a ride out of there.[303] I had to spend the night there and catch a bus back the next day (Sun). I expected to make Pocatello Sat. nite but it's farther than I thought. If I ever get that much time off again, I'll know how to make it.

The trip wasn't a complete failure tho, because I really enjoyed myself in Twin Falls. There aren't any servicemen around there, and the gals really mob you. Find out what time the buses leave Pocatello for Mt. Home.

All ratings are frozen so we go overseas as a corporal.

Bevo is flying a B-26 down in Tex, and Butch is flying 17's in Las Vegas. I think I'll start flying next Wed. Believe it or not, I'm getting tired of lying around.

Twin Falls is a lot better town than Pocatello. I went to Mass there Sun. Write soon.

Love, Bob

U.S. Air Corps

Friday

Dear Mother, Dad and the Brat,

---

[303]Twin Falls is 114 miles west of Pocatello.

Received both of your letters and although I am not as late as previously, I am still later than I had intended under my new resolutions.

Sorry pappy worried you out of your trip Mother, but it is your own fault for babying so much and spoiling him. Isn't that right, Roger?

Received a letter from Helen today and she says that her mother just had a bad operation. That is, about two weeks ago, and she had her breast removed and a muscle under her arm and other cancerous places. It really sounds pretty bad, and I feel sorry for Mrs. Timmons. [304] She has always been pretty nice to me and I like her very much.

My students never cease to amaze me with their boneheaded stunts they pull in an airplane and my voice is getting very froggy from swearing at them. I know what I did myself at school, but it was never anything like the stunts they pull. And you know how much patience I have. We get along well enough though, and I think they all like me and don't hold any grudge for bruised knuckles where I crack them on occasion.

Was scheduled for a navigation mission to Los Angeles over this weekend but it isn't coming off. I think four of us will drive to Amarillo tomorrow, instead. Tomorrow is our day off. (The one that comes every three weeks.)

---

[304] Helen Chandler Biner's mother divorced her father and remarried a man named Lou Timmons.

We have had two wonderful days of rain yesterday and today. No flying and a chance to cool off. Wednesday was a cool day, and the thermometer read 108° in the shade, so help me! So you can readily see what this lovely country is like. At least in Africa we could dress for weather.

I'm glad Grandma is better and I would like to get up there myself to see them all. Tell Betty I'll really write her now, I'm not so sure that she isn't the one who owes me a letter! That is all the news for now, hope I have some sooner next time.

My love to you all, Bill

P.S. This is not for Fritzy! Dad, see if you can't get her a bike for her birthday. I'll pay for it. If you can't let me know soon enough.

Bill decided that he did not want to be an instructor after all. His sister said he was bored in Texas, and wanted to return to action. He volunteered to go to France, where liberation by Allied troops was in full swing following the epic D-Day invasion of June 6, 1944. On June 9, 1944, Bill was transferred from the Midland school to a base in Childress, Texas to prepare for redeployment. His parents were not pleased to hear the news and his mother was worried sick. So he lied.

According to Fritzie:

"He told us he would not be flying any combat missions but would have a support job. We found out after he had to bailout just before the war ended that he had been flying as a bombardier-navigator on a B-25, the Mitchell Bomber, which was also known as "The Flying Coffin".[305]

This would explain why his next letters, mostly from France; say nothing about the fifty missions he completed. He did tell Paul and Julia Jones and George and Helen Biner that he was returning to combat, but they kept his secret safe from his parents.

Bill would arrange to see his parents one final time before he left for Europe. He sent a Western Union telegram from Amarillo, Texas to his father in Pocatello, Idaho on August 8, 1944. It read:

Have reservations for the family at Newhouse Hotel Salt Lake Thursday be there urgent love – Bill.

While Bill is preparing to go far away, Bob is relishing the fact that he is so close to home.

August 2, 1944

Dear Mom, Dad, Bet & Fritz,

---

[305] Actually, most of the missions during Bill's second tour of duty were aboard a B-26. But the nickname for the B-26 wasn't much more reassuring than the Flying Coffin. It was called "The Widowmaker."

I got your letter to-day Mom. It's too bad you weren't home when I phoned last nite. But Pop and I had a nice little chat. The line was buzzing all nite.

I spent the nite in Boise again. I wish I was this close to Pocotello. About the only thing we do there is dance and hit a few of the pubs.

They sell a lot of Hartz beer[306] there, but I've only been able to get Aero Club[307] once.

I don't want you folks expecting me home each week-end, because I just can't make it. However, the rumor is, we may get a few days furlough when we finish up here. I sure hope it's true, but I'm not counting on it.

Love, Bob

August 13, 1944

Dear Mom, Dad, Bet & Fritz,

I've been kinda getting behind on my letter writing this week. They have really been keeping us busy. We have been flying a lot of high altitude and when you wear an oxygen mask for four or five hours it gets pretty rough.

---

[306] Hartz Beer was made by the Silver Springs Brewery in Port Orchard, WA where Bob's father served as brewmaster before landing his job in Pocatello.
[307] The beer his father brewed in Pocatello.

We have been up since 4 this morning, so I didn't get a chance to go to Mass to-day.

That was sure a surprise about Bill going overseas. However, there is nothing to worry about so that must make Mom kinda mad.[308] The way things are going he's going to miss out on the war all together.

What does Maxine think about it or did he say? I have until to-morrow noon, so I think I'll just go to a show to-night and take it easy. Were in our second phase now, and the work is getting a little tougher.

I'll write again soon.

Love, Bob

Bill reported to Kearns Air Base near Salt Lake City on August 9, 1944. He wrote another letter home before boarding a train to yet another camp and finally to New York, where he would ship out.

Hotel Utah
Salt Lake City
August 15, 1944

Dear Folks,

---

[308] Bob suggests that his mother likes to worry about her boys.

Late as usual but you will forgive me again, I know. There has not been any news given out here as yet so I still don't know where I am going or anything else.

Pappy Heinz shipped his family back to Chicago and came here too, so I feel pretty good about the whole thing. L.R. Hardy, our Mormon assistant engineer is in town and I had a little reunion with him Monday night.

I have drawn all kinds of equipment and had my papers etc. straightened out and all I am doing until Monday, when we have a lot of classes to attend, is loafing around.

Pappy and I are going to see Crosby or *Double Indemnity* [309]tonight (if we don't go to the Aviation Club instead). I was lucky to get a berth in the tourist coach coming down here, so I was able to get some sleep.

If it is possible to get a two-day pass, Pappy and I may try to get to Pocatello for a night. We will see if it can be arranged. There isn't any more news to give out, but I will keep you posted on what happens to me as it happens.

Love to all,

---

[309] *Double Indemnity* (1944), starring Fred MacMurray, Barbara Stanwyck and Edward G. Robinson was directed by Billy Wilder and produced by Buddy DeSlyva.

Bill

P.S. Did you get your China?

August 17, 1944

Dear Mom, Dad, Bet & Fritz,

I got your letter yesterday Bet. I'm way behind on my letters but we've been working pretty hard. We flew high altitude yesterday. There were no waist windows in the plane, and I was really cold.

This is Thurs. Pat hasn't called or anything. We fly till 10 tonight anyhow and I have classes all day to-morrow. We flew as far as the air base in Pocatello the other day but we didn't fly over the town.

They are really working us in this second phase, but I think we'll be here for the full training period. I'm still hoping I'll get enough time off to get home someday, but not at the rate we're going now.

It's still plenty hot here, but the nights are really cold.

Has Bill left yet? He'll probably go to a P.O.E.[310] *before he leaves the states.*

Love, Bob

---

[310] Point of Embarkation.

Aug 22, 1944

Dear Mom, Dad, Bet, & Fritz,

To-day I got a hair-cut. It was the second one I had since I left Pocatello. The barber really went hog-wild, and when he ended up he was standing in hair up to his ankles. I feel better but will probably freeze at high altitude.

I got a couple of nice letters to-day. One from John and one from Tom. Tom didn't say where he is, but I think he is in Fresno now. He expects to head back to the Pacific soon. He said Red had a baby premature, but it died. John seems to be doing O.K. They are rationed to six bottles of beer a week, but he has his own and three other guys.

We were scheduled to fly to-day, but were up on our missions and we got most of the day off. We fly again to-morrow noon. I was in town Sat. night, and tried to find a birthday present for Ignats. Most of the stores were closed, but I hope to get in one of these afternoons. I never do get anything for the little mutt on time.

Did you see Pat last week-end?

Write soon.

Love, Bob

Aug 27, 1944

Dear Mom, Dad, Fritz, & Bet,

I guess I'm really getting behind on my letter writing. I got your letter Sat but I've been busy.

To-day we went on a 6 hr. cross-country flight. We flew from here to Spokane and then to Portland and back here. We didn't land at any of the places but we flew right over Yakima and I saw Ellensburg but we were too far off to see any of the town. Mt. Rainier really looked good from the air. We were flying at 10,000ft and there was a blanket of fog over Portland at 1000ft so we didn't see Portland either. Our crew was the only one in our phase to fly the mission, so you know we're really on the ball.

We went to Twin Falls last Thurs. nite. Fred and I got a ride from a guy who was taking a load of empties right to the Brewery, but we didn't have enough time to go all the way. I told the guy to look you up, Dad.

We had a big water fight the other day, but Smitty ended up with three stitches, so we quit.

Our little Bumps is really getting up in the world. I don't know what she'll like, but I'll look around whenever I get in Town.

If you have any extra time and material, Mom, we all like those cookies with the pieces of chocolate in them.

This has been a pretty long letter for me.

Love, Bob

Tuesday (probably early September, 1944)

Dear Mother, Dad & All,

I'm writing this letter from camp, but will mail it Wednesday when I get off with Pappy to go into New York. The reason being that these paddle-feet here censor our mail and they are being silly about what we can say.

After I wrote my last letter I was going to phone, but never got the opportunity. They had us loaded on the train before I could look around. It was a long, sooty trip. We went by way of Chicago, Washington D.C. and Philly. We got here early Sunday and Monday, Pappy & I went into the Big Town to see what all the world talks about.

Broadway didn't impress me much. It looks like an overgrown honky-tonk district. The crowds amaze you though. At two in the morning you can hardly walk on the sidewalk the raff[311] is so thick.

We took in Greenwich Village and were disappointed. Went to Leon & Eddies[312] and the

---

[311] As in riffraff.

[312] Leon & Eddies' was a popular nightclub and restaurant on West 52nd in NYC. Started by Leon Enken and Eddie Davis it began as a Prohibition-era Speakeasy.

Astor Roof,[313] etc. All the tourist spots. Tomorrow we are going to take it easy and see a play. I think it will be *Carmen Jones*[314] or *School for Brides*.[315] Both seem to be doing a good business. There are about 15 plays including Mae West's[316] right now and if one likes the Ink Spots[317] or the Andrews Sisters[318] or anyone you can think of all you have to do is look up the address. It is really some town. The buildings form gigantic canyons and the cab drivers are right out of the movies. Such characters yet! I'm tellink youse![319]

Was surprised to hear about Dad's new prospects.[320] Hope something good comes from it Roger. If you have the wanderlust like me I know you will be looking forward to it. Be sure and let me know right away.

---

[313] The stately Hotel Astor, now long gone from the New York landscape, had a magnificent rooftop garden.

[314] A 1943 musical starring Muriel Smith with music by Oscar Hammerstein II.

[315] Directed by Howard Morton, *School for Brides* opened on Broadway August 1, 1944.

[316] Mae West (1893-1980) was a world famous American actress, playwright and sex symbol.

[317] The Ink Spots, from Indianapolis, was a popular R & B band during the 1930s and 40s.

[318] The Andrews Sisters were singing siblings from Minnesota very popular with U.S. troops during WW II.

[319] This is Bill's second humorous attempt to sound like he is from New York or New Jersey. See page 304 "Wipe youse off the map."

[320] Bill's father continued to work for East Idaho Brewing until 1946, but was looking for a bar to own and operate.

Please don't cash a check on Ft. Sam Houston. I'll send the $75 when I get my back pay. It will be after I get overseas.

We still don't know when we are leaving or where, but the story going around now is that we will be in the new air force of occupation that will be set up when Germany quits. That wouldn't be hard to take at all. Pappy and I are already planning on a French Chateau for our residence.

I wrote Bob from Salt Lake. Write me at this address. It's all I can tell you now.

All my love, Bill

Lt. W.D. Biner 0733517
Casual Sqd. A-3
APO 16447A c/o P.M. NYC, NY

Sept 1, 1944

Dear Mom, Dad, Bet, & Fritz,

Well, I made it O.K. and I got a little sleep besides. I got a letter from Bill to-day. He said he expected to leave the next day. He still doesn't know for sure where he's going, but he thinks it'll be England.

We have a mascot now. She's part fox terrier and part cocker. We call her Kahki & she's sure cute. We had a regular dog-tag made for her.

I got paid 19 bucks yesterday and I paid out 14, so I think I'll be a little short till I get my flight pay. I could use 10. We fly at 3 in the morning, so I think I'll try & get a little sleep.

I'll write again.

Love, Bob

Sept 9, 1944

Dear Mom, Dad, Bet, & Fritz,

I got your letter to-day Dad and I guess I've been slipping a little too.

I got the telegram O.K. last Thurs. I spent Thurs. nite & Friday in Boise. We didn't fly to-day like we were supposed to so we have to-night off & also to-morrow. I'm not going any place, tho because I have a lot of letters to write and a big washing to do.

We only have about 25 more hrs. to fly, but I suppose we'll be here for the full month. The rumors are flying fast about what will happen to us, and there is even the possibility that we may go in B-29s but I don't put much stock in it.

That's really too bad about Grandma. I think it'll do her a lot of good if you can get down to see her. Tell Fritz I still haven't forgotten about her and Sloppy Joe.

I'll write sooner next time.

Love, Bob

Sept 14, 1944

Dear Mom, Dad, & Bet & Fritz,

I got your letters yesterday and the cookies to-day, Mom. The cookies are really nice and the whole crew sends their thanks.

We didn't fly yesterday, so I finally got in town before the stores closed.

That sweater is about 3 sizes bigger than what you asked for Ignats. Smitty tried it on for me & it was too small for him, so it should fit just about right.

I guess Bill will have a pretty good deal over there. Who knows, he may come back with a French wife.

The wind is blowing to-day and for once, it's really cold. I sure hope we don't fly to-day. It gets too cold on these high altitude missions.

How does Bet like her job? It sounds pretty good to me.

Love, Bob

Sept 17, 1944

Dear Mom, Dad, Fritz, & Bet,

I got your letter to-day Mom. I spent a quiet Sat. nite on the post, & for once I really feel like flying. We haven't many more missions to go, and in spite of everything I kinda like this post.

We've been having some rainy weather the last few days. I guess I got used to the rain in Seattle, because I like this.

I got another letter from Sauve the other day. All he ever tells me is bad news. Weezy & Nancy R. both got married. Corky Carmody was killed in France. He flew a P-38.[321]

I went to the 12:00 Mass to-day, so I slept till 11:00. I'm broke again Dad. Did you write to that Seattle bank for a statement yet? I could use another 10, but I don't want it unless you can cash a check in Seattle.

The Superbombers [322]play in Boise next Sat. I already bought a ticket, now I hope we don't fly.

[321] 1st Lt. Cortland "Corky" Carmody was killed in France on August 6, 1944. Corky's brother, L.G. Carmody, was also a member of the U.S. Air Corps. L.G. Carmody survived the war and attended Central Washington College in Ellensburg where he was an All-American in football. He was drafted by the Washington Redskins in 1947.

[322] The Superbombers was the 2nd Air Force football team out of Colorado Springs. They belonged to the Pacific Coast Service Football League and played in the 1943 Sun Bowl.

They are playing the Walla Walla Oct. 12. That's where Pennington is.

Write again.

Love, Bob

Sept 24, 1944

Dear Mom, Dad, Bet & Fritz,

I got your letter Friday Mom, and Dad's letter yesterday. Yesterday was the big game, but as luck would have it, we flew. I guess it wasn't much of a game anyhow.

I really put out a big washing to-day. I'm getting to be a regular old maid.

We start processing to-morrow, so you can see we haven't much time left. A couple of weeks at least. I would sure like to get home again, and I'm sure going to try, but they are keeping us pretty busy.

Did Fritz get her sweater? It was insured, so let me know.

Thanks for the money Dad; I was kinda running low on cash. You write a check.

It has been kinda chilly here lately, but I think it'll warm up again. I don't know why you expect a letter from Bill so soon. You don't know but what he's doing is a lot of traveling.

Write soon.

Love, Bob

A few days later Bob and his crew were transferred to Topeka, Kansas where they were to get equipped for deployment.

On September 11, 1944, Bill Biner departed the United States for his second tour of duty. He arrived in England on September 19, 1944. Paris had been liberated a month earlier. Bill was assigned to the 453rd Bomb Squadron, 323rd Group. His Army Post Office (APO) was in newly liberated Reims, France. On September 29th Bill was cleared to resume missions by the squadron surgeon Captain Victor F. Albright. The following undated V-mail, probably from late September or early October, 1944, was written in France.

453rd Squadron, 323rd Group

Dear Mother, Dad & All,

Well, I finally have a permanent APO and address. I didn't want a mix-up in my mail like the last time I was over.

Pappy and I are still together and we are having a wonderful time sampling this very good French wine. We hunt out the little towns away from everything and we always are lucky. Good Champagne is very cheap in these towns and we can get a good meal to go with it. Our transportation consists of two bicycles and a knapsack. We always carry candy for the kids. It goes over big with the parents. The weather is a little wet and chilly, but not as bad as England. While in England Pappy and I took in Oxford and its pubs. Didn't get a chance to go to London. Right now we are trying to get to Paris if we can get a few days off. Oo la la! Will try to write tomorrow. My love to all of you.

Bill

Topeka, Kansas
Oct 11, 1944
Dear Mom, Dad, Bet, & Fritz,

Hi folks, I've been here two full days now. We had our personnel processing to-day.

I went in and saw the town last nite, and to-night we are going to try to go to Kansas City. As you know Kansas is a dry state. We don't know how long we'll be here, so we're going to take advantage of all our free time.

They have the open post policy here, for all combat crews. Any free time we have, we can take off.

We have a nice non-com[323] club here, and we have a special room for combat crews called the Esquire

---

[323] A club for non-commissioned officers. Bob was a corporal.

Room. Varga did some special large art for the walls.[324]

We may get a three-day pass, but I doubt if I'll be able to make it home. Our co-pilot had appendicitis the day before we left Mt. Home, so we now have a new co-pilot. He has only had 4 hrs. on a B-24, but I think he'll be a pretty good man.

I'll write soon.

Love, Bob

Oct 16, 1944

Dear Mom, Dad, Bet, & Fritz,

I got your letters to-day and I was really glad to get them. You two really sound better. I'm telling you right now if you haven't heard from Bill, there is a good excuse. You don't know but he may have travelled by boat.

It looks like my good times here are coming to an end. Our pilot told us we would leave here either Thurs. or Friday. I don't think I'll be telling you any military secrets if I say I'll probably go by boat. I don't know when or where, but it may even

---

[324] Alberto Vargas (1896-1982) was a Peruvian artist famous for his pin-up girls and voluptuous nudes. Needless to say, his work was very popular on bases during World War II.

take a month, so if you don't hear from me, don't think I don't want to.

I don't think much of Kansas, but Kansas City is really a town. Of course it runs into a little expense going to & from on the train, cabs, etc. but I guess we won't have many good times on this side. The money I sent for will buy me a bunch of things to take with me, cigarettes, soap, and a bunch of stuff. It will probably be quite a while before we leave the state. Write here.

Love, Bob

Oct 19, 1944

Dear Mom, Dad, Bet, & Fritz,

I got the money O.K., the cookies and candy and Bet's letter. The cookies & candy are really neat, Mom. There wasn't one of them broken, and we all enjoyed them.

We have from now till Sun. morning off, so to-night we are heading for Kansas City again. We go there whenever we can, it's really a nice town, and it reminds me a lot of Seattle. If they would only give me a few more days off I could almost make it home. I've been in the army too long to expect a good thing at this stage of the game.

We got all our over-seas equipment yesterday, but none of it indicates what theatre we're going to. I guess we'll get some more when we get to P.O.E.

I guess Ignats was never built to be a farmerette; she's going to be an artist anyhow.

We took a picture of the crew yesterday, but Smitty was in town. I'll send you the picture as soon as I get it developed. Meanwhile here's one of Frie & me. It's a bum picture of Frie.[325]

Write soon. Love, Bob

Undated V-mail from France. Probably Oct. 1944

Dear Folks,

I am keeping up my good resolutions as you can see with this quick follow-up of my last letter.

The weather here is getting progressively worse as the days go by. I don't have a sleeping bag like I did in Africa and Italy and I feel the night pretty much. However, I am feeling much better than I did at Childress. I've lost all my excess weight already and I am getting lots of sleep. The food is not fattening but it is much better than I ever had in my old outfit.

Pappy and I are being spoiled by an old Frenchman and his son who run a little bistro in a little town hidden away here. We have been bringing the kids candy bars every time we go in and the men cigars. Now we are one of the family

---

[325] Donald Frie was the upper gunner in Bob's B-24 crew.

and get the best wine at rock bottom prices and steak dinners that no one else is able to get. We get a big kick out of sitting around, drinking sparkling wine and trying to improve our French and his English.

Yesterday Pappy and I took a quick trip into Paris to see the sights and we really did. I was expecting something, but I wasn't prepared for it when we got there. I thought Naples was nice, but Paris is beyond description. The city is full of beautiful parks and fountains. The fountains are not running now but it doesn't spoil the effect too much.

We got a terrific thrill walking down the Champs Elysee.[326] On one is the Arc of Triumph[327] and at the other the Place de Concord.[328] It is the widest and most beautiful street I have ever seen. We had some Champagne at the famous Crillon Hotel

---

[326] Champs-Elysees is one of the most famous boulevards in the world, with some of the most expensive real estate.

[327] A monument at the western end of Champs-Elysees built between 1805-1836 to honor the war dead from the French Revolution and the Napoleonic Wars. It is also the site of the Tomb of the Unknown Soldier from WW I.

[328] Place de la Concorde is a popular public square designed in 1755.

Bar[329] and then Pappy wanted to climb the Eiffel Tower. I stopped that.

If you come over here, you shouldn't miss it. I wouldn't mind coming back myself and going to school. In fact, I am thinking about it very seriously. Looks like I am running out of paper so I had better close for a while. Hope you are all fine and all my love to you.

Bill

Oct 24, 1944

Dear Mom, Dad, Bet, & Fritz,

Just a short note, while I'm waiting. We're leaving to-day and that's all I know.

I got your letter to-day, and yesterday I got a package from Aunt Molly. She sent me a nifty white scarf and some good candy. I'll write her & both grandmas when I get to P.O.E.

If we leave from the East Coast, I'll have a good chance of going to France. But they also leave there for China & India, so when you get my A.P.O. you know I'll be in either of three or thirty places.[330] As I said before, we'll leave by boat, so

---

[329] The Crillon Hotel, at the foot of the Champs-Elysees in the Place de la Concorde, opened in 1907 in a magnificently renovated 1758 building.
[330] Bob was on his way to the Old Buckenham Air Base near Norwich, England.

don't be surprised if you wait a good long time for a letter. The only reason I'm telling you this now is because our mail is censored at P.O.E.

We spent a 3-day pass in Kansas City, and had a good time even if it was expensive. By the way Dad, have you written to the bank in Seattle yet? I wish you would, because I want to know if they're getting the allotments or not. It always pays to make sure. Don't forget.

I'm glad Bill is having such a good time. Who knows, I may even be able to look him up. I'll write as soon as I get to P.O.E. and don't do any worrying. Love, Bob

---

Oct 26, 1944

Dear Mom, Dad & All,

Well folks, here I am on the east coast. I can't tell you where I am, I can't tell you about the trip, and I can't tell you what I'm going to do.[331] I guess you'll have to wait till I go over-seas so I can write a letter with something in it.

Oh yes, I can also say I expect to go over-seas in the not too distant future. One thing I will say is I don't like this place as well as Topeka. One of the

---

[331] He was in East Brunswick, New Jersey getting ready to board the *SS IIe de France*, the same liner that took his brother to his second tour.

big reasons is we get details here. I pull K.P. tomorrow.

I'm going to try and catch up on all my letter writing. As long as I can't say anything, I may as well start another letter.

Write soon.

Love, Bob

Oct 29, 1944

Dear Mom, Dad, Bet, & Fritz,

The only reason I haven't been writing much is there isn't anything to write about. When you don't get any more letters then you'll know I'm on my way.

I went in & saw the sights last nite. I rode the subway, and did everything I could. I wasn't too impressed tho.[332] I pulled K.P. the other day, and I'm still tired. It's the first work I've done since last July.

I got another letter from Tom to-day. He didn't get any letters for a couple months. I hope I don't have to wait that long.

Love, Bob

---

[332] He visited New York City.

Within a week both Biner brothers would be in
Europe flying missions for the U.S. Air Corps.

V-Mail from France
Nov. 3, 1944
Dear Folks,

Just got some of my back mail; some of it as late
as September 3rd. Three letters in all. From the
tone of them Mother, you sound like you did when
I was over the last time and I wish you would stop
worrying. I am really having a big time here and
am in as much danger as I would be in Pocatello
listening to some of Dad's jokes.[333]

Also had a letter from Betty Morgan. I guess it
was because I wrote to her for the Ellensburg
news. She informs me that Betty Webster now
has a baby boy, which may or may not be news to
you. She also said that the Kelleher's received
news that Jack was killed somewhere over here in
France.[334] Must be pretty tough on them.[335]

---

[333] In fact, Bill had already flown in several dangerous
missions, dropping 1000 pound bombs on a bridge in
Sinzig, Germany and on the German towns of Merzig,
Sarrlautern (Saarlouis) and Reichenbach. His parents
remained unaware of his missions.

[334] John "Jack" Kelleher, Jr. (1921-1944), was the son of
John Kelleher and Selena Preece of Ellensburg. A staff
sergeant in the 137th Infantry, 35th Division, he was
injured twice during the invasion of Europe following
D-Day. He was injured on July 12, 1944, in France and
after recovering in a military hospital in England

As for where my typewriter is, as you can plainly see, it is in front of me at this moment. I'm sorry it isn't around for you to use again, but Betty should have hers there if she hasn't hocked it yet. My watch was not working right and when I was in Salt Lake I managed to get hold of an army job that is a honey. No use wearing my own when I can get my time off the government.

At this writing I should have approximately $565 in the bank. It should develop into quite a tidy sum by the time I get back. I got on the boat with seven dollars and Pappy had about the same. When we got off we had run it up to about three hundred between us. At one time we were changing one hundred dollar bills for the boys. The last night out we ran into a little tough luck and dropped some of our ill-gotten gains, but it was a pretty profitable crossing on the whole.

---

returned to combat. Injured again on Sept. 20[th,] he died from his wounds on Sept. 23, 1944 and is buried in Lorraine, France. He was posthumously awarded the Purple Heart. Jack was a basketball and track star at Ellensburg High and later Washington State. His brother Joe Kelleher (1925-1985) was a naval officer during World War II and is buried near his parents in Ellensburg's Holy Cross Cemetery.

[335] Bill would have upset his own mother if he had confided in this letter that he had officially resumed missions on October 28th. He served a navigator during his first three missions and then served as bombardier on the next 30.

Yes, Mother, I have a lot of postcards for you, but I haven't found out the censorship rules for sending them yet. All in due time. You already have French money, it is the same as we used in Africa, so there is no use sending any. I believe they have a rule against it anyway. We are stabilizing the Franc and it makes it tough for us when we want to buy anything because we are actually only getting a third of our pay when it is figured out. C'est la Guerre!

Had a letter from Bob today but it was very short. Send his address as soon as possible because I want to write to the little squirt. It was swell that he got home even for so short a time.

I am gradually getting things figured out so quit worrying yourself Mother. I have that to do on my own with no kibitzing.[336] Love to all, Bill

France
Nov. 9, 1944
Dear Mother, Dad & All,

I'm sorry I can't use the typewriter but I cut left index finger yesterday when we were sawing firewood for our tent. The saw slipped while two of us were holding the log on the horse and I got a good gash to put Sulfa[337] in. It ought to be O.K. in

---

[336] Getting unwanted advice when you're trying to work.
[337] Antibacterial sulfonamides to stave off possible infection from the cut.

a couple of days. Wood and coal have become very important now. It looks like it will snow most any day. I'm wearing John L.'s[338] now and I really need them.

I think I could get home sometime after Christmas, if not before, but I don't know whether I want to or not. This is the only way I can save any money and I don't feel it is time to leave yet anyway. I want to go home a civilian if I can. I don't think I could stand the army over there again. Pappy may go though. He's getting homesick for his family. Sorry I missed your anniversary again. Maybe next time.

My love to all,

Bill

V-MAIL from England
Nov. 13, 1944
Dear Mom, Dad and All,

I got two letters from you today Mom, and I think that is pretty fast. The last one was dated the 3rd. I've seen a lot of the country, but all of it has been from a train window.

This is a pretty fair post that I'm at now, but I don't think I'll stay very long. We just stay here for orientation, then move on to another post. The weather here is something like Seattle, but it's a

---

[338] Long johns.

lot damper. I haven't been to town to try the warm beer yet, but I intend to do so as soon as possible.

Love, Bob

Staff Sergeant Robert Joseph Biner

Bob recalls that he was "stupid" when he got to England. Most of the Americans were young, between 18-25 years, and they were cocky.

"I really wasn't afraid. The war was going pretty well. That's where the stupidity came in. It never occurred to me that we wouldn't come back from a mission. Our gear was heavy and hot so when we got in the air we'd take off our flak jackets and parachutes. We were reckless. We just didn't know. At briefings we were told about conditions and targets but never about other planes being shot down. You didn't think about the possibility of being shot down." Bob also admits that ground troops might have been envious of the Air Corps men. "They thought we got special treatment, and we did. There was a hell of a lot more reality in the infantry when every step you take you're a target. We didn't have to carry a damn mess kit and all that crap. We ate in a mess hall all the time. We had a base; a place to sleep. They were out in the open. But I never felt any animosity from the ground troops. They appreciated us."

France, November 13, 1944

Dear Folks,

Just a few lines in answer to your last one with Bob's temporary address in it. From the sounds of it I think he is in England someplace, but you never can tell. It could be Italy.[339]

Enclosed you will find a check from a friend of mine that I would like you to deposit for me. I lent him the money on the boat when I was flush. As you can see, he has the same bank. If you can cash it, go ahead and keep it. Another thing; how about sending me a money order for about $75 so that I can get out of the hole? The last two pay days I have owed about that amount and I can't seem to get ahead. It hasn't been the result of poker playing, because I haven't played a game since arriving. It is just the high cost of living and too much time off.

Pappy was in Paris over the Armistice holiday[340] and he came back with many tales to tell. It was the first time they have been able to parade freely in four years and I guess they really went hog wild. He said it started about ten in the morning and was still going at eight o'clock that night. De Gaulle[341] and W. Churchill[342] were there and the

---

[339] Bob Biner was at the Old Buckenham Air Base near Norwich, England. He would soon fly 17 missions over Germany as a belly gunner and waist gunner on a B-24. Bill flew the 2nd mission of his second tour on November 9th.

[340] November 11th commemorates the signing of the armistice that ended World War I. The 1944 Armistice Day celebration in Paris remains one of the great events in the city's history.

[341] Charles de Gaulle (1890-1970) was the leader of the Free French Forces and future president of France.

people went wild. So many people were standing on the roof of a Buick next to Pappy that the roof caved in.

I haven't been to Notre Dame yet but expect to on my next trip in whenever that is. Probably the end of the month. Pappy went to Mass there Sunday and he said it was terrific. The stain glass over the altar is very beautiful he says, and the acoustics wonderful. However, he said the ceremony wasn't as fancy as the Cathedral in Reims, where the ushers dress like Rear Admirals and the collection takers, Brigadier Generals.

Just heard the news over the radio of the English sinking the Tirpitz.[343] They have been after it for quite a while now and I hope it was worth it.

I am going to send all my presents to you Mother for redistribution. I can't get a piece of paper to save my neck. It is one of the many scarce items around here. Another is string. Looks like I am running out of paper and news so I will close.

---

[342] Sir Winston Churchill (1874-1965) was the Prime Minister and primary source of inspiration for the beleaguered British people during World War II. A man who needs no introduction, he was one of the greatest figures in world history.

[343] On Nov. 12, 1944, after several failed attempts, the Royal Air Force finally destroyed the massive German battleship Tirpitz off the coast of Norway. 21 RAF Lancasters attacked, making several direct hits with armor-piercing six-ton bombs.

Write often and don't forget the money order (postal).

Love to all, Bill

V-MAIL from England
Nov. 16, 1944
Dear Mom, Dad and All,

I got another letter from you yesterday. The reason I couldn't tell you much about New York, because I only spent a few hours there. I didn't see much of the town, because we went to a dance, and then right back to camp.

Little Ignats must be a pretty busy girl. When is she going to take over the Mayors job?

I should be moving to a new base pretty soon, and I'll probably get a new A.P.O. I haven't been to town yet, because its 4 miles away, and I don't feel like walking it. How's Bet doing now? Is Pat still there? Willy is having quite a time; I wish I could go there.

Keep writing. Love, Bob

Nov 20, 1944

Dear Mom, Dad & All,

I finally got my new A.P.O. address, and I think this will be fairly permanent. The living quarters aren't as good as the last place, but we don't pull any K.P. or stuff like that.

We live in Nissen huts, and they aren't as warm & cozy as they look from the outside. We have a stove about the size of a thimble. I'm not crabbing tho. The boys in France would think I'm living like a king.

It seems we still have some schooling and local flying before we ever go on a combat mission. This outfit really has a good record, so don't worry.

I still haven't been to town yet; just lazy I guess and short a few pounds. Everything is rationed around here. We get 5 packs of cigarettes a week. Also 5 candy bars. The candy is sufficient, and I brought enough cigarettes to keep up for quite a while.

If you can Mom, I wish you would send me my fur slippers as soon as possible. It doesn't look as if I'll be able to get anything before Xmas. What could I get Ignats?

The blackout is still on here in England, and it really gets dark at night.

Write soon.

Love, Bob

Undated V-mail probably from Nov. 1944

France

Dear Folks,

Just received your letter and am ever so glad to get it. The other two were from Julia and Helen. But that is what I expected. You remember the last time?

I don't know how I am ever going to save any money around here. I get quite a bit of time off and every place I go to costs so much darn money. I just got back from a two-day pass to Paris and it cost me eighty-five dollars. However, I did get a few bottles of perfume for Christmas presents. The next time I go I intend to stock up some more and finish all of my shopping.

Chenel 5[344] is almost impossible to get. All the Americans want it and have bought out all the stores. There is plenty of Molonyeux[345] and Schiparreli[346] and Lucien Lelong,[347] etc. though so people will have to be satisfied with that.

---

[344] The popular and expensive perfume was introduced in 1921 by the legendary French fashion designer Gabrielle "Coco" Chanel (1883-1971).
[345] This perfume was introduced by the English fashion designer Edward Molyneux (1891-1974) as a friendly rival to Coco Chanel's #5.
[346] A line of perfume started by Italian designer Elsa Schiaparelli (1890-1973).
[347] Lucien LeLong (1889-1958) was a French designer who introduced 27 different fragrances.

Julia told me about Leo passing away. He certainly didn't have much of a chance in life, did he?[348]

If you told me that Betty is working it must be in another letter that hasn't arrived yet. Is Pat staying in Pocatello now? You say he is doing over Fritzie's room.[349]

I can't tell you much about what I am doing but I'm doing staff work here and it really is a snap.[350] We are living in tents again but have it fixed up pretty nice. Wooden floor, door, stove, etc. German prisoners have just finished gravel walks all around the camp and they come in pretty handy with all this rain and mud. It is getting much colder now and should snow pretty soon. They say it is snowing in Belgium now.

If you want to send me something that I can use it is a wool sweater. A V-neck job that I can wear

---

[348] Leo Vincent Biner was the son of Albert and Mary Kreider Biner. He was born in 1919 and suffered from poor health and mental retardation. He died on August 31, 1944, six weeks before his 25th birthday.

[349] Charlton Paschal "Pat" Fulton, Betty Biner's new boyfriend and future husband. Betty met Pat Fulton while both worked for the Lend-Lease program in Pasco, Washington.

[350] Bill is not being straight with his parents. He was, in fact, engaged in many dangerous missions. His most recent missions included bombing German positions in St. Vith and Houffalize, France and destroying German bridges in Nonnweiler, Keuchingen and Eitorf, Germany.

under my blouse if I want to. Not a sweater-vest but a regular pullover. I don't need any candy because I stocked up on that before coming over here and we get a couple of bars a week rationed to us. However, you can send some cigarettes if you want. They are always a little scarce.

Glad to hear that Fritzy is taking piano lessons. Hope she turns out better than the rest of us at it. I'll send Grandma Lynch some perfume for Christmas and it might help to cheer her up. I'll have the States smelling like the Rue de la Paix[351] before I'm through.

Hope you can make it down to Los Angeles – both of you. I would not mind being there myself right now. Chopping firewood is not to my liking. Well, no more for now.

All my love, Bill

While Bill was dropping bombs, Bob was busy as a belly gunner. After his plane crossed the channel the turret would be lowered and he would climb in. He was able to rotate and shoot down, but never above horizontal. When they approached bombing targets he would be lifted from the belly to serve as the "armer gunner." In other words, he pulled the pins to activate, or arm, the bomb fuses before the bombardier dropped the load.

---

[351] A fashionable shopping street in Paris.

Photographs show Bob and Fritzi with their
father, the brewmaster Billy Biner.

Nov. 27, 1944

Dear Folks,

I am really running out of material to write about so I guess I will have to write up my monthly visits to Paris and the like for want of better material. Have you received any of the post cards yet that I have sent off and on? I have a book of Paris street scenes for you that I will send along in a package whenever it is filled with what I want to send.

Got back Sunday from my last two-day pass and I didn't spend so much money this time because I couldn't borrow much. Too near the end of the month. That money order will put me just right. I owe sixty-five dollars and I can assure you it won't happen again.

This time I went to the top of the Montmartre[352] where the Sacre Couer[353] stands and next to the Eiffel Tower, the best view of the city can be had there. It was a beautiful day, sun shining and all and you could see almost the entire city. Quite a sight. The church itself is very beautiful and quite new in respect to most of them.

---

[352] The highest point in Paris, France at 130 meters.
[353] The Basilica of the Sacred Heart on the top of Montmarte.

Saturday there was another terrific celebration in town. This time it was St. Catherine's Day. In France that is sort of a French Sadie Hawkins Day. All unmarried girls of 25 years participate and it goes on all night.[354] They wear outlandish hats and march all over in groups snaring young males for parties and dances. I guess I didn't use enough Lifebuoy[355] because I was left out in the cold.

Saturday night we all went to the Follies Bergere[356]and it was really something. The man who designed the scenery was really terrific, or rather, his scenery was. The acts were very good and their star comedian, M. Dandy, was as good as I have seen.[357] The theatre itself is something you would only find in Paris and the seats are very plush and comfortable.

---

[354] Women who reach the age of 25 without having married are known as Catherinettes in France.
[355] Lifebuoy was a soap brand that popularized the slang term B.O.
[356] The Folies Bergere is a Paris music hall established in 1869 and still in operation today. Many famous singers, dancers and comedians performed there, including W.C. Fields, who was a close friend of Bill's uncle, Paul Jones. The great African American singer/dancer Josephine Baker was a regular at Folies Bergere.
[357] Bill is probably referring to a clown who performed at Folies Bergere in the 1940s under the name Dandy the Irrepressible. His actual name remains a mystery.

Sunday, after Mass, I went out to the Trocadero[358] on the subway and got a good close-up view of the Eiffel for the first time. I started talking to a Frenchman who was giving his little girl an airing and he invited me to lunch. I didn't go because the Red Cross has restaurants for us and the French citizen doesn't get much. He said the situation was improving now that the railroads are running again, but I don't like to impose on their hospitality.

There is a pair of book-ends I would like to get some time. On one an old tramp is crouched down with a bottle to his lips and on the other an old hag is peering around with a club in her hand. They both have red roses and are the neatest book-ends I have ever seen. I don't know whether they are wood or ceramic. Next time I'll try to bargain for them.

No more for now. Weather is still cold and wet and windy. Have a little cold but am taking vitamins so everything is O.K.

Love, Bill

Dear Mom, Dad & All,

I'm getting kinda lazy now that I'm not getting my mail, but it should catch up with me pretty soon.

---

[358] A hill across the Seine River from the Eiffel Tower. It's most prominent structure is the Palais de Chaillot.

I still haven't done any flying, and now I'm getting a little impatient. I'd like to get my missions over & get home.[359]

I went into town last nite for my first time. It seems funny groping around the streets in a blackout that's really black. The pubs have a little red sign in the window and if it weren't for that everything would look dead. The beer, which is called mild or bitter, tastes a little flat. It's dark & has about the same kick as ours. It sure keeps me running to the back tho.

Everything looks so old I can't get over it. I still think they could use a good plumber.

We finally made buck, but we have to go before a board to get our staff ratings. From what I've heard it's pretty stiff too. It's a little early to worry about that tho.

We have a pretty nice chapel here, and we also have a Catholic chaplain.

Keep writing. Love, Bob

---

[359] Bob found ways to amuse himself while waiting for combat missions. He readily admits to sneaking up to his Nissen (Quonset) hut, at the Old Buckenham base during the night and running sticks along the outside of the corrugated metal sides, which sounded like machine gun fire to the unsuspecting GIs inside. Bob and some of his buddies would also fire their pistols in the air in an attempt to scare their sleeping buddies. It didn't win them any fans, and occasionally resulted in the temporary confiscation of their firearms.

Dec 4, 1944

Dear Mom, Dad & All,

I'm sorry I haven't written sooner; I hope you haven't been worrying. Just lazy.

We finally finished our first mission.[360] *We really have a good pilot & crew, so if that means anything, we should come out O.K*[361].

I've only been to town a couple of times. There isn't much to do at night because you can't see anything. We're due for a pass pretty soon which will enable us to take in London. If the money holds out.

My morale has really reached a new low. I've only received about three letters since I've been here. I hope it all catches up pretty soon. By the way, you don't have to use V-mail. Not enough room to

---

[360] Bob tried to say something about his first mission, but it was censored. The first mission was on Nov. 30, 1944 to Hamburg, Germany as a belly gunner on a B-24 named *Lace*. They bombed a marshalling yard. Bob remembers getting a few scattered bursts of flak from enemy fighters. Eventually the turrets were removed from the B-24 and Bob became a waist gunner.

[361] The crew of the *Lace* and later the *Maid of Fury* was pilot Warren L. Brown; co-pilot Rueben O. Peterson; navigator James Musgrove; bombardier John L. Black; nose gunner Frank Lane; engineer Wiley Fortson; upper gunner Donald Frie; tail gunner Virgil Vance; radio operator Lowell Smith and belly gunner Bob Biner.

write. How long does it take my mail to reach you?

What is Bill doing in France? I sure wish I could be with you for Xmas, but maybe I'll be able to make it next year.

Merry Christmas & love to you all, Bob

Dec 10, 1944

Dear Mom, Dad, Bet, & Fritz,

There isn't much to write about, but just so you won't worry.

I haven't any more missions yet, but our 48 hr. pass is due in a couple of days[362]. I guess we'll all go to London. It's really cold over here. If you can find any sweat socks I wish you would send them to me. Also a box of Ritz and some cheese. We usually make something to eat in the barracks.

I've received one letter from Grandma and also one from Sauve. All my mail should be catching up with me pretty soon. I sure hope you're getting my mail O.K. Keep writing even if you aren't getting my letters regularly. This Xmas rush is pretty tough.

---

[362] Bob did fly in his second mission on Dec. 6th aboard the *Maid of Fury*. They bombed a viaduct in Minden, Germany. He called it a "milk run" which simply means it did not meet enemy fire.

They really have a nice Red Cross Club here. They have games & food & stuff, the only trouble; it's pretty far to walk from the hut. I'm sure getting lazy.

There isn't much to write about, and I have to get to bed early. I'll write again as soon as I come back from my pass. Love, Bob

---

Undated V-mail from France. Probably Dec. 1944

Dearest Folks,

Don't know whether my mail or yours is being lost or delayed, but I haven't heard from you in about six weeks now. In fact, outside of a card from Tommy, a birth notice from a friend and one letter from Maxine, I have received no mail from anyone.

Well, I have all the perfume I want to send now, but my book-ends were bought by someone else when I got back to town, so my list is still incomplete. We have train service going to Paris now, but they are not heated and we travel at night so it's no pleasure. I get in for two days every fourth week which is plenty. Pappy and I got stranded hitching back from Reims a while ago and we slept all night in a haystack and ate a sugar beet for breakfast. Some fun!

Haven't heard from the Runt in quite some time. How is he and Great Britain getting along? I can get him all the artist supplies he wants here if he'll tell me what he wants. How about sending me some cheese or salami or both. We are eating poorly again and I am hungry all the time. Hope to get twenty letters tomorrow.

My love to you all, Bill

Dec 15, 1944

Dear Mom, Dad, & All,

I just got back from old London, and I'm ready to go home any time now.[363] London really isn't so bad. We saw all the sights, and had a lot of fun, but none of it is as good as what we have in the States.

We took a four bob tour[364] of all the places of interest. St. Paul's Cathedral was really interesting. A guide took us through and showed us the paintings, sculpture, bomb damage, and the tombs of the great historical figures. From there we went to the bombed area, London Bridge,

---

[363] Before leaving for London Bob flew on his 3rd mission, aboard the Lace, hitting a supply dump in Bitburg, Germany. According to Bob, "This was a tactical mission in support of the ground troops a day after the great counter offensive (Battle of the Bulge). On the way back we were diverted to a Navy Base due to fog at home field. Had ice cream and beer." Apparently the Navy base was close to London because he was there with his crew the next day.
[364] A bob was a British pound. Apparently the tour of London set Bob Biner back four pounds.

Tower of London, Parliament, Westminster Abbey, and Buckingham Palace.[365]

Most of the people were quite aware of the Yanks. They are all eager to oblige and get as much as they can out of us. We had a lot of fun riding the tube[366] and that was the only thing they couldn't rob us on!

I looked all over town for some Toby jugs, Mom, but it seems they only make them for export. They are quite rare over here, but I may be able to pick some up in an antique shop.[367]

None of your letters have arrived yet, but I got one from Sauve & one from Scotty Kelleher the other day. Scotty told me his brother Jack was wounded last Sept. and died three days later. Jack was with Patton. Did you read about it in the paper?

Send me Doc's address, also Grandma Biner's.

Love, Bob

In France
Dec. 21, 1944

---

[365] Bob doesn't mention one of the best benefits of staying in London. Since the Army Air Corps did not issue sheets or pillow cases, Bob convinced a chamber maid in a London hotel to sell him a set. He slept much more comfortably because of it.

[366] The Tube is the subway system of London.

[367] Harriet Biner passed her Toby collection on to her daughter Betty. When Betty passed away in 2009 every son and grandson inherited one of the Toby jugs.

Dear Folks,

Just received your V-mail of November 28 and yesterday I received a letter from Betty that was mailed on October 18. The first two letters in a long time. Apparently there are some more in-between because you talk about some machinery Dad. What machinery? And where is my money order?

Enclosed are two snaps taken last month on our leave. The other fellow isn't Pappy. You can tell it is early in the morning and we are still sober.

It looks like my packages will arrive sometime after Christmas. The way the letters are coming, though, it will be a long time after. Pappy hasn't heard from his wife in over three weeks, so I guess the condition is universal.

Have been feeling pretty blue the last few days over this new German drive. It seems like they will never give up. I am beginning to think that every town in Germany will have to be razed before they throw up the flag. I hope you people aren't too optimistic about an early peace. But then, I can see the newspapers at home still treating things pretty calmly.

Would like to be at home and have some Tom and Jerry this Noel, but maybe next Christmas it will be different. It is hard to realize that this is the third Christmas I have spent in the army. Next month I start drawing five percent more money for time in the service. It is called old-foggie pay. And that's the way I feel right now. I think I'll burn every piece of army clothing I have when I get out and buy the loudest civilian clothes I can find. Crosby will look like a conservative when I am through.

Am doing a little writing in my spare time but am not getting anyplace. It is good practice though, and I will have some notes when I get through.

Still haven't heard from Bob, but guess he is pretty busy and having a good time looking England over. Wouldn't mind being over there now myself. Getting tired of living in a tent again.

We are not near the little unnamed town where we got steaks and good wine anymore. In fact, it has been a long time since we moved so I am hungry all the time again and this army food seems to get worse by the day.

Never mind about buying a sweater, Mother. I got hold of one in the P.X. in Paris. But anytime you cook up a batch of cookies, send them along. Not the kind that break into dust in transit, but some of those German cookies like Grandma Biner used to make. I think you know what I mean. Speaking of Grandma Biner; have you been down to L.A. yet Dad, or have you given up the idea? Any time you want to write out a check you know you can. Just as long as you keep track of it.

Well, there doesn't seem to be any news to pass on so I might as well close.

Love to all,

Bill

Bill flew three missions in early December on the 1st, 2nd and 9th.   After a two week break he returned to the skies over Germany.   He participated in missions on Christmas Day, the day after Christmas and on December 29th.   These missions, and two more in January, were in support of Allied ground troops attempting to halt Hitler's last desperate, and ultimately futile, counter-offensive in the mountainous Ardennes region of Belgium.   The counter-offensive became known as the Battle of the Bulge.

Dec. 27, 1944

Dear Mom, Dad & All,

I got a letter from you yesterday and it sure helped the old morale. It was the only one in over a week.

Well, Xmas is gone, and I didn't even miss it. The day before we played Santa Claus to the Germans.[368] I went to midnight Mass and the next

---

[368] On Christmas Eve, 1944 Bob and his crewmates flew to Mayen, Germany and hit a railroad and crossroad. According to Bob, "We really knocked the place off the map. (It was the) biggest single mission of the 8th Air Force to date in direct support of the Army in the

day we had turkey and all the trimmings. It was a lot better than what the boys in the foxholes had.

We had a white Xmas, but it wasn't from snow. The frost is about an inch thick, and it really looks nice. It sure is cold here. I'm writing about two feet from the stove, and I can see my own breath. Five blankets and my overcoat keeps me warm at night.

If you want to send me something you can send food. Any kind of canned meat or beans or anything like that, just as long as it doesn't take any points.

I've got a couple more missions, but we've sure got a lot to go.[369] Don't worry, because all the missions so far have been milk runs.

Let me know how long it takes my letters to arrive. Love, Bob

---

In most of Bob's missions his crew flew at 20,000 feet and targeted marshaling yards, depots or

---

German break-through." The mission took eight hours. The bomber was the *Lace.*

[369] Bob had completed four missions by this time. He was in two more before the end of the year. On Dec.30, 1944, Bob and his crewmates were sent to hit railroad yards in Euskirchen, Germany. It was overcast and Bob recalls that they took some flak and missed their target during a five hour and 10 minute mission. On New Year's Eve they bombed a railroad bridge with four 2,000 pound bombs in Koblenz, Germany. The crew won the Air Medal after this mission.

factories. But when engaged in the Battle of the Bulge they would fly much lower, targeting the advancing German ground troops. American bombers flew during the day and rarely had fighter jet escorts during this stage of the war since the German Luftwaffe had already been decimated by Hitler's arrogant and foolhardy insistence on fighting on so many fronts simultaneously.

The belly turret turned as the gunner operated his guns. But the gunner was stuck if there was any trouble. He could not pump himself out of the turret. When Bob's crew became lead plane the belly turret was needed to hold the bombsight, enabling Bob to become a waist gunner.

When asked if he was happy with the change from belly to waist Bob could only say, "Hell yes!"

1944-45, was a cold winter in England and Bob had difficulty getting comfortable in his Nissen hut on base. His cot had one blanket and no sheets. The hut was made of corrugated steel, had no insulation and was heated by a single, small cylindrical woodstove. There were no windows in the hut due to the blackout. Two flight crews, about 18 men total, shared a hut. They were generally kept in the dark when it came to the fates of other crews in other huts.

Part Four: 1945

Jan. 11, 1945

Dear Mom, Dad & All,

This isn't going to be much of a letter. The only reason I'm writing is so you won't worry. We've just been lying around. I haven't any more missions since the last time.[370]

I received your Xmas card to-day, also one from Bill. This reminds me. I looked all over London last time, and I couldn't find anything for Ignats. You can't even buy a hanky without a ration card. They don't make much of anything over here. I'll keep looking for something though.

We had enough snow to make a snow man, but it doesn't look like much.

The "Jerrys" are playing "There's No Place like Home". If they want to make me homesick, they're succeeding, but that won't help them any.[371]

---

[370] Perhaps Bob discovered that his brother had been hiding his missions from their parents and decided to do the same, or perhaps there is a missing letter, but Bob was on a seven-hour mission aboard the *Maid of Fury* on January 7, 1945. They bombed Zweibrucken, Germany through overcast skies.

[371] Jerry was a nickname for the Germans. Bob is referring to a German radio station playing American

Frank Lane our nose-gunner went to the hospital the other night, and had his appendix taken out.

I have another letter to write, so I'll cut this short.

Write soon. Love, Bob

Jan. 17, 1945
V-MAIL
Dear Mother, Dad & all,

During the past week I have received a great many of my back letters. Some as far back as November, the first week of November that is. As yet, none of my packages have arrived, either Christmas or request packages outside of the one from Maxine that I have already told you about. They ought to be along soon though, unless they have been lost, which is quite probable.

The letter with the money order in it has arrived and thanks for sending it. I haven't had to cash it yet and will just keep it in reserve in case I am lucky enough some time to get a trip to England. Which reminds me? Did you ever receive that letter with the twenty-dollar check? They have cut out our passes to Paris now so I ought to be able to set a little aside. Also, I start drawing an extra five-percent this month for fogey-pay as I think I told you last time.

music and using propaganda to demoralize U.S. troops. According to Bob, it didn't work. Most American soldiers found the German radio efforts laughable.

This new drive of the Russians looks too good to be true, but if all they say about it is correct and they keep it up, the war is likely to be over this spring. I certainly hope so. This darn wet and cold is beginning to get me down. Also, it looks like I'll be a first John for the rest of the war and that doesn't please me very much.

Your clipping about Jeanne wasn't much of a surprise but I am glad you sent it along. There is a little story connected to it that I'll tell you when I get home sometime.

If Dad hasn't gone to Los Angeles yet why don't you both go? The Bank at San Antonio shows about a thousand now and I would like you to take what you need as a Christmas present. I can hear your objections from here but if I was back home I would see that you take me up on my offer. Maybe Betty can pound some sense into your head. And don't stint on yourself. Take two or three hundred and have a good time. My earning power is good for a long time yet and I'm not worried about the future. You don't need a lot of money to go to school under the Army plan.

Haven't heard from the Runt yet, but I guess our mail is getting mixed up somewhere. At the first opportunity I will get over to see him but he will probably be on his way home before that. They say the missions out of England are pretty easy now and they are flying them pretty fast.

Please don't try to send me any cigarettes because I have sufficient now and I know how hard it is to get them back there. I know Bob has plenty too, so don't send him any. In fact, he gets more than I do.

Got a kick out of hearing about Fritzy going to dances already, but when I think about it I was learning to dance when I was in the 8th grade and sneaking a drink of cherry wine on the side.

Well, more later, and I hope there won't be such an interval next time.

All my love to everyone, Bill.

Jan 19, 1945

Dear Mom, Dad & All,

Nothing much new has happened but I just don't want you to worry. We've just been lying around the hut doing practically nothing. I received the funny papers the other day. I really enjoyed them. If you get any more send them on.

We're getting some special training right now. It has its compensations, but it also may keep us over here a while longer. However, I would rather be here than the Pacific. The way we're going on the Russian front we may be home sooner than we expect. I sure hope these boys keep it up.

The pilot put me in for staff, but now we have to put in ten missions before we can go before the board. Tough.[372]

All the snow is gone now, but it's still cold & wet.

I'm kind of running out of stationary. If there is any handy I would sure appreciate it. I hate to always be asking for stuff but that's about the only way I can get anything. If I get a chance I'm going to send home a money order to pay for some of this stuff.

Gotta get some sleep. Write soon.

Love, Bob

P.S. Enclosed are a couple of bucks for Ignats. I'd send more only that's all the American money in the hut.

Jan 20, 1945

---

[372] In truth Bob needed only one more mission to reach #10. He flew in his eighth mission on January 14th and his ninth on January 15th. They were both highly successful, but dangerous. On the 14th they hit an oil storage dump in Ehmen, Germany. According to Bob, "It was well concealed, but we got some good hits. We passed near Hamburg and took some flak. Wiley (Fortson) and I put on our suits (flak suits) then." The mission took seven hours. On his ninth mission they hit marshalling yards in Reutlingen, Germany. Bob recalls that, "The target was visual and we really knocked it out. We also took half the town." The mission lasted seven and a half hours.

Dear Mom, Dad, & All,

This is going to be a real short one. Not enough happens in the two days to even bother about.

We got caught in a snow storm on a practice mission, but with the pilot we have there wasn't a thing to it. I received your letter last night, plus the one from Mrs. Mordhast.[373] She really goes into detail. I can't understand why you didn't get a letter from me. They must have gotten into the Xmas mix up.

We have another pass coming up in a couple of days. If it weren't for London this would be a really dull place. Can't think of a thing to ask for this time. Write soon.

Love, Bob

V-MAIL

Jan. 26, 1945
England
Dear Mom, Dad, and All,

This will be short, but I'll write an air mail as soon as I can. I just got back from a pass yesterday. I had a good time as usual, and I think our allies are getting better every pass.

---

[373] Lillian Moordharst was the next-door neighbor of the Biners in Ellensburg and just 38 at the time of this letter.

I received the Xmas box just before I went on pass, and the gloves really came in handy. The hair dressing is just what I wanted, and of course it made me irresistible.

I went before the promotion board tonight, and should get the results in a few days.

Thanks for everything and will write soon.[374]

Love, Bob

Jan 27, 1945

Dear Mom, Dad, Bet, & Fritz,

I received the Xmas box and letter from you just before I went on pass. Many thanks to all for everything. Both pair of slippers really came in handy. Also the gloves and hair tonic. The fruit cake didn't last a minute and it was sure good. The cigarettes are always good, but if the shortage is as bad as the papers say you better save them for yourself. We get enough in our weekly rations.

I'm really proud of you folks. I know you'll like your plane ride down, and while you're at it I hope you enjoy yourself. Give Grandma & all the folks

---

[374] Bob does not mention a mission he took on January 21st. It was a very dangerous mission in complete cloud cover to Heilbronn, Germany. The bombers hit a marshalling yard, but two planes had to bail out on the return. The mission took eight hours and temperatures dipped to 45 below zero.

my love. Don't forget to see the Poolers and above all have a good time.

We are training for lead crew right now. It means a little extra time and practice, but all in all I think we are getting a pretty good deal out of it. This now puts us about a third of the way through.

The whole crew received the Air Medal the other day. You know what it looks like.

It has really been cold here lately. The long underwear really came in handy. I never thought I'd wear 'em, but now I can't get along without them. I warm a brick every night to keep my feet warm and it really does the trick.

Write soon.

Love, Bob

P.S. Please send some cookies. Preferably the ones with chocolate chips. Don't forget to use a strong container.

V-MAIL
Jan. 30, 1945
Dear Mom, Dad and All,

I just received your letter, Mom, saying you just returned from the hospital and Ignats was doing O.K. It was the first I heard there was anything wrong with her, and I hope it was nothing serious. I'm sure sorry to hear you missed out on the trip

Mom. I know how badly you must feel, and I hope we can make it up to you when we get home.

In case I didn't tell you before, I got the Air Medal the other day. It's quite common, but even so I'm kinda proud of it.

Write soon.

Love, Bob

V-Mail
February 4, 1945
Dear Folks,

Received two letters from you. The first one told me about the plans for flying to L.A. on the 20th and the second one started right out by saying you had just returned from the hospital and that Fritzi was coming along fine. There must be a letter in-between that I haven't received and telling me what happened. From what I can guess at, was it appendicitis?

It certainly was a tough break for you Mother, but maybe we can work something out when I come home. The way the Russians are moving these days that won't be far off.

Still haven't received any packages so I guess they are gone for good. I know darn well that they could not have been all in one shipment. Some should have come through.

Finally heard from Bob yesterday and he seems to be enjoying himself. He says he has a fifth of them over now and has seen nothing spectacular yet. I can believe that too, with the milk runs they have been having.

Betty Morgan writes that Mary Webster was killed in Oklahoma flying a B-25. I wish they would stop the women from flying such hot ships. [375]

I'm anxious to hear all the news about my big sister and bear up, Mother; we'll get you to L.A. yet.

My love to all, Bill

Feb 4, 1945
Dear Mom, Dad & All,

I haven't had any mail for a long time but I'll try to keep up. I should get quite a stack when it finally arrives. We've just been loafing around lately. We've been to town a few times, but there isn't much doing there.

---

[375] Mary Webster (1919-1944) was from Ellensburg, WA. She joined the Women's Auxiliary Service Pilots (WASP). On Dec. 9, 1944, she was a passenger on a UC-78, a twin-engine Cessna known as the Bobcat. The plane encountered a massive cold front some 9000 feet above Tulsa, Oklahoma. The wings quickly became heavy with ice and the plane crashed, killing all aboard. Mary was not the pilot, but an online obituary states that she was the last WASP killed in the line of duty.

I've managed to put on about fifteen lbs. and I sure don't have room for it. I can hardly button my blouse and pants.

I want you to take the money order Mom, and buy yourself a present or anything you need.

I made staff the first of this month.[376] That's as high as I can go as long as I'm flying. I'm going to raise my allotment to seventy-five this month and if I have anything extra I'll send it home and have you buy war bonds.

I'm sure sorry you couldn't make the trip Mom.

What's the latest from Bill? Write soon.

Love, Bob

V-MAIL
Feb. 9, 1945
Dear Mom,

I received your letter today and finally found what the matter with Fritz was. I'm glad to see it wasn't anything serious.

I received a letter from Bevo the other day. He is over here, as a co-pilot. I'm going to try and look him up. I picked up a nice cold, but it isn't enough to keep me off operations.

---

[376] Bob was promoted to the rank of staff sergeant.

I'll get those post cards the next time I go on pass. That should be in a couple of days. Gotta hit the sack early. Write soon.

Love, Bob

Feb 12, 1945

Dear Mom, Dad, & All,

I just got back from London again and I had three of your letters & also a package waiting. One letter was written the day after Xmas, but the rest were about the middle of Jan. The cheese was sure welcome also the sausage. I'm wearing a pair of the socks right now so you know how I needed them. That sure is tough news about Tom Bass. What was he flying? Do they know anything about it?[377]

I'm sending you a little package in a couple of days. I'm also getting something made for Ignats. I hope I'm not duplicating anything Fritz's hasn't finished yet. I haven't any more missions since the last time.[378]

I got Bevo's letter that you sent, also another from Les. I just missed him on pass by one day. He is going to be a Pappa.

---

[377] 2nd Lt. Thomas A. Bass, son of Alton & Nellie Bass, was killed in action.

[378] On January 28th Bob was in a mission to Dortmund, Germany. His squadron bombed a synthetic oil plant and took heavy flak in a seven-hour mission.

I want Dad to tell me all about the trip. You didn't do the Highland Fling[379] again did you, Rodge?

I received a letter from Bill & we are both in favor of getting home as fast as we can. Don't forget to send the stationary cause I'm really running low.

Write soon.

Love, Bob

Feb 19, 1945

Dear Mom, Dad, & All,

I received another box from you yesterday and it really makes me feel good. It was the Ritz & cheese. The nuts were really good & in fact I enjoyed everything.

We really took it easy to-day. I slept till noon, ate, wrote one letter, went to church, ate again & now I'm writing again. Pretty tough life, eh? We have a pretty nice chapel here. Have Mass every day, and when we fly the chaplain gives us communion right at the briefing room. It doesn't seem like another Lenten season could be here again. This makes the third I've spent in the Army.

To-day was really swell. It seemed just like a spring day back home. It was warm enough to walk around without a coat. I haven't flown a mission for a long time, but I'm not complaining.

---

[379] A Scottish dance.

I'm still waiting for that letter from Rodge, telling me all about his trip south. I suppose he's a real flyer now. I see in the paper where they are going to take away some of your malt. How is that going to affect you, Dad?

I received a real nice letter from Mrs. Kelleher the other day. They flew down to see Joe. I got another from Aunt Rose but I seem to have lost their address.

The Russians are sure going ahead, and I hope they keep it up.

Before I forget it, I want to wish Betty a happy birthday. Of course she'll forget all about it by the time this gets there. I'm gonna find something nice to send her, even if she has to wait three or four months. I have something I'm sending Ignats too. Keep the letters coming.

Love, Bob

P.S. Please send some more cookies. Bob

Feb 23, 1945

Dear Mom, Dad, & All,

Sorry for the delay, but I just got back from another pass. This was an extra pass, and our regular one is coming up in a few days. I talked to Bevo on the phone, and I think I'll get to see him on this next pass.

I went to Cambridge on this one and soaked up a lot of the local color. Cambridge is really a beautiful place. It's full of colleges and everyone is a sight. They are all made of white stone. They are half covered with moss and ivy, and they really look impressive. The upper classmen wear long black capes, and the under classmen wear a scarf around the neck and slung over their shoulder. They also wear the little striped caps.

The town is lousy with antique shops, but none of them have any Toby jugs. I tried them all, but it seems they're quite rare. It was fun trying tho. They have a lot of silverware Mom, so if you'll tell me what you like, I can get just about anything.

I haven't flown for quite a while, but I'm in no hurry. I doubt if I'll be home before this war ends, so don't be making any prophecies.

I'm glad Rodge likes the air. I suppose that'll be the only way he'll travel from now on.

Another thing – flying over here for us is twice as safe as it was a year ago, so don't worry.

Keep the letters coming.

Love, Bob

La Belle, France

February 24, 1945

My Dears,

I sorry there has been such an interval between my last letter and this one but there has been a reason. The past two weeks I have been packing and unpacking and moving and then starting all over again. I also flew down to the South of France for a few days on a trip and naturally I didn't write from there. The beautiful sunshine made me wish I was back in Casablanca again. It was pretty hard to come back here to the mud and rain.

I also took a couple of trips to Belgium and intend to take more. You can get most everything you want there even ice-cream and chocolate éclairs. And I always thought the Belgium's were having it rough. Maybe I was in the wrong part of Belgium. Expect to take a trip to Brussels in the near future and I'll give you an account of the trip when it comes off.

The enclosed pictures were taken in Belgium and I was sober both times. Have some beer coasters I picked up in the taverns that I will send in the box. Belgium beer is pretty good considering the French stuff but there isn't much to it.

Was really very shocked to hear about Bill Flynn. [380] I can't understand it. I didn't think cancer would hit you that young. Do you think it was from too much drinking?

---

[380] William F. "Bill" Flynn was a friend from Ellensburg, Washington. He was born in 1912, the son of Thomas and Mary Burke Flynn. He died in the Aleutian Islands on Dec. 20, 1944.

Glad to hear you liked your trip by <u>plane</u> (notice the spelling, Mother) Dad. It's the only way to travel. Was that train wreck in Utah and reason why you went by air? I would have liked to have been there at the Jones' with you and sampling some of their rare Scotch.

A friend of mine sent me a book for Christmas, <u>Lost in the Horse Latitudes</u>,[381] and there was a chapter in it about Paul. It was pretty good. He called him a whisky salesman and the world's best tangent talker. You ought to get hold of it, it's pretty funny.

Received a beautiful scarf from Molly and Fred and leather traveling chess and gin-rummy set from the Jones'. Helen sent a nice fruit cake. They all came within the last week so maybe yours will get here after all. I had just about given up hope.

Thank you very much for the Valentine Fritzy, you always remember the kid brother, don't you? The photos were very good and very welcome. Was going to buy a camera in Belgium but they want too much for them. They also have some very good radios for sale but I don't know how I would send one home. They run around $120 but are beautiful models. One of my room-mates bought one and we get U.S. Stations on it.

I will try to get the box off soon but it won't be

---

[381] <u>Lost in the Horse Latitudes,</u> by humorist H. Allen Smith (1907-1976), includes chapters about the author's years as a writer for Paramount. There are hilarious chapters about W.C. Fields and Paul Jones.

complete. I still have a good many things to get so I guess I'll have to send another later.

No more for now, will write again sooner. Love to all---

Bill

V-MAIL
Feb. 25, 1945
Dear Mom, Dad, and All,

This is just a short one, because I'm going on pass, and I don't want you to worry. I haven't flown for so long I'm beginning to feel like a ground pounder. [382] As long as we're getting all these passes, I don't mind it so much tho.

The mail hasn't been very good this week, and I'm still waiting for Pop's report. I'm still waiting for one from Ignats too.

Did you get the medal yet? What do you hear from Bill? Write soon.

Love, Bob

---

[382] Bob flew on a total of 17 missions. His crew took extra training to be a lead plane, but he neglected to record his final six missions. During his most dangerous mission his plane was hit and almost crippled. Bob felt the plane jump and noticed a hole blown through one wing. The aileron cables were bent by the blast but not broken and the plane was able to land safely.

March 1, 1945

Dear Dad, Mom, & All,

I received your letter to-day, Dad, and one from Mom yesterday. I've been waiting to hear about your trip and I'm glad to hear you had a good time. I'm only sorry that Mom couldn't make it too.

There's not a lot to write about now. We haven't flown a combat mission for about a month so you can see I won't be home any too soon.

It's getting much warmer now, and it sure looks like spring. The other crew in my barracks is finished now, so I guess they'll be home for Easter. I sure wish I was going with them.

Bob Hope is on the radio now. The radio really comes in handy. They give us most of the best programs. I got your Valentine to-day Ignats & you're mine too. Keep the letters coming and don't worry. Love, Bob

---

March 5, 1945

Dear Bet & All,

I received your letter to-day Bet, and I sure was glad to get it. Yea, this isn't too bad a place. The people are pretty friendly, even if they are usually looking for a drink. The women of course look better all the time, but the American gals have it all over them. The gals over here don't look too nice in clothes but you can actually blame that on the war.

There are a couple of nice dance halls in London, and they have some pretty good bands, but even over here they have too many jitterbugs.[383]

Now that it's getting warm the country is really beginning to look nice. It's hard to explain, but it looks just like the movies. They still have the farm houses with the thick straw roofs & just about everything looks as if it had been around for a couple hundred years.

The only thing I'd like to see before I go home is Paris. I've seen it from the air, and it really looks nice. It sure is spread out.

We finally got another mission in. It was our first lead mission, and we did pretty well. We saw plenty of stuff and as far as I'm concerned that's all I want to see.

I sure hope Bill gets a chance to come over. We get a 48 hr. pass every two weeks & it would sure be nice if we could have a few mild & bitters together.

The house must look pretty nice now. It's a lucky thing for Rodge that Pat was around. I really feel sorry for him tho. He must be living a dog's life

---

[383] The Jitterbug was a wild, shaking swing dance popular in the 1930s & 40s. Its name is derived from the word jitters.

with three women nagging at him all the time. I wouldn't blame him if he took a few nips now & then.

So you're a bird woman, too. Just as long as you take an occasional ride its O.K. but when this war is over, I'm staying on the ground.

I got the funnies the other day. Seeing as how they are the only thing I can understand I enjoy them better than anything.

What would you enjoy from England, Bet? I have something for Ignats I was supposed to mail a month ago.

Write soon.

Love, Bob

P.S. Enclosed is a money order for Mom.

V-MAIL
March 14, 1945
Dear Mom, Dad and All,

I'm writing V-mail because I'm going on pass again, and haven't much time. We got a couple more in, so now we have fifteen more to go.

This is a beautiful spring day. It's warm enough to go around without a coat, and that's pretty good for this time of year. I haven't heard from you for a week, so I'll expect a bunch on my bed when I come back. I still haven't mailed Ignats back. Keep forgetting it.

Write soon and often.

Love, Bob

March 19, 1945

Dear Mom, Dad, & All,

I'm in one of those moods where I have to force myself to write and I can't think of a thing to write about. I received a birthday card to-day from Aunt Rose, and that is the only thing I have received in over two weeks. I know it isn't because you're not writing as everyone is in the same position, but it's hard to write when you don't get any mail.

We have a new crew with us in the barracks now, so of course we are the old vets. I think I have a good set-up but I'm not getting the missions in soon enough to suit me. At least we're on the down grade.

I went to London again on the last pass. I didn't do much but go to shows. I saw None but the Lonely Heart, [384]Something for the Boys,[385] and Then Tomorrow the last day. I went to the National Art Gallery. It's really a huge place, and

---

[384] None but the Lonely Heart (1944) was a film starring Cary Grant and Ethel Barrymore.
[385] Something for the Boys (1944) was a musical starring Carmen Miranda.

I didn't get to see hardly any of it. The next time I go I'll have more time & get in on the lecture. All I saw this time was an exhibition of war paintings. It covered about six rooms.

I've been sitting in a daze for the last ten minutes, so I'll quit.

Love, Bob

P.S. Please send some cookies.

The following letters by Bill, written from France in March & April, 1945, during the climatic action in the European theatre, conveniently fail to mention the numerous missions he was engaged in. Of course, he never intended to tell his parents that he was flying missions again. The cover was blown when he was shot down on March 21, 1945, in an engagement that earned him the Distinguished Flying Cross.

On March 2, 1945, Bill dropped 500 lbs. on a railroad yard in Butzweiler, Germany. The next day he dropped another 500 lbs. on a bridge in Simmern, Germany. He bombed a road block in Colbe, Germany on March 9th. Two days later he bombed another rail yard in Herschback, Germany. On the 15th of March he dropped 1000 lbs. on a marshaling yard in Neunkirchen, Germany. Siegen and Bad Durkheim endured his accuracy on March 17th and 18th respectively. On the 19th he hit Wuppertal, Germany with 1000 lbs.

and dropped another 1000 lbs. on Geseke the following day.

On the day he had to bail out he was flying in his fifth mission in as many days.

Sunday
France
Dear Mother, Dad & All --

It's raining like a son-of-a-gun here, as usual, and I am sitting by the fire – for which I am thankful. The boys up on the front aren't getting any fire but what the Germans are shooting at them. It must be one h--- of a mess there.

I was in Paris last Sunday and Monday and had a grand time rubbernecking and drinking Champagne. The only souvenirs I picked up were postcards. All the shops are closed Sunday and Monday. Monday in France is something like a Bank Holiday. The next time I get there I expect to come away with some presents. Jewelry and perfumes are plentiful but at a very high price.

The French themselves have more money than they know what to do with and so the prices are very high. One man told me that since there was very little to buy, everyone had more money than before the war. Drinks are high. One glass of Champagne costs 80 cents. The same for Cognac. It is one spot where the American soldier is not the "rich guy".

I get a big boot out of riding the Paris Subway, or Metro, as they call it. It is a very excellent one and you can go anywhere in it. Soldiers ride for nothing and I have taken full advantage of it. I have yet to see any bomb damage to the city itself, but you can see bullet holes in all the shop windows and nicked brick where the street fighting took place.

A surprisingly number of people speak pretty fair English and my French is improving every day, so I get along pretty well. Window dressing on some of the smart shopping streets is really excellent. Some of the best I have ever seen. The cloth etc. looks good, but a Frenchman said that it really wasn't. Good coloring, but short on wear. Most of the people wear composite and wooden soles on their shoes although you wouldn't notice it. The women's shoes are very chic and they wear terrifically high fronted turbans.

The beer has a good color Dad and an excellent head, but there is hardly any taste to it and it is very, very weak. Which reminds me, some of the English beer I had in England surprised me. It wasn't bad. Other beer was very poor.

Am still looking for mail but don't expect it for a while. Don't worry about me, because I am in no danger whatever and am enjoying myself immensely. This beats Africa and Italy all hollow.

Tell Betty I'll get her manuscript off soon. Hope you are all feeling well.

Love, Bill

P.S. Has Fritzy received any of her magazines yet?

Undated V-mail from France
(Probably late March, 1945)

Dear Folks,

Just received two letters from you. A V-mail from February 11th and a regular air-mail of February 23rd. You figure it out; I can't. I also received the Christmas packages yesterday but I was out of town for two days. Thanks so much for the compliment, Mother, but my feet really aren't that small. However, they won't go to waste as I am going to send them to Bob. I can't even get my toes in them. I have bigger feet than Dad, remember?

Everything else was swell though, although the gloves were a little tight. Here's hoping I don't lose them like I lose all my gloves. Thanks a million for everything because it was swell and really worth waiting for. Also got a package of cookies and candy from you. The candy came through in pretty good shape but the cookies were all crumbs. Cardboard boxes are no good for anything like that. One box was so smashed that I don't know how it ever got to me.

That was a horrible thing to say about Fritz; that she looked like me. You must not think much of her looks. If she was over here she wouldn't have to worry about swimming. I don't think it will ever warm up. Right now it is raining and it's cold and there are no lights. I am typing with the aid of a flashlight. Some trick.

Couldn't keep up the flashlight stunt any longer, so this is the next day and today I got a request package. Salami, cheese, etcetera's. Tres bon[386] and thank you very much. If cheese and things you send cost you any points then don't do it. I think there is one thing that doesn't cost anything and that is A-1 or 57 sauce. [387] Could sure use some of it if you could send it. Also, don't try to send me any more cigarettes as we are getting all we need now after the purge.

Had a letter from Helen telling me all about the reunion and how proud Grandma was to have most of her lugs together. She said FDR and the English took a beating but all in all it was fairly calm. Sounded like I really missed something by not being there. Especially that part about going to Lucy's. I could use one of their steaks and some of that garlic bread right now. Not to mention their good Scotch.

---

[386] Very good.

[387] Some readers might be surprised that these meat sauces were popular back in the 1940s. In fact, they are both much older than that. Heinz 57 dates to 1892 and A-1 sauce was introduced in 1831.

Helen also told me about Tom Bass. It is hard to say what has happened to him, but prisoners are not often reported until five or six months some time. They may get word anytime that he is O.K. Bob wrote and said that they were training for a lead crew which is a pretty good deal as they won't fly so often and it is better for them all the way around.

Hope you get a deal there in Cal. Dad, maybe Albert will come through with something. It's about time you got back in the bosom of the family, and besides, I intend to live in California when this is over.

Think I'll get the packages off this week. Will send one direct to L.A. so you won't have to bother with it.

Love to all, Bill

On March 21, 1945, Lt. Bill Biner was engaged in an extraordinary bombing mission, but true to form, the humble and thoughtful soldier spared his parents the gory details. In fact, he doesn't write home about it at all. But a report from the headquarters of the Ninth Air Force on May 25, 1945, revealed some of the details:

Distinguished Flying Cross.- By direction of the President...and in accordance with the authority of the War Department, a DISTINGUISHED FLYING CROSS is awarded to:

WILLIAM D. BINER, 0-733517, 1st Lieutenant, Air Corps, 323rd Bombardment Group. For extraordinary achievement against the enemy on March 21, 1945. While serving as bombardier of a B-26 type aircraft, Lt. BINER, flying in conjunction with allied crossing of the Rhine, demonstrated outstanding airmanship and a high degree of technical skill. In the face of concerted enemy antiaircraft fire which severely damaged his aircraft, Lt. BINER, nevertheless remained at his vulnerable position and despite this hazard, he released his bombs on the objective with telling effect. The outstanding courage, tenacity and presence of mind displayed by Lt. BINER in the face of enemy fire and a seriously damaged aircraft, contributed in large measure to the success of the mission and reflect great credit upon himself.

By command of Major General Weyland.[388]

March 23, 1945
Dear Mom, Dad, & All,

Well kids, the army finally came through. I was just beginning to talk to myself and act a little queer. Believe me; it came in the nick of time as it's been about a month since I've heard from anyone.

What do you mean why did Mrs. K write me? I guess she wrote because she wanted to and believe me I'm darn glad to get a letter from anyone. Mail

---

[388] General Otto P. Weyland (1903-1979). After World War II, General Weyland served as Commander of Far East Forces during the Korean War.

call is the biggest moment of the day around here. After to-day my morale is about 100% better. Before to-day we were all jumping down each other's throat at the slightest thing. Now we're all one happy family again. And while I'm on letters I'll tell you it doesn't make any difference what you say it's just the idea of getting a letter from home. The censors around here are pretty strict. I also got a nice letter from Aunt Julia. I didn't know you sent the locket to Julie. I'd forgotten all about it.

We're enjoying a beautiful spring here. The place is really beginning to look nice. To-day was warm enough to go around without a shirt. Of course I don't expect it to keep up.

I haven't heard from Bill for a heckuva long time. I guess I'll give him another chance. I still haven't been able to get together with Bevo. I got a letter from him to-day and he tells me Butch is over here now. I'd like to see his ugly pan too.

I got the chaplains letter that you sent. He's really a good egg. Did you get the medal or any of the money orders yet?

Keep the letters coming.

Love, Bob

March 25, 1945

Dear Mom, Dad, & kids,

I received two letters from you yesterday, Mom. One was dated the 2nd and the other was dated the 11th. The last one got here in pretty good time. I also got the box. The stationary is swell. The cookies really came at the right time. We get four candy bars a week, but they're gone long before the week-end rolls around and we all dove right in. I haven't tried the soup yet, but it sure looks good.

I'm learning to play your game – pinochle[389]. I'm a pretty shrewd player, but I just don't get the cards. However, even with my bad luck I think I could take Rodge to the cleaners.

We finally got a ship and are going to name it – Leading Lady, for obvious reasons.

Write soon.

Love, Bob

March 29, 1945

Dear Mom, Dad & kids,

I just received two more letters from you. One was a V-mail & the other was written March 4.

I'm just glad you got to see Joe. I hope he never gets in this war. They've had enough troubles. I'm glad to see you got my Air Medal. I was getting worried for fear it was lost.

---

[389] Pinochle is a trick-taking card game.

Well I'm going on another pass to-day. I've got a slim chance of meeting Bevo. Every time we think we have it all planned something comes up. I'm also going to try and see if I can get in touch with Bill Lambert.

I'm also going on a "flak" leave in a few days. We go to a rest home & take it easy for a week or so. I'll get in a little golf, etc. and probably get a little fatter. I must weigh about 145 now and everyone calls me "fatty". I'll see if I can pick up something for your book, Mom.

Did Joe tell you Bob Whipple was married? He married Bunny Hultgren. Looks like all the boys are going nuts.

Well, I have to start getting ready for pass.

Keep writing.

Love, Bob

April 1, 1945

Dear Fritz, Bet, & Folks,

I got your letter to-day Ignats, and boy you're sure improving. What's this about people dropping out of the house? I didn't think Rodge mixed them that stiff.

Well yesterday was Easter Sat. so I suppose you ate all the stuff you said you would. It's a lucky thing you're thin and don't have to worry about your waist line and don't worry about your feet, just tell them they're no bigger in proportion than the rest of your frame.

To-day is Easter, and I was very disappointed when I woke up. The bunny didn't leave a single egg. Then I went to a field right next to the hut. There are a lot of cotton-tails there, but the things I found were too small to be eggs and besides they didn't taste like eggs at all. I just can't understand it.

Please note the change of address. I'm just in a different sqdn on the same field. This place is a penal colony compared to the place we just left. I could go on for hours on all the hardships here, but I won't bore you with all my troubles.

I just returned from London again, but this time my recreation was slightly limited, it being Holy Week & all. I didn't even visit my favorite pubs.

As usual I couldn't get together with Bevo. I guess he didn't get his pass. I also tried to find Bill Lambert. Someone must have given Joe a bum steer. I had the Lt. in charge phoning all over the place, but they don't have any record of him in any of the cesoc offices.[390] I still haven't mailed your bracelet Ignats, but I'll try & remember. I also got some postcards, but I'll bring them with me.

---

[390] In the US Army list of acronyms, CESOC stands for Communications/Electronics Staff Officer Course.

Love, Bob

P.S. I had the soup Mom and it was sure good.

P.S. I got your letter, too, Bet, & I'll try & answer soon.

La Belle France
April 3, 1945

My Darlings,

Just got back from my first leave to Paris since the December breakthrough. Everything is much the same except that it is more beautiful now with Spring here and everything in bloom. In the woods outside of town they have acres of wild daffodils growing and people peddle out and gather baskets of them and bring them to the city. It is really quite a sight.

What I enjoyed most about the trip were the wonderful meals at the Red Cross Officers Club (one of many) and real beds to sleep in. Also, first run movies in a swank theatre. Had to leave the day Crosby was coming in, something about Waves with Betty Hutton.[391]

Finally got my boxes off. Sent one to Helen and Julia and one to you. Forgot to put in the instruction sheet but the only thing you need know is that the scarf is for Fritz. I bought the ties when I was a little fried on Pink Champagne

---

[391] Here Come the Waves (1944) was a light comedy starring Bing Crosby and Betty Hutton.

so will try to find something better for you Roger. "Obie brought out the green light" and I didn't' know they were so bad until I saw them in the morning light. You can give them to the Salvation Army if they will take them.

Things look very good over here and I'm eagerly looking for an early peace. I hope nothing stops the boys this time because they really have the Krauts on the run. The French think Patton[392] is the greatest American since Woodrow Wilson and most of us agree. The Germans don't care too much for him I'm afraid.

The runt ought to be finishing about now, although he may not be doing much flying. I see heavies fly over here all the time and I guess they have things pretty much their own way now compared to the old days. Hope they don't have any ideas about keeping me here when it's over. I'm pretty disgusted about no promotion and want to get home as soon as I can. All my old buddies back in Texas are one grade higher now but then they may go back to the S. Pacific – who knows.

I suppose the midnight curfew has curtailed your night life quite a bit, eh Roger? Too bad. No more for now. This ought to reach you a month before

---

[392] General George Patton (1885-1945) was one of the most significant military leaders of WW II. Controversial and eccentric, he led the Third Army through the invasion of Normandy with a quick advance to Lorraine, liberating many French citizens in the process. He also played a critical role in the Battle of the Bulge. He was killed in a car accident in 1945 and is buried in Luxembourg.

the package. The coasters are ones I pick up pub-crawling in Belgium.

Love to all. Bill[393]

V-MAIL
April, 6, 1945
Dear Mom, Dad and All,

Here I am with nothing today and yet I have to force myself to write. I'm at the Post Home now and the easiest way to describe it is, "It just ain't the Army". We're at a sea-side resort, and can do just about anything we desire. The Army and Red Cross furnish us with just about everything, even civilian clothes. The only thought that's worrying me now is it only lasts seven days. Even the beer is better here, and naturally I'm putting on more weight.

Don't expect another letter from me till I get back to the base. I feel too lazy.

Love, Bob

---

[393] Bill does not mention that he was shot down on March 21st, but he will in a letter a month letter. He returned to the air three days after he was shot down, bombing German troops near Wiedenbruck, Germany. On April 9, 1945, Bill dropped 500 lbs. on a marshaling yard in Naumburg, Germany and two days later on April 11th, he bombed Bamberg, Germany with a 1000 lb. load.

April 13, 1945

Dear Mom, Dad, & All,

Well I'm back again, but I don't feel much like writing. I'm really homesick to-day and I sure hated to come back to this sqdn.

I just heard about the Pres. Death last night, and I could hardly believe it.[394] I feel as if I knew him personally. I personally think he was our greatest president.

We spent eight days at the flak home,[395] and we really had a lot of fun. The only thing we had to do was enjoy ourselves. The place was a regular summer resort, and we had the biggest hotel in the town. We could step out the door right into a cab and go anyplace we wanted to. There were no M.P.s and anything we wanted they supplied. The beer was better than any I've tasted over here, and there were more women than you could shake a stick at.

The war news is really looking good, so I'm hoping. Got more letters to write.

---

[394] President Franklin Delano Roosevelt died from a cerebral hemorrhage in Warm Springs, Georgia on April 12, 1945.

[395] Flak Home was a curious slang term for the rest area that Air Corp soldiers were sent to when they were in desperate need of some R n' R, as Bill was after being shot down.

Love, Bob

April 18, 1945

Dear Mom, Dad, & All,

To be truthful I don't know why I'm writing. I'm really bitter about this mail situation. I've received one letter from home since the day I went on flak leave. All the other fellows have been getting mail, and I'm wondering if it's entirely the fault of the post office. Mom isn't the only one in the family who knows how to write I hope. I'll admit I don't write too often, but I also have about fifteen other people to write to.

With the war going the way it is things over here are plenty unstable. I don't know what will happen to me, but things are cooking. When the war ends here, don't build your hopes too high, because I just don't know.

I haven't flown for quite some time, but I'm getting plenty to keep me busy. We report for work detail at 0800 every morning, and in this sqdn they really work us.

The last few days we've been having a mild heat wave. The whole country has suddenly turned to green & blossoms and I mean it's really beautiful. It's certainly a change from last winter. I got a bunch more post cards Mom, but I think I'll just bring them home with me. I have too many to mail. We also took some snaps, but it takes a lifetime to get them developed over here.

Well I gotta hit the sack. Don't forget to write.

Love, Bob

April 20, 1945

Dear Folks,

Just had a bit of good news thrown at me today. Sometime in the next week or so I am getting a week's leave to England and I am very happy over the whole thing. I'll be able to do a little Pub-crawling with the kid. Maybe he can get off for a couple of days and we can see London together.

I saw very little of England the time I passed through, outside of one night in Oxford and one night in Stafford, and so I am looking forward to the trip for more than one reason. Now that the V1 scare is over and the blackout lifted it ought to be a good holiday.[396]

Enjoyed your letter Roger and wish <u>you</u> would write more often. Glad to hear you have become the "Thin Man" but don't let your dieting get out of control. Speaking of food reminds me. If there are any canned meat or fish or anything that you don't

---

[396] The V1 and V2 were pilotless, rocket-powered German bombs used with deadly effectiveness against the citizens of Great Britain. Nearly 3,000 people were killed in London alone by these warheads, which were the precursors of the modern cruise and ballistic missiles.

need points for I wish you would send it along.
Our food seems to get worse by the week but guess
it can't be helped. The way it is prepared has a lot
to do with it I guess.

The weather here now reminds me of California
and I am getting a little color back in my face.
What a beautiful time to end the war. For the life
of me I don't see how they can still put up any
fight.

If you could see the endless stream of bombers
that fly over day and night going to Germany you
wonder how it didn't end a year ago. I have seen
some of the captured Rhine cities and from what I
saw the only thing the Germans can do is level the
rubble and start from scratch. Contractors will be
the new-rich in the post war Reich.

Some of the stories that are coming out of
Germany are pretty hard to visualize because we
have a different philosophy and are in the essence
a kindly race. I cannot fathom the German mind
but ten years of insidious propaganda has made
the majority of them more barbaric than even the
Japs. Some of the pictures coming back from
captured towns where there were concentration
camps and political prisons turn the stomach.

The way they have starved and maltreated our
prisoners makes my blood boil. If I ran a German
camp back in the States, I'm afraid I would be up
for Courts Martial before I ran it a week. The
crowning irony is the finding of Red Cross prisoner
packages in private German homes. I'll leave it to

your imagination how the dough's[397] treat these civilians.

I like to think the Germans are going to remember the American soldier with fear for a long time to come and I'm sure they will.[398]

Just figured up my accounts and I'll have twenty-two hundred in the old sock if I stay here until September. That wouldn't be too bad at all, but hope I get home before that.

Yes, I hear from Maxine a couple of times a week and I write almost as much.

Hope my package gets home for Mother's Day, Mother, although you are standing short as far as the contents concerned. Will find something suitable for you one of these days. Haven't been able to get to Brussels to get any lace yet, but may get the chance someday.

---

[397] Short for doughboys, a slang term for American soldiers that dates to the Mexican-American War.

[398] Although Bill neglects to mention it, he was personally contributing to that fear. On April 16th he completed his 80th mission of the war, an extraordinary achievement for any airman. He dropped 2000 pounds on an ordinance plant in Kempten, Germany. The next day he dropped another ton of bombs on Magdeburg, Germany. A day later, on April 18th, as the German high command hunkered down in their Berlin bunkers awaiting the end of their self-imposed nightmare, Bill Biner bombed Neuburg, Germany. Hitler was fantasizing that German troops would come to his rescue from the south. Biner and the other Allied airmen were making sure it would never happen.

Will close this now and write Bob to start looking for me.

Love to all, Bill

April 22, 1945

Dear Mom, Dad, & All,

I'm sorry for the big delay, but as any fool can plainly see I've moved again. It's a different field this time, and if I'd stayed a day longer at the last place I'd have your mail. I'll soon be back to the old routine and won't be bothered with this eight o'clock work call stuff. If we don't fly or go to ground gunnery, we can get all the sleep we want.

I met Jake States,[399] one of my old buddies from Mt. Home, so I'm really glad I came. Jake got a package yesterday that was mailed Dec. the 4th. I don't suppose I'll be getting any more mail from you for a decent long while, as they say over here. The last letter I received from you was written on Easter. Yea, I went to church on the post on Easter. By the way Mom, that Father Beck you mentioned is the chaplain at this field. Jake slept beside him for a long time and he says he's really a character. I hope I get to meet him while I'm here.

---

[399] Emanuel "Jake" States, born 1922, the son of Emanuel and Emma States, was from Montana and remained a close friend of Bob Biner following the war.

I don't know how good the chow is, but they have a nice theatre in the post. As a lead crew we will get a 48 hr. pass about every ten or eleven days.

Tell Bet I received the Readers Digest from her the other day, and thanks a lot.

It's time for church now.

Love, Bob

April 24, 1945

Dear Mom, Dad & All,

I received two letters from you to-day, so I feel pretty good. I also heard from Marie Bevacqua and Unk Fred & Molly. Unk Fred says he's quitting the USO to take care of his business.

Everything here is O.K. so far. The chow isn't quite as good, but I'll take anything to get out of that chicken sqdn I was in.

I'm going to see the chaplain to-morrow night, and incidentally the cover on the Extension is of Fr. Beck and the chapel here. He's quite a wheel around here, and the boys say he pulls a lot of weight.

The chestnut trees are in bloom here now, and it sure reminds me of our front yard in Nelson. As I said before it's sure beautiful around here.

The cookies haven't come yet but while I'm on it, you better not make any more with this new rationing set-up you don't have enough as it is. Besides, I just got a bunch of candy. I can't send any money home this month because I spent all I had at the flak home, but the end of the month is almost here, so I'll try next month.

Keep the letters coming.

Love, Bob

Bob Biner, belly gunner, with his crew in England. Bob is 3rd from left in front row.

May 3, 1945

Dear Mom, Dad & Kids,

It's been a few days since I've written and I guess you know by now where I've been. In case you haven't heard from Bill yet, I'll tell you all over again.

Bill phoned the Red Cross here last Friday afternoon. I wasn't here at the time, but I found where he was staying and Father Beck helped out by getting me a four-day pass. I arrived there Sunday morning and we had three days together. We didn't do much but eat, sleep, and visit pubs, but we didn't care to do much else. The weather was kinda rotten so naturally we had to stay indoors most of the time. We really consumed a lot of beer but don't worry Rodge, we still think you make the best there is.

By the way Happy Birthday Dad. It's kinda late I know and you'll get something nice after the 10th of this month. And all the best on the 13th to you, Mom. You've had something in the mail for almost three months.

Don't start looking for me to be home in a hurry. No one knows what's going on, so there's no telling how long I'll be here.

Keep writing and all that stuff. Love, Bob

P.S. Enclosed are a few labels I picked up.

May 6, 1945
V-Mail
Darlings,

I've been to London to see the Queen, but she wasn't in. However, I did spend three grand days with Bob at the Flak Home in Southport[400] and the boy knocked me out with his Pub antics. He always calls the barmaids "Irish" and pulls a Dublin brogue on them and of course being English they resent it, but that doesn't stop our Bob.[401]

We had a picture taken at the hotel and I'll send it as soon as I can get hold of an envelope.

This has been a very exciting day. The day I have been waiting for ever since coming over this second trip. Everything here in England has stopped for two days so we can't fly back to France. (How I would have loved to spend tonight in Paris!)

I have a good many stories to tell you in my next regular letter but for now I can tell you I had to lie to you and that since I have been over here I have flown thirty-three extra missions.[402] I couldn't tell you at the time but nevertheless I had to do it. I

---

[400] Southport is a beautiful town on the northwest coast of England.

[401] Bob defends himself by saying, "I was probably three sheets to the wind."

[402] Bill finally admits to his parents that he has been flying missions. Of the 33 only five were on German targets outside of Germany. The other 28 missions were on marshalling yards, bridges, railroad yards, airfields, an oil dump, an ordinance plant and a town across Germany.

hope it had something to do with this early and great victory. Until I get leave to France.

All my love to you. Bill.

May 10, 1945

Dear Mom, Dad, & All,

I'm sorry for the delay, and I don't even have a good excuse. I haven't been busy, just too lazy.

We're two days past VE Day[403] now and I don't feel any different now than before. Thursday night was a big night in this country and they declared a two-day holiday. We were lucky enough to get a pass, so we went into Norwich.[404] The place was conspicuous for the lack of G.I.s. Most of the bases were restricted that night, but we had a real time. Naturally everyone was mad with excitement and there were big bonfires all over the city. They had the search lights turned on the cathedral spires and it really looked beautiful. We ended up by

---

[403] Victory in Europe

[404] Bob and a few of his pals took leave in the city of Norwich before the Old Buckenham base restricted movement on VE Day. Bob was among the few Americans who witnessed the unabashed joy of VE Day in Norwich. Bob recalls bonfires, fireworks, dancing, kissing and drinking in the streets. But because of restrictions imposed after he left the base he could not find a ride back and walked the several miles from Norwich through Attenborough back to Old Buckenham.

walking back to the camp. There was no Liberty Run that night and all the taxi companies were enjoying the holiday. We got in about three and my legs were so numb I could hardly walk.

I haven't received any mail for quite some time. I guess they are getting it around at our old address.

We are going to start voluntary classes in a few days. They have different classes to keep us busy while we're waiting around. We don't know how long it'll be, but it may be quite some time.

Write soon. Love, Bob

May 11, 1945

Dear Mom, Dad, & All,

I just wrote yesterday, but since I got a letter I'll write again. I received the letter you wrote on the 1ˢᵗ. I guess it was the first letter you sent to the new address. I'm still waiting for the letters from my old address to catch up, but I think that was pretty good time on this letter.

I suppose Ignats will have graduated by the time this letter arrives and I sure wish I could be there to see her. Naturally she's the smartest and best looking gal in the class. I suppose she's right up to her neck in a lot of extra work & stuff. Where is she going to go next year?

Now that the war is over there is naturally a lot of rumors going around, but it's best to forget them because none of them amount to anything.

We only had seventeen missions in when the war ended. We needed one more for another cluster, and that would have been five more points towards discharge. Whatever happens tho we'll probably go to the Pacific sooner or later.

The weather the past few days has really been nice and I hope it keeps up.

Did you get the letter from Bill yet? I hope he sent the picture. How do you like it? Keep writing.

Love, Bob

Lt. Bill Biner, with his 2nd crew in Northern France, 1945. Bill Biner is second from right in the back row.

Maastricht, Holland
Sunday, May 13, 1945

Dear Mother,

Since this is Mother's Day I thought I ought to address this letter solely to you. Roger won't get his chance because I'll probably be home by Father's Day. My group had moved when I got back from England and I have since transferred to another group and am waiting my orders from Hdq to go home.[405]

We are in Holland now, near the town of Maastricht and not far from the German border. We have an officer's club here that serves American draught beer – that is, it is made by the Army and its plenty alright. All I am doing now is sun-bathing and waiting for the club to open in the evening.

My pilot is going home tomorrow but my orders haven't come through yet. If I could go to school in Paris for six months I would stay, but there is not a chance to do it. You have to have a passport, civilian clothes, army permission and a suitcase full of money if you want to visit Switzerland, so if I don't make it you'll know why.[406]

As I mentioned in my last letter I have pulled

[405] Bill was transferred to the 559th Squadron, 387th Bomb Group. He will confide in a future letter that it does not measure up to his previous groups.
[406] Since his paternal grandparents, and his dad's older brothers, were born in Switzerland, Bill's father probably encouraged him to visit relatives there.

some more missions while over here – thirty-three to be exact. Pappy got in twenty-eight. I had to lie to you folks but I couldn't help myself. I wanted to do it but I couldn't have you worrying again. It has been the best thing in the long run because I think I'm through for good now. Would like to have made an even hundred but will settle for the eighty-three I have.[407]

Just before I went to England we got shot up pretty badly and I had to bail-out but I never got a scratch so the old luck didn't desert me.[408] I have also been put in for the D.F.C.,[409] but it hasn't come through yet. This is beginning to sound like a confession isn't it?

I gave some of the nylon panels away for scarves but the bulk is going to Maxine. She said you people can have some too if you want it. I told her to dye it black and put some lace on it. (The Paris influence!)

It's all over now and I don't regret a thing. All the boys I left in the States have been promoted but I've seen most of the western world and I wouldn't trade that for anything. Besides, they'll be going Japan-way and I'll be sitting it out in the States.

---

[407] Bill's final mission was a bit of a birthday present for Hitler. He dropped 2000 lbs on a marshalling yard for jet fighters in Memmingen, Germany on April 20, 1945; the last birthday Hitler would have.
[408] Bill was on a mission to Haltern, Germany. He explains the episode in the letter dated May 26, 1945.
[409] Distinguished Flying Cross. The award came through on May 25th. See March 21st for details.

From all Bob told me he really has it easy. I think he said he only had nineteen and none were really rough. He's mowing lawns and things like that now. He wants to go home but I told him to stay where he was for now because he is really better off than he would be at home. I can tell you now that I came over on the "Isle de France".[410] Bob did too. I would like to fly back and make it two by sea and two by air. Maybe I'll get back in time for the wedding?

Hope you people are stacking up on bottled goods because I have a great thirst and we have to celebrate our V.E. Day the Biner way. Have an idea Japan will fold pretty soon now so it may not be long before that discharge paper shows up. Then it's back to school in sunny California.

Hope you'll forgive me Mother now that it is all over. I'll paddle you if you don't when I get home.

No more for now. Will write soon again and give you the latest dope. Maybe I can remember some more details then.

My love to you, Bill

---

[410] A large French ocean liner built shortly after World War I.

May 14, 1945

Dear Bet, Fritz, & All,

I don't know what's happened to these sisters of mine, but whatever it is – I like it. I received your letters from you, Bet, and one from Ignats. I'm tellin you it really boosts the morale, and I need it.

Yesterday was Mom's Day so I naturally went to Mass & communion for mine. They had some cards for the occasion, but they ran out before I could get one.

When is the big event supposed to take place? I sure wish I could be there but the army can't always see things my way. I told them we would need someone to take charge of Rodge and clamp down on his toasts, etc., but they won't tell me a thing. Bill told me I met Pat one night at Grandma's but I sure can't remember – can you?

If all the reports are true, Ignats must look something like this [a sketch of a girl with giant feet and long arms is on the letter]. But I can't believe it. I think Pat is just spreading rumors.

I haven't been off the ground for a long time, but they find plenty for us to do. We have roll-call at 7 every morning, and then they put us to work. It's a good thing we don't work all day, because it stays light till ten. We have double summer time over here.

The pictures were taken last winter and we're wearing heated suits, so it's not all fat.

Keep the letters coming. Love, Bob

V-MAIL

May 20, 1945
Dear Mom, Dad, Bets, and Fritz,

I received two letters from you. Bet, as I said before it sure is great to get a letter every day. I supposed my mail will be all mixed up again, as were moving to a new base. I don't know what the deal is or anything. We've been moving so much I'm beginning to feel like a Nomad.

We got our first pay today since March. After two trips to the Flak Home all I did was hand it out. Don't ask me any questions about Bill; I'm just an innocent bystander. If things turn out right I may be home this summer, but that's just a guess. I'll send my new address when I get there.

Love, Bob

Rosieres, France
May 26, 1945
Dearest Folks --

Well, here I am still in France and no nearer home. We moved back from Holland Tuesday and so far I haven't been able to get anyone to send me home. I'm not doing anything but getting in a lot of sack-time but they may put me to work teaching bombsight maintenance to enlisted bombardiers. I haven't even put in my four hours for flight pay yet and it doesn't look like I will get a chance to now.

Pappy and a bunch of our old group are having a big time disarming the Luftwaffe in Germany. I've sent my old C.O. a letter and maybe he will do something for me. This garrison life is beginning to get me down and I am anxious to get home. Who knows, maybe I could get a discharge once I got home?

If I have to stay here for a few months I am going to try to get to one of the Universities for a little free education – preferably the U of Paris. I suppose one has to have pull to do that, and my pulling power is nil, as usual.

My D.F.C. hasn't come through yet and I suppose I'll be disappointed on that score too. C'est la Guerre!

I really did the smart thing in the long run by coming over here this second time, because now they have come out with the order that anyone who has served in the two theatres doesn't have to go to the Pacific unless they volunteer. And all the taste for volunteering has gone out of my system. I am beginning to think that being over-patriotic doesn't pay. It has taken me a long time to figure that out, but I know it now.

Was in Paris for two days, we aren't far here, and the town is full of liberated prisoners. Some had been there since 1942 and they were certainly anxious to get home. Who wouldn't be? Who isn't?

Concerning my bailing out last March: We were going up to support the Limey crossing north of the Rhine and when we hit the Rhine River they really started throwing the flak at us. We got a bad hit right away and started a little fire which eventually went out – right under my fanny – but we kept going. We were under almost constant fire for forty-five minutes and our ship, which was brand new, looked like a sieve by the time we got back in friendly territory. It was shot up so badly we couldn't land so that is why we hit the silk. I bailed out at seven thousand feet and it was the longest few minutes I have ever spent in my life. I landed in a plowed field and hit pretty good – right next to a country pub. By the time the ambulance arrived I had been held up and searched by two French police fearing I was German and secondly, I was feeling very high from the cognac the pub owner was thrusting on me. The doctor fed me good American Rye and Pappy and I started on some Scotch. You can see how it ended. All this happened without getting a scratch. I really wished I had broken a leg afterwards because two days later we went back to the same area. Came out better that time, but I aged on the trip.[411]

No more for now darlings. Will try to have more cheerful news next time. Incidentally, the L.A. relatives know all about the above.[412]

Love to all, Bill

---

[411] The editor of this collection would love to find out exactly where this "country pub" was located. Bill dropped his bombs on Haltern, Germany, a few miles southwest of Munster, Germany. As his crew attempted to fly their badly crippled B-26 back to Rosiers, France they would likely have passed the Rhine River near Rheinberg, Germany and the Maas River near Venlo, Holland. It is unlikely that they made it all the way to France before bailing out. More likely Bill landed next to "a country pub" somewhere in Belgium. It would be of great satisfaction for the editor and his family to know if the pub still exists. The irony that the beer-loving son of an American brewmaster would land safely next to a drinking establishment is a most cherished family anecdote.

[412] It is amusing how Bill nonchalantly informs his parents that his relatives in L.A. have known about his missions while they were kept in the dark.

Lt. Bill Biner, left, in Rosieres, France, 1945
Sgt. Bob Biner, right, and Don Frei in England.

V-MAIL
May 31, 1945
Dear Mom, Dad and All,

I hope you haven't been looking for me. I just got back from a 72 hr. pass, as that explains the delay. I didn't have the dough to go to London, so I spent my pass in Norwich. There isn't much doing there, but I did meet an Ellensburg boy. I met Jack Marx[413] in the Red Cross Club. He's been over here for more than two years. He's a pretty good boy, but we didn't have much to do, so we just went to a show. Betty knows him.

---

[413] Jack Marx was a 1939 graduate of Ellensburg High School.

It's after ten and it's still light out. We only have about seven hrs. of darkness. If you start getting impatient just think of me without any mail.

Love, Bob

June 2, 1945
Rosieres, France
Dear Bob,

I should have written to you sooner but you know how it is. When I got back to Vallencieneo,[414] our group had broken up and I was assigned to this outfit, which at that time was stationed in Maastricht, Holland. We are on D.S.[415] but are expecting a permanent transfer any day now. I hope it doesn't come through because this Group is too eager to suit me and Rosieres is out in the sticks and transportation anywhere just isn't. Besides, the ground-pounders[416] are getting all the passes now.

I may become a ground-cruncher myself. Right now I have a deal working where I only have to fly four hours a month and only with old pilots. If they change their minds and want me to fly steadily, practice missions, I will refuse to fly

---

[414] Valenciennes, France, on the northern border with Belgium, was liberated by U.S. troops on Sept.2, 1944.
[415] Detached Service: off on an errand, or simply reporting for duty at another unit or location.
[416] Ground pounders or ground crunchers were ground-based troops; Infantry soldiers.

426 | The World War II Letters of Bill & Bob Biner

altogether. This plane is now obsolete and I can't see risking my ass in it. With my record I don't think they will do anything.

The big question right now is how to get home. All our old staff, including Pappy, is in Augsburg, Germany and I am sweating a letter to my C.O. By the time you get this I hope I am on my way!

If I do get to go and fly to London we will get together again if I can arrange it. At least I will call you on the phone. Received a V.E. letter from Mother and she says every time the phone rings she thinks it is me. These civilians will never understand army machination.

Hope you aren't scheduled for the CBI[417], and don't start volunteering. Take it from me, it doesn't pay. And don't forget the folks. We haven't been paid yet and I'm way in debt. Funny where the money goes. Would like to be in Paris today but can't borrow anymore or I won't have anything to go home on if my orders come in.

Take care of yourself and drop me a line – I'll probably still be here.

Love, Bill

V-Mail
June 7, 1945

---

[417] China-Burma-India theatre of operations, generally regarded as the most dangerous destination in World War II.

Dear Mom, Dad and All,

Just got back from another pass. It must seem like that's all I do. Well it just about is. If I didn't I would go mad for sure. The other two groups I was in have both gone home, but they just keep setting us back.

They set a date for us to leave and the next day they set the day back some more. Between that and the mail, I'm as low as a snake's belly. I've read everything that's worth reading, but I finally ran out. Now for nothing better to do I'm forced to write letters. It can't be many more weeks, so keep your chin up. Love, Bob

Bob Biner, 2nd from left, with Danny Gaunt, Bevo & Tex.

Lt. William D. Biner, right, with his buddy, Pappy Heinz.

June 18, 1945

Rosieres, France

Dear Folks —

Just received your May 22nd letter and am glad you are not mad at me for flying more missions. I was always afraid something would happen so you would find out the hard way but my luck held out.

Also got a letter from Auntie Rie today thanking me for the perfume. She wants me to visit when I get back. Hope it can be arranged.

This brewery trouble seems to have a familiar melody about it. I don't remember a single manager who didn't start out as a "Prince-of-a-Fellow" in the eyes of the household and end up a Simon Legree![418]

I still have nothing definite on going home, so don't expect me until I call on the phone. This run-around is beginning to get me down, and the life we are living now is far worse than when we were in combat. When the army needs you, you are a fine fellow. After the crisis you are a tramp.

Three of us sneaked to Paris over the weekend and the highlight of the trip was going up in the Eiffel Tower. The elevator ride scared me but the view was well worth it. I didn't have much money but I

---

[418] Simon Legree was the notorious slave-master in the Harriet Beecher Stowe classic Uncle Tom's Cabin.

managed to get rid of most of it. Prices are still going up. A drink in the cheaper places costs at least $2.

We were late getting to the Gare du Nord and we hit it on the run. We gave the Frenchies an example of American footwork by catching the train as it was half way out of the station. The last car was the baggage car and that is what we caught and rode to Amiens sitting on a box in the open doorway and drinking gin with the baggage man – and waving at the pretty girls along the road and at the stops. Just like hoboes.

Last Saturday I went to Arras and was presented with the D.F.C. by General Mays. There were fifty men altogether getting different awards and it was quite impressive. After, we stood in line and the local Bomb Group passed in review and we received the salute, á la movies. Each man had his picture taken at the time of award but I don't know whether I'll ever get hold of one.

Glad to hear Fritz got out of the eighth on the first try. She had better luck than Betty or me.

Hope my next letter has good news in it. This garrison duty is driving me batty – we even have full dress parades on the runways. Some fun. And me with almost double the points to get out of the Army.

Well, good night all. Love, Bill

V-MAIL

Dear Mom, Dad, and All,

I forgot to tell you last night not to write any more letters. It's not that I'm on my way home or anything, but the way we're moving around, I'll never get any mail anyhow. I expect to move again in the near future, and after that I may head for home. Right now we're working on the plane that we hope will someday carry us to the States. We have plenty to do, so we don't have many spare moments. I sure miss the mail tho. I was getting a letter about every day and now it's stopped short. Start saving those points.

Love, Bob

June 20, 1945
Rosieres, France
Dear Bette,

Well, I am finally writing to you and I hope you appreciate the effort.

It is a very warm and sunny day and I'm sitting outdoors trying to get a little tan so that I won't look like an Easterner if I happen to hit California this summer. Wish – Wish!

Still sweating out orders to go home and not having much luck. When I think about the way I have missed out on everything – promotions, etc. – I get a little browned-off with everyone around here and make myself obnoxious. All my old buddies that stayed home this time are at least Captains and still home. Probably some are on their way into civilian life now. That is something I am really going to work on that when I get home.

The boys around our living area have acquired dozens of puppies recently and now someone got a batch of baby rabbits. It's beginning to look like a dog farm, but anything to keep occupied.

The army is trying to set up a school program but it is doing it the usual army way. Right now we are taking classes in subjects they quit teaching cadets years ago. Just to keep us from lying in the sack too much.

This Rosieres is a typical dirty little village and miles from nowhere. After living with the Dutch for a week or so it is hard to appreciate French dirt. From my tone you can see I am getting tired of France and I don't mind admitting it. See that there is a good stock of ham steaks and eggs in reserve because I'm really going to tear into some when I get home.

When is your big day going to come off? Or have you run into more snags? Maybe I'll be in on the celebration, I hope.

Give my thanks to Pat for you-know-what and I'll make it up to him when I get home. One way or another. (The best thing I could do for him would be to scare him away from you). I know you'll appreciate that.

Take it easy Priscilla and don't forget the ham 'n eggs.

Love, Bill

Now that the European operations were over, Bob Biner continued to participate in practice missions in anticipation that he might yet be sent to join the fight against the Japanese in the Pacific or in the China-Burma-India Theatre. Two days after this letter was written US forces won the Battle of Okinawa, but it was costly. 12,500 American soldiers were killed and another 35,500 wounded. But for the Japanese the battle was devastating as 162,000 soldiers and civilians were killed. A week later US forces retook the Philippines. The end was now in sight for the Japanese Empire, making it more unlikely that Bob would be transferred to the Pacific. Bill had already flown in far more than the required number of missions and would have had to volunteer for extended duty, but Bob could have been sent. Fortunately, he was not.

Betty Biner, the older sister of Bill and Bob Biner, worked for the Lend-Lease program during the war. She married her boss, Charlton Paschal Fulton, and was the mother of ten children. It was Betty who saved all of the letters written by her brothers during their terms of service in the US Air Corps. Betty passed these World War II letters on to her son Joe, the editor of this book. Betty Biner Fulton died on Joe's birthday in 2009. Her passing was the inspiration to publish these letters for posterity.

June 26, 1945

Rosieres, France
Dear Folks, et al –

First of all, let me excuse myself Pop, for missing Father's Day. There isn't much in these countries that one can buy, especially for the male race, but maybe I can run across something you can go for. Until then, let yourself be consoled by the thought that you are the father of two great heroes of World War II. And I mean – heroes!

Had some good news yesterday. Found out that my name is in to go home and the orders should be out this week. When they come (the orders) I will go to a receptions center in Paris for an indefinite period of time before boating for the Etats Unis (USA). It may take one week or four to get out of Paris. You may realize this when you think of the number of men returning to the States at this time.

Anyway, I'll love every minute of the trip back. In fact, I'd love every minute of jail after leaving this Group. You have never been in the Army so you won't know what it is like, but this Group is the most chicken outfit I have ever been in. An officer is just so much riff-raff and an individual with a good record is no better than an individual with a rotten record. It is the final blow against my patriotism and all I want to do now is get out of the Army and back into civilian life. What a great day that will be.

I am entrusting you people with the task of stocking up a reserve of Scotch, Gin, etc. for the glorious homecoming. I'm hoping to be back for my 25th birthday – one decade of dissolute life. I have a good chance of making it for that epic day, but don't count on it.

Didn't go anyplace this weekend because I was confined for missing athletics and a ground school class – you really know the war is over when that happens. One of the reasons I love this place.

Haven't heard from Bob since I left England but I assume he is alright. Thought I would look him up again on my way home but I don't think I'll be going through Old Blighty[419] on the way back. Probably will en-boat at Cherbourg or some other port here in France. Hope he leaves for home soon himself.

No more for now chubbies, will write the latest developments as they happen. Hope the good news comes tomorrow or Thursday.

All my love, Bill

June 30, 1945
Rosieres, France

---

[419] A sentimental nickname for Great Britain used by soldiers abroad.

Dear Mother, Dad & All –

Just received the good news that my orders are on the way and it makes me feel like a liberated prisoner. We had an inspection yesterday and the entire squadron has been restricted for the weekend. Just as if we got passes and transportation to some town of any size. What a laugh!

I have cleared the post and my bags are packed. Right now I am waiting at the line like a runner for the starting signal. The orders should be in tomorrow and we will then leave for Paris where the wait is indefinite. I believe we will catch a boat out of Le Houvre or Cherbourg but don't know definitely. Anyway, I will be out of this group and that is as good as being at home.

Wouldn't mind putting in a week or two in Paris as I have never really seen the city and so there is a lot of unfinished rubber-necking in store for me if I do stay awhile.

You will receive a "termination of address" V-mail, probably before you receive this, so do just what it says. Don't mail any more letters. I will continue to write but don't answer because they will never reach me. Don't forget to send that money order to LT. Parrish. I hope you haven't sent it in a letter addressed to me.

Don't expect me home as soon as you receive this because, if you remember, it took me two months to get home from Italy, and we didn't have the huge redeployment situation then that we have now. Just consider me as on the way and don't give it another thought. It may be August or October. Who can tell?

Haven't' heard from Bob yet since I left England. Hope he is on his way home or preparing to go. What a grand gathering we could have if we got home at the same time! No more for now. Enjoyed letter Roger and am glad you aren't mad at me – so you say. Will write the latest developments as they happen.

Love to all, Bill

V-MAIL

Dear Mom, Dad and All,

I thought I better write before you get any ideas. I'm at a new base now, but we got mixed up with the Post Office. Before we left we had to give a forwarding address. As a result, I'm not getting our mail, and some of my letters may be coming back. Don't get the idea I'm on my way home or something has happened to me. However, I do expect to leave before many more weeks. They took me off the crew and put me on one that had a man short. The boys are here too, so I don't feel too bad. I'll try to write again tomorrow.

Love, Bob

The Biner brothers made it back to the states almost simultaneously, much to the relief of their worrisome mother, Harriet. Bill returned on July 17, 1945, and was once again stationed in Santa Ana. But the only duty he was preparing for was his marriage to Maxine Gray. Bob returned shortly after Bill. He was initially sent to Ft. Douglas, Utah and then to Deming, New Mexico. Now out of danger, the faithful sons nevertheless continued to write home.

Aug. 9, 1945

Dear Mom, Dad and All,

How do you like this for a quick trip? We left Ft. Douglas Monday evening, and arrived here yesterday. The only trouble I've had so far is our bags haven't arrived yet. My uniform is almost black, and the only thing I have with me is my toilet articles.

We should start a two-day processing tomorrow. I'm not sure how things are going to turn out, because we're just about on the line. Guys under 18 missions may be sent to the Pacific, but we may keep out on our combat hours. We have the required 110 hrs. After we process we may be around here for two or three weeks. As soon as I'm classified I can tell you if I'll be stationed in the States.

It's been raining all day, and naturally I don't have my rain coat yet. This field is really crowded. It's not big enough to handle us all, and we have to stand in the chow line for at least an hour every meal.

Vance and Frie are the only guys of my crew that I have seen. Vance gave me the pictures we took at the Flak Home, but there are too many to send in an envelope so I'll send them off one of these days. I'll just send a couple in this letter.

The patch on my eye was for a cut I got when I was fooling around that day. The other picture was taken at Southport. I'll write soon.

Love, Bob

Aug. 11, 1945

Dear Mom, Dad, and All,

We've been sitting around the last few days listening to the news broadcast. I hope by the time this letter arrives the whole thing will be over. Things have certainly been going fast since I left for home.

I still haven't processed. This field is really in a state of chaos. There are about forty thousand men here and this field is only capable of handling about half that number. If the war does end, this place will really be a mad house.

I haven't been able to get any towels yet but there should be some in soon. I supposed Bill is in Spokane now really having a time. Will you look around the house for my pen? I left it there by mistake. Also send Betty's address. I can't remember the street number. How is she getting along? I'll bet she'll be out of a job in a week or so.

Ignats should be starting school pretty soon. You better send her a sweater or something for her birthday. Don't forget to write and don't be looking for me if the war ends.

Love, Bob

Santa Ana Army Air Base
Officer's Mess
Tuesday Nite
Dear Folks,

I'm sweating out a call to Maxine's and I thought this would be a good time to write a few lines.

Read your letter yesterday at George's and I wish you had explained the article in the Bulletin. It sort of leaves me up in the air. Is it bad or good?

Sunday, Pappy & I went to Paul's with the G. Biner's for dinner and we had a great time. Pappy entertained Grandma with German for quite a visit and she enjoyed it immensely.[420] The party

---

[420] Juliana Truffer Biner, who was born in Switzerland, spoke German and French. She was 83 at the time of this dinner party.

lasted quite late and Julia got you-know–how before we left. I even did the Samba[421] with her.

I was screened yesterday and they told me I could get out but it would take me at least three weeks. The $500 a year bonus is coming through but I probably won't be paid here. Pappy expects to get out in a week, but he's not sure.

This place is lousy with officers and G.I.'s trying to get out and with all the red tape it is a slow process. I have a swell room and the weather is wonderful so I am not having it so tough. Also, the food is the best. Am having the G.B.'s and the Jones' out for dinner Saturday if they will come.

No more now. Love to all,

Bill

Sept. 5, 1945

Dear Bet,

I supposed Mom has told you by now where I am but in case you haven't heard I'm in Deming, New Mexico. This is probably the worst air base in the U.S. and I don't think I'm exaggerating. It's impossible to find a place to stay cool. In fact, it is so bad I can't even sleep in the daytime anymore.

The only reason why we are here is to wait till they call our number for discharge. There are still

---

[421] The Samba is a fast-paced dance of Brazilian origin.

plenty of guys here with 85 points, so you can see our morale isn't any too high. They just lowered the points to 50 – I have fifty-eight, so I'm hoping they'll get around to me before Xmas.

How do you like your job, and how will it be affected by the end of the war? What are you doing for fun and when in the heck are you going to get married? Say hello to Pat for me and ask him if he needs any cigarettes. If he does, I can send some up.

Don't forget to write. I'll be expecting a little from ya. Love, Bob

P.S. When is the folk's anniversary?

Sgt. Bob Biner after the war with his sisters Fritzi and Betty.

Undated letter from Los Angeles, probably late Sept. or early Oct. 1945

Wednesday

Dear Folks,

I haven't picked up my mail out at the base since Friday so I may have a communication from you, but I owe a letter anyway.

Julia phoned yesterday and made plans for a breakfast at her house. She couldn't get the extra help so she has decided to have it at the Beverly Hills Hotel.[422] Some swank affair. Too bad you broke your teeth Willie; they might not let you in without them.[423]

I picked up my Baptismal certificate yesterday and the priest said Father Donahue died about seven years ago. [424] I got a kick out of reading the register.

Phoned Maxine Sunday and she told me that you three and Bob were coming down. That's the best news I've heard yet, but what day are you coming down? I think Maxine and her Mother are coming

[422] The Beverly Hills Hotel, which opened in 1912 and is still in operation, was a famous hangout for movie stars, and when Bill was there it was partially owned by Loretta Young and Irene Dunn. Howard Hughes lived in the hotel during the 1940s.
[423] Bill is poking fun at his Dad and calls him Willie.
[424] Bill was born in Los Angeles and Father Donahue performed the Catholic baptism.

on the fourteenth. I haven't got a place to stay yet but I have prospects and there are always private entrance rooms in converted homes to be had all over town.[425]

Am going back to Santa Ana today and stay there until the weekend unless something keeps me there. Pappy gets out today and he will leave tomorrow morning. It took him a little over a month. Of all the inefficient places. Frank Cranz is in town and a civilian.

George, Helen and I went to visit the Poolers last night. Betty and her baby were there. John is still in Germany. Well, enough for now. Will be anxious to hear from you.

Love to all,

Bill

Lt. William D. Biner married Maxine Gray on October 20, 1945 at St. Mary Magdalene Catholic Church in Los Angeles. His brother, Sgt. Robert Biner, served as his Best Man. Bill's parents and his two sisters came down from Pocatello. During the visit Paul Jones took Fritzy and her cousin Sheila Biner to the Paramount Studios where they had their picture taken with Bob Hope.

---

[425] Perhaps Bill wanted a place for Maxine after they got married; a place he could call home. But he still had several months of duty ahead.

October 1, 1945

Dear Mom, Dad & All,

I'm sorry for the delay, and I don't have any excuses either. It seems the more time I have the less I do. I went to a high school football game here last Friday. It wasn't too good a game and it only made me homesick for the burg.[426]

I guess I must have forgotten about the ten bucks, but I got it O.K. I'll probably have to wait another month or so for my Sept. pay now. This is really mixed up. They still have men around here with a hundred points or more. They're going to have to improve a lot if I'm going to be home for Xmas.

The nights have suddenly turned cold, all in a week. We even had the heat on all day Sunday. I finally heard from Bet. She sent Bill's and Aunt Mollie's letters. I was just getting ready to write her a nasty letter. Tell Ignatz I haven't forgotten about her, but still haven't been able to go anyplace.

Write soon. Love, Bob

Sgt. Robert Biner remained in Deming, New Mexico for most of October, although he did receive a furlough to attend his brother Bill's wedding on October 20th where he served as Best

---

[426] Ellensburg

Man. He received his honorable discharge on November 14, 1945 in Boise, Idaho.

A Letter to Bill's parents from Maxine.

November 13, 1945

Dear Folks:

It is 7:00 and we are in our room at 16767 Ballinger Dr, Pacific Palisades, listening to Fibber McGee. We had another busy day spent at the rationing board, tire inspection station and then over to Helen's to pick up our mail.

Got your letter of the 8th, and I'm so glad Bob will be home for Thanksgiving. Be sure to say "hello" to him and our congratulations on his getting out of the service.

I want to thank you for your lovely wedding presents. And blue is my favorite color too! We are using both the blanket and the comforter in our new room. And, I used the darling clothespins yesterday (Monday – wash day) the twenty-four pins, so you can imagine what a big wash I had! And Bill had our car "the rocket" greased yesterday.

It's really quite an automobile, except that Bill worries every time he starts out in it that we will never reach our destination. The tires are in pretty bad shape, so we may get some in a few days through the rationing board.

We are still looking for a larger place to live. We are both getting tired of eating out and even I'm willing to get down to cooking in a kitchen of my own! But, this room is much better than the place we were in last week, and in the rocket we can look around from here.

When we went out to Julia's Friday – we got your blankets, a pair of figurines from Paul, Julia and Grandma, the six bone-handled steak knives from Grandmother and Grandfather Lynch, and a silver coffee service from Fred & Mollie Lynch. All the gifts are lovely and I can hardly wait til we get a place of our own where we can use our things.

Had a letter from mother today and she doesn't think Lambert will go back to school at Gonzaga.[427] It's very cold up there and Mom was going to start housecleaning yesterday. Dad's going to Seattle for a salesmen's meeting for a couple of days.

Now I am going to have to cut this letter short tonight because I have a dozen thank you notes to write. Will write in a few more days.

Love to all, Maxine

---

[427] Maxine is referring to her brother, Marine Cpl. Lambert J. Gray.

Bill Biner returned to Spokane to finish his education at Gonzaga University, earning his LLB (Bachelor of Laws) degree in 1950. But his heart remained in southern California. Upon graduation he moved his young family to Los Angeles where he secured a job as a claims adjuster for Farmers Insurance Group. He led investigations, conducted negotiations and had authority to settle claims.

Bill volunteered for the Air Force reserves following the war and remained on active duty for the next ten years. He was formally and honorably discharged from the United States Air Force as a Captain on July 22, 1955. A former football player, Bill remained athletically involved in golf and swimming. He also dreamed of becoming a short story writer and exchanged some stories with his older sister Betty.

Maxine gave birth to four "Baby Boomer" daughters; Barbara, Susan, Karen and Joan. The family lived in the La Crescenta area of Los Angeles County. Bill died on October 29, 1981. He was just 61 years old. Two crutches he relied on to get through the stress of the war years, tobacco and alcohol, may have contributed to his premature death. His loving wife Maxine passed away less than two years later at the age of 62. They are buried in the Holy Cross Cemetery in Culver City, not far from the graves of Bill's parents, Billy and Harriet Biner, and from one of his favorite uncles, George Biner.

Bill is survived by all three of his daughters and eight grandchildren: Dominic and Christina

Jimenez, Billy Burke, Kyle, Jaime and Stacy Beckman and Steven and Robert Tucker.

Bob Biner was discharged on November 12, 1945, as a Staff Sergeant. After the war he returned to Seattle and enrolled in the University of Washington as an art major earning a BA in Art Education. He taught for four years at North Central High School in Spokane, Washington and then, following the death of his father in 1953, moved to Whittier, California to be closer to his widowed mother Harriet. Bob Biner taught art classes for 32 years at East Whittier Intermediate School, a school attended by Richard Nixon in the early 1920s. Bob earned a Master's Degree at Long Beach State in 1957.

Bob Biner was 39 years old when he married Louise Claire Andos, a fellow teacher at East Whittier, on August 4, 1962, in Fullerton, California. As of 2013, Bob and Louise continue to live in Yorba Linda, California, and are the parents of Timothy, Mary and William Biner and the grandparents of Isabella and Olivia Biner.

Bob volunteered as the director of a credit union for over 30 years and continued to volunteer at his church following retirement. A lifelong golfer, he still played golf every week into his 90s. On January 31, 2013, Bob Biner celebrated his 90th birthday. At his birthday celebration that weekend were his wife, children and grandchildren; his beloved sister, Fritzi Bernazani, and most of his many nieces and nephews from the Bill Biner, Fritzi Bernazani, and Betty Biner Fulton families.

Robert Joseph Biner died on May 18, 2019 in Yorba Linda, California. He was 96 years old. He was preceded in death by his wife Louis Andos, who died on February 19, 2016. Bob was honored with a military burial at Holy Sepulcher Cemetery in Orange County. He is survived by his three children and two grandchildren.

Back row, left to right: Fritzi Biner (who would later marry Paul Bernazani), Betty Biner Fulton, Billy Biner, Lt. Bill Biner, Charlton "Pat" Fulton.

Front row, left to right: Maxine Gray Biner, Harriet Lynch Biner and Sgt. Bob Biner (who would later marry Louise Andos).

ADDENDUM

Theophil Biner, paternal grandfather of Bill & Bob Biner, was the son of Alois Biner, an independent-minded judge and member of the Valais Canton parliament in Switzerland. A hotel he built in the town of Randa still stands. Theophil was also a builder and several homes in Boulder, Montana were built by Biner, who also helped build the Olympia Brewery in Tumwater, Washington. Biner was a multi-talented man who spoke four languages and was a gifted musician. He was also an entrepreneur who realized that the Irish & Cornish miners who flocked to the copper boomtown of Phoenix, British Columbia, would be thirsty after a day in the mines. He built the Phoenix Brewery and sent two of his sons to Milwaukie, Wisconsin to earn their brewmaster degrees. Theophil Biner died in Los Angeles, California in 1926 at the age of 70. He is buried in the Calvary Cemetery, Los Angeles.

Juliana Truffer Biner, paternal grandmother of Bill & Bob Biner, came from a family of mountain guides. After immigrating to Montana Territory, she braved sometimes hostile interactions with Native Americans and raised a family of nine. Ironically, her youngest child, Julia Biner Jones, lived until 2006, 106 years after her closest sibling in age, Emil (1899-1900), passed away! Juliana's children were talented musicians, writers and artists. All of the Truffer-Biners were known for their sense of humor and fondness for good food and drink. Juliana was still drinking and smoking as an old woman. She died in 1950 at the age of 89 and is buried next to her husband at the Calvary Cemetery, Los Angeles.

Daniel Samuel Lynch, maternal grandfather of Bill & Bob Biner, was the first of his large clan born in America. His parents, Cornelius and Bridget Harris Lynch, arrived from Ballyduff, Waterford, Ireland a month after the end of the Civil War. They settled in Michigan's Copper Country, where many other Irish miners had settled. The Lynch family suffered from unspeakable tragedies, as one brother fell to his death off a cliff, another was severed by a train and a third committed suicide. But the remaining brothers moved on to Butte, Montana and then Alaska where they formed The Lynch Brothers Diamond Drilling Company and became famous for their critical work determining the proper placement of dams all over the world. Dan was a drilling supervisor known for his good cheer, excellent culinary skills and hard cider. He died in Seattle, Washington at the age 84 in 1951 and is buried in Seattle's Calvary Cemetery. The story of the Lynch Brothers can be found in my book, Dam Right! Fred Lynch, Oscar Kendall and the Lynch Brothers Diamond Drilling Company, published in 2017 and available through Amazon Books.

Mariette "Mate" Kendall Lynch, the maternal grandmother of Bill & Bob Biner, was the daughter of Jackson Kendall, a Union veteran, who fought with the 30th Wisconsin during the Civil War. Her grandfather, Asa Kendall, fought in the War of 1812, and was the cousin of Amos Kendall, postmaster general of the United States and closest advisor to President Andrew Jackson. Mate's great-grandfather, Joshua, was a soldier during the American Revolution. Her mother's pedigree was even more daunting. Harriet Chipman Kendall was the grand-niece of U.S. Senator Nathaniel Chipman and U.S. Representative Daniel Chipman, both from Vermont. She was a direct descendant of John Chipman, who married Hope Howland, the daughter of Mayflower pilgrim John Howland.

Mate Kendall was a stern woman, not particularly affectionate, who became extremely dependent on her husband during her old age. Around 1910-11, Dan Lynch slipped off to West Africa to lead a drilling operation for The Boyles Brothers Diamond Drilling Company. He knew that Mate would not approve of the idea so he intentionally kept it from her until a day or two prior to his departure. Mate was livid, especially since her husband would be gone for the better part of a year. Determined not to let him pull such a stunt again she feigned helplessness upon his return and spent the rest of her life as a self-imposed semi-invalid.

The "invalid" Mate outlived the doting Dan; but not for long. In her final days she reported visits from her departed husband. He would stand in her doorway checking in on her. She died on January 13, 1952, less than two months after Dan; a final testament to the fact that she could not live without him. They are buried side by side in Seattle's Calvary Cemetery.

William Henry "Billy" Biner, the father of Bill & Bob Biner, was the son of Theophil Biner and Juliana Truffer. He was a champion amateur boxer in British Columbia. After graduating from Hantke's Brewers' School in Milwaukie, Wisconsin, Billy worked as a brewer at ten different breweries between 1911 and 1946, in British Columbia, Mexico, Washington and Idaho. In 1947 he bought the Leipzig Tavern in Portland, Oregon and operated it until 1952. The tavern is still popular in the Sellwood district of Portland. Billy and his wife Harriet sold the tavern and moved to LA in 1952 to be near their son Bill. Billy found work at the North American Aircraft Company but died from a heart attack on January 5, 1953. He was 63 years old. Billy Biner is buried in the Holy Cross Cemetery in Culver City, California.

Harriet Veronica Lynch Biner, the mother of Bill & Bob Biner, was the daughter of Dan Lynch and Mate Kendall. She was born in Portland, Oregon in 1892; the first of the family to be born in the

Pacific Northwest. Harriet, the daughter of a miner, met Billy Biner in Phoenix, British Columbia in 1914. They had six children, four of whom survived childhood. After her husband died in 1953, Harriet, known as Nanny Biner to her many grandchildren, divided her time between the families of her four surviving children: Betty Fulton, Bill Biner, Bob Biner and Fritzi Bernazani. Famous for her homemade bread and maternal care, Nanny Biner was deeply loved by the 25 grandchildren she left behind when she died of colon cancer at the age of 85, on April 14, 1978. She is buried next to her husband in the Holy Cross Cemetery in Culver City, California.

Paul Meredith Jones, was born in Bristol, Tennessee on March 14, 1897, the eldest of the four children of John and Flora Jones. Bristol was founded in 1854 on what had been a plantation and it is now known as the "Birthplace of Country Music." Jones himself got out of the country, but part of his charm as a down-to-earth Hollywood producer was that the country never completely left him. He produced 37 Hollywood movies, including the popular "Road" movies starring Bob Hope and Bing Crosby. He also wrote and directed films. But the most intriguing bit of trivia about Paul Jones was his friendship with the great, and notoriously anti-social, comedian W. C. Fields. Hollywood silent screen actress and historian Louise Brooks, in her excellent 1982 memoir Lulu in Hollywood wrote:

"After a famous person dies his biographers feel free to give him a glittering list of intimate friends. Anecdotes are so much tastier spiced with expensive names. Bill Fields' list grows with every telling. So far as I know he had no intimate friends and loved only one person whose name, Paul Jones, is meaningless to practically everyone."

The editor of this work clearly remembers a visit from Uncle Paul, and his wife Julia Biner Jones, to the Fulton home in Portland back in 1965, a year before the death of the Hollywood producer. As the editor recalls, Jones was a dapper, funny-looking man, who was good-natured and seemed to find pleasure in all that he saw. Jones and his wife Julia Biner, the sister of the brewmaster, had one child, Julia Ann. Jones died on Dec. 29, 1966 in North Hollywood, California at the age of 69. His wife survived another 40 years, dying on August 30, 2006; two months' shy of her 103rd birthday.

Charlton Paschal "Pat" Fulton, who married Betty Biner in 1946, was from a railroad family. His grandfather had been an engineer on the Lincoln funeral train. His father was the agent of the depot in Chehalis, Washington. His brother Leland became vice-president of Northern Pacific. Pat Fulton also worked in the transport business and was put in charge of a Lend-Lease office in Pasco, Washington. There he met Betty Biner, 18 years his junior. They raised a family of ten children in Portland, Oregon. Pat Fulton was the nephew of Newton and Tommy Paschal, the brothers of his maternal grandmother, and the subjects of my first book <u>From Beardstown to Andersonville, The Civil War Letters of Newton & Tommy Paschal</u>, published by Heritage Books, Inc. in 1998 and again in 2011 with additional information.

Elizabeth Jeanne "Betty" Biner, the oldest child of Billy & Harriet Biner, graduated from Central Washington College and was an aspiring writer, until ten children took up all of her time. Following the death of her husband in 1980 Betty became a Jesuit volunteer and managed the Tundra Women's Coalition, a safe house for abused Native American women in Bethel, Alaska. After moving to Seattle to be near her daughters and grandchildren, Betty held numerous volunteer jobs with Catholic charities and the Democratic Party. She took annual breaks to travel the world and had a great appreciation for different cultures. She continued to be a tireless and generous volunteer and an active member of St. Joseph Church until her death.

Betty had an infectious charm and everyone who met this tiny, vibrant woman fell in love with her. Her children and grandchildren revered Betty as the loving matriarch of a large, diverse and close-knit family. She had a tremendous sense of humor and Fulton family gatherings with her were always full of laughter. She was a passionate progressive in her world-view and was never afraid of expressing her opinion. Betty will always be remembered for her intelligence, generosity, curiosity, courage and compassion. Pat and Betty Fulton had ten children: William, Charlene, Charles, Mariette, Leslie, Joseph, Daniel, Robert, Frederick and Thomas. Betty died on November 25, 2009, two months' shy of her 92nd birthday. She is buried near her grandparents, Dan and Mate Lynch, in Seattle's Calvary Cemetery.

Fredericka "Fritzi" Biner, the youngest child of Billy and Harriet Biner, graduated from Marylhurst University in Portland. She married Paul Joseph Bernazani and had eight children: John, Joseph, Mary, James, David, Elizabeth, Rita and Daniel. Fritzi and Paul both worked for the federal government and their jobs enabled them to raise their large family in various parts of the world including Germany, Japan and Greece. They settled in the Washington D.C. area where many of their children currently serve the United States in military or diplomatic occupations. Son James collects military paraphernalia and his private museum includes the bomb pin from the 100th mission of the *Berlin Sleeper*. Like her siblings, Fritzi Bernazani is full of good-humor, progressive ideas and appreciation for food, drink and travel. And like her father the brewmaster, Fritzi is an expert on beer! As the youngest child, Fredericka had to endure a number of pet names from her older siblings, particularly from her brothers, Bill and Bob Biner. She was known as Fritz and Fritzy, Ignatz and Bumps. Sometimes they called her Freddy. Today everyone in the family knows her as Fritzi, the beloved matriarch of our large and still growing Biner-Lynch clan.

Dan & Mate Lynch with their grandchildren. Fritzi is held in the middle behind her sister. Betty. Bill sits in front with his admiring brother Bob looking at him on the right. Also pictured are Jack & Danny Lynch, sons of Kendall Lynch.

Bob Biner, left, and Air Corps buddy Bevo Bevacqua.

Don Frei, Frank Lane and Bob Biner prepare to leave on a mission from Old Buckenham Air Field in England. Below, Bevo and Bob in England.

INDEX

Cover Photos: 1. The Berlin Sleeper and Crew 2. Bill & Bob Biner in front of the family home in Ellensburg, WA

Dedication photo: Sgt. Robert Joseph Biner.

Page 6: 1. Billy Biner as amateur boxing champion of British Columbia, circa 1910. 2. Dan & Mate Lynch with sons Fred & Kendall at a mining camp in British Columbia, circa 1910. 3. Bill Biner as Gonzaga University football player.

Page 17: George Biner

Page 18: Paul Jones & W.C. Fields

Page 25: Bill Biner at boot camp.

Page 103: Juliana Truffer Biner

Page 104: Bob Biner in Cedar City, Utah.

Page 114: Lt. Bill Biner

Page 200: The crew of the Berlin Sleeper.

Page 246: Harriet Lynch Biner as a young woman.

Page 247: Christmas card by Bill Biner.

Page 342: Staff Sgt, Bob Biner

Page 351: Fritzi and Bob Biner with their father.

Page 409: Belly gunner Bob with his crew.

Page 414: Bombardier Bill with his crew.

Page 423: Bill in France. Bob in England.

Page 426: Bob with Air Corps buddies.

Page 427: Bill and Pappy Heinz.

Page 433: Betty Biner.

Page 442: Bob, Fritzi & Betty Biner.

Page 450: The Biner Family after the war.

Page 459: Dan & Mate Lynch with grandchildren.

Page 460: Bob Biner and Bevo Bevacqua.

Page 461: Bob Biner in England with crewmates.

Page 476: Bob & Louise Biner. Bob with granddaughters.

Page 477: Bill Biner and daughters.

Back cover photos of the editor, Joseph Fulton, and his book From Beardstown to Andersonville, by Debra Hascall.

All other photographs are from the Fulton/Biner/Lynch family collection except Paul Jones & WC Fields, page 18, courtesy of Paul's daughter, Julia Ann Cusick.

Bob and Louise Biner on Bob's 90th birthday in 2013, celebrate the publication of this book featuring the letters that Bob and his brother Bill wrote home during World War II. Bob and his granddaughters Isabella and Olivia Biner.

Top: Bill Biner with daughters in the 1950s.
Below: Susan, Barbara & Joan Biner celebrate
the publication of their father's letters in 2013.

Coming in 2020
from Originario Productions

UNDER A FULL HEAD OF STEAM:

The Famous Fulton Family of Fairfield

By Joseph Edward Fulton

Printed in Great Britain
by Amazon

45095930R00273